The Responsibility to Protect

The Responsibility to Protect

Ethical and
Theological Reflections

Forming the Ecumenical Mind and Addressing Ethical Dilemmas
on Prevention and Protection of People in Peril

Geneva, 21-23 April 2005

**Semegnish Asfaw, Guillermo Kerber
and Peter Weiderud,** *editors*

World Council of Churches, Geneva

CCIA Liaison Office at the UN Headquarters
777 UN Plaza, Suite 9D
Ne-York, NY 10017
USA
Tel. +1212 867 58 90
Fax +1212 867 74 62

Cover design: Rob Lucas
Cover illustration: Alex Maffi

ISBN 2-8254-1470-0

Printed in France

Contents

Foreword

In January 2001 the Central Committee of the World Council of Churches received a document entitled 'The protection of endangered populations in situations of armed violence: toward an ecumenical ethical approach'. The document requested the churches to further study the issues it raised. Some of the more relevant studies subsequently undertaken by the churches include the Church of Norway's 'Vulnerability and security' (2002) and the Evangelical Church in Germany's 'Steps on the way to peace: points of reference on peace ethics and peace policy' (2001). There was also a meeting of the Historic Peace Churches, entitled 'Just peacemaking: towards an ecumenical ethical approach from the perspective of the Historic Peace Churches' (2001).

A summary of these contributions was discussed by the Commission of the Churches on International Affairs in 2003 and presented to the WCC Central Committee in September 2003. This document pointed out the need to reflect on the ethical and theological criteria for discernment; the significance of the notion of human security in all its dimensions; and the importance of further developing the connections between sovereignty, human rights and international law, and the issue of just peace and the use of military force as a last resort.

A minute was adopted by the Central Committee which stressed the importance of the issue of the responsibility to protect as a permanent topic under consideration by the WCC since its foundation. It asked the CCIA to develop a study on this issue, to be presented at the next WCC Assembly in Porto Alegre, Brazil.

A session on the responsibility to protect was part of the 2003 UN Advocacy Week organized by the WCC/CCIA in New York in November. In April 2005, 21 experts from around the world gathered in Geneva to discuss 'The responsibility to protect: ethical and theological reflections'. Among them the two rapporteurs of the International Commission on Intervention and State Sovereignty, Hon. Gareth Evans and Amb. Mohammed Sahnoun and personalities like former ICRC President Dr. Cornelio Sommaruga, former UN interim High Commissioner for Human Rights Dr. Bertrand Ramcharan and Dr. Konrad Raiser. It is the report of this seminar that you are now holding in your hands.

The responsibility to protect is a controversial issue in most intellectual and political circles. While some believe that force should be used when it can alleviate or prevent large-scale human rights violations, others hold that military intervention, even for humanitarian purposes, can only make things worse, and instead the preventive capacity of those in need should be strengthened.

Churches too have participated in this debate. While some defend a pacifist position that condemns any form of military action, others find justificatory criteria for armed intervention. In addition, some believe that any war is evil and requires time for repentance, even if the conflict is deemed necessary and unavoidable.

CCIA studies show that although churches have different views on the use of force for human protection purposes, they agree on one thing: the importance of preventive efforts designed to avoid or tackle a crisis before it escalates. Prevention is key. Churches in close contact with populations are well aware of the early warning signs of conflict. They can thus help alert the appropriate authorities as to potential sources of human rights crises, or even deal with the matter themselves.

The seminar in April 2005 stressed the need to form the ecumenical mind on the use of force for humanitarian purposes. It noted that churches support the emerging international norm for the responsibility to protect as a means of tackling human insecurity and halting human suffering. Subsequently, the WCC welcomed the inclusion and endorsement in the Outcome Document of the UN World Summit in September 2005 of the principle of the responsibility to protect civilians from genocide, war crimes, 'ethnic cleansing' and crimes against humanity.

CCIA studies also show that churches are not prepared to claim it is never appropriate or necessary to resort to lethal force in order to protect the vulnerable. The resort to force is first and foremost the result of a failure to prevent what could have been prevented, given appropriate foresight and action. Having failed, and having acknowledged such failure, the world then needs to do what it can to limit the consequent peril.

Churches are aware that the resort to force for humanitarian protection may sometimes be the only option. It cannot guarantee success, but sometimes it has to be attempted in order to help those in a desperate plight. The use of force should be limited to the short-term objective of mitigating and alleviating imminent threats and suffering. Long-term objectives require other means. If force is used, it requires the acceptance of the local population and the simultaneous provision of humanitarian relief.

Peter Weiderud
Director,
Commission of the Churches on International Affairs

Introduction

The late 1980s and 1990s witnessed more and more interventions for humanitarian purposes. There were many reasons for this, such as the increasing number of non-international armed conflicts, the erosion of sovereignty, the need to contain refugee flows resulting from domestic wars, and the need to protect internally displaced people to name only a few. With this in mind, the General Assembly of the United Nations adopted two major resolutions (GA resolution 43/131 on 8 December 1988 and GA resolution 45/100 on 14 December 1990), thus forming the legal cornerstone of humanitarian intervention and assistance to populations in need.

However, this approach arose mainly from a nation-state perspective. A number of consultations and negotiations also took place that led to the introduction of a new concept – the responsibility to protect (R2P) – proposed by the International Commission on Intervention and State Sovereignty in its 2001 report. For the first time, the debate shifted from the viewpoint of the interveners to that of the people in need of assistance, thus redefining sovereignty as a duty-bearer status, rather than as absolute power. Hence, states can no longer use the pretext of sovereignty to perpetrate human rights violations with impunity, but instead have an obligation to protect their citizens and ensure their basic rights by preserving their dignity, well-being and safety.

Churches have often been involved with issues of civilian protection in all kinds of emergencies. In most cases, churches are the main point of contact for the local population in need of protection. They thus have an important role in prevention and providing assistance, healing and reconciliation – locally, nationally and internationally.

The World Council of Churches has been involved with the R2P issue for some years. In 2001, the Central Committee of the WCC met in Potsdam and adopted a document entitled 'The protection of endangered populations in situations of armed violence: toward an ecumenical ethical approach', whereby it requested the Commission of the Churches on International Affairs to report back on the issue, which it did in July 2003. In its report, the CCIA asked the International Affairs, Peace and Security team to follow-up on the issue and to prepare a report for the WCC General Assembly in 2006. With this in mind, the IA team organized its April 2005 seminar on 'The responsibility to protect: ethical and theological reflections'. The seminar gathered 21 participants from around the world, with a wide variety of expertise and professional backgrounds: theologians, scholars, researchers, academics and policy-makers.

This seminar had a dual objective. It aimed to advise the WCC on the R2P issue both from a theological standpoint (including ethical considerations) and from a political perspective: international affairs, governance and diplomatic and legal views. The content and recommendations of the seminar will be translated into a policy proposal for the Worl Council of Churches' 9th Assembly in February 2006 (Porto Alegre, Brazil). The seminar gathered 21 participants from all around the world, with a wide spectrum of expertise and professional background: theologians, scholars, researchers, academics, policy-makers.

This publication contains the papers presented by seminar participants. The positions expressed in these papers are the personal views of the authors and have not been edited. It is hoped that this publication will be used as a basis for consultation and action by churches, church-related groups, theologians, academic researchers, those engaged in interfaith dialogue, and all those involved in the issue of R2P.

The CCIA is grateful for those experts who honoured us with their presence and freely shared their time and knowledge. Our thanks also go to the ECOGIA–Red Cross Conference Centre for its warm hospitality.

Semegnish Asfaw
Consultant,
International Affairs, Peace and Human Security

Proceedings of the Seminar

Participants began by discussing a public session on the seminar theme, held at the Ecumenical Centre. An introductory evening session was devoted to discussion of Christianity's different approaches to war. This was followed by four major sessions:

- The Responsibility to Prevent
- When National Authorities Fail
- Criteria for Intervention
- When International Authorities Fail

There were four working groups to each session. Panellists, moderators and rapporteurs for each session gathered in small groups with other participants to discuss and elaborate their respective topics. Rapporteurs were assigned the role of summarizing and highlighting the discussions held during the sessions and in their working groups. Their reports were shared with all the participants on the last day of the seminar and are included at the end of this publication. It is to be noted that each participant spoke in a personal capacity.

The seminar was very lively and all the participants actively engaged in the discussions. It was an extremely fruitful experience. We reiterate our thanks to all the participants for their brilliant contributions to the issue of the responsibility to protect.

Semegnish Asfaw

Words of Welcome

Samuel Kobia

It is an honour and a joy to have the opportunity of welcoming you to this afternoon's seminar here in the Ecumenical Centre. We are pleased to welcome in this hall today representatives from different missions here in Geneva, a number of NGOs, the United Nations and other international organizations, some members of our governing bodies, the Central Committee of the WCC, and some of the staff colleagues of the World Council of Churches, in addition to those of the International Affairs team. It is thus my pleasure to welcome you, and I look forward to the deliberations this afternoon and during the next few days.

I recall that in December 2001 the UN General Assembly received a report entitled 'The responsibility to protect'. This was the result of the work done by the International Commission on Intervention and State Sovereignty. The report looked at a set of criteria to be applied when dealing with cases of humanitarian intervention. Earlier in that year, in January 2001, the WCC Central Committee had adopted a document entitled 'The protection of endangered populations in situations of armed violence: towards an ecumenical ethical approach'. This was almost a year before the UN General Assembly adopted the ICISS report, and in the years since then we have seen churches in a number of countries eager to address this issue of human security within the broader fellowship of churches.

In 2002 the Church of Norway carried out a study which led to a publication around the theme of 'Vulnerability and security'. The Evangelical Church in Germany also had a series of studies around the issue, entitled 'Steps on the way to peace: points of reference on peace ethics and peace policy'. Most of this work has been taken up by the Historic Peace Churches. These are churches which, for a long period of time, have used non-violence as a way of helping to resolve conflicts. The Historic Peace Churches had their own process under the theme 'Just peacemaking: towards an ecumenical ethical approach'.

All this occurred within a period of three years, between 2001 and 2003. Several processes were going on, sometimes in consultation, but at times also discovering each other along the way. Hence, the issue was taken up seriously by the churches at different levels within the churches' constituency, but also within the Central Committee of the WCC. Within the WCC, it is the Commission of the Churches on International Affairs which has organized this seminar and whose staff have been coordinating the work around the ethical and theological reflections on the issue of human security, leading to the adoption of the title 'Responsibility to protect'. Human security means the security of people not only in terms of physical security, but also in terms of their economic and social well-being, respect for the dignity and worth of all human beings, and the protection of their human rights and fundamental freedoms. It is an area that has provided a framework for ethical and theological reflection, but which has also taken us beyond such considerations by bringing together people from different walks of life to help reflect on this very important issue.

It is within that framework that we come together this afternoon, in order to share what has emerged out of these processes, including the work of the Central Committee of the WCC in 2003, where there was again a discussion that stressed the importance of the issue of the responsibility to protect as a permanent agenda within the work of the WCC because it touches all aspects of human life. We are therefore pleased to provide the space for exploring the critical issue before us.

Ethical and theological views vary, of course, in the different churches, and sometimes we have quite divergent views on this issue. At times, ethical and moral issues are more divisive than doctrinal issues within the churches, but at the same time there is some commonality when it comes to addressing specific ethical dilemmas. An example is the ecumenical approach to challenges posed in recent years by military engagement in different parts of the world. In this engagement we have had varying degrees of success and failure; success especially because of the accent we put on the sanctity of human life and the sacredness of life based on our common belief that human beings are created in the image of God. It is that commonality within the churches and the faith communities that inspires and encourages us to continue the discourse on the issues mentioned above. We should not only focus on the responsibility to protect; we must also ask the question, 'how do we prevent?'

Conflicts are responsible for the insecurity we are talking about. It is almost like talking of a medical ethics, in which prevention is better than cure. Untimely and inappropriate treatment of a human body can be catastrophic, and this can become a serious ethical issue, particularly if you have the means to prevent the disease from spreading. The mission of prevention has therefore emerged powerfully to inform the process we undertake. If we have the possibility of intervening ahead of time and not waiting until a conflict happens, we should rather opt for the former. While external intervention is necessary in many situations, we should nevertheless be equally concerned about increasing the capacity of local people to intervene themselves, in terms of prevention as well as protection.

The Responsibility to Protect:
Moving Towards a Shared Consensus

Gareth Evans

The issue we are dealing with at this seminar has been one of the centrepieces of international relations discussions since the end of the Cold War: what should be the response of the international community when faced with situations of catastrophic human rights violations within states, where the state in question claims immunity from intervention based on longstanding principles of national sovereignty? It is a question right at the intersection point of international relations, law, policy, ethics, human rights and human security. This topic has the lot: it is one of enormous complexity.

The evolution of the concept of the responsibility to protect, as a way of organizing conceptually the response to this problem, is a fascinating exercise in intellectual history in its own right. What we are seeing now is the emergence, almost in real time, of a new international norm, maybe ultimately a new rule of customary international law, of really quite fundamental ethical importance and quite fundamental novelty in the international system. We are not there yet, but we are on our way, and there is a critical need to maintain the momentum of this evolution: the forces of resistance to these ideas are still quite strong in the international community.

In understanding the stages in the evolution of this policy response, the best place to begin is the UN Charter of 1945. This was overwhelmingly preoccupied with the problem of states waging war against each other, and the Charter produced a really quite stunning innovation to the extent that it outlawed, across the board, the use of force, the only exceptions being self-defence in confronting an attack, and when authorized by the Security Council, a new international institution given unprecedented authority to act in cases of threats to international peace and security. On the question, however, of external force being applied in response to an internal catastrophe, the Charter language if anything pointed the other way, with its clear statement of the principle of non-interference in Article 2.7: 'Nothing should authorize intervention in matters essentially within the domestic jurisdiction of any State'.

The inclination to read the Charter as very limited in its reach was reinforced by the breakout of the Cold War almost immediately after the UN began. Post-Second World War inclinations – carried right through to the 1990s – were to call the principle of national sovereignty really quite sacrosanct. This was much reinforced in the decolonization era with a very rapid increase in the member states joining the UN system: states newly proud of their identity, states conscious to some extent of their fragility, and states who saw the non-intervention norm as one of their few defences against threats and pressures from more powerful international actors seeking to promote their own economic and political interests. And this was extremely inhibiting to the development of any sense of an obligation to respond in protective or other ways to situations of catastrophic internal human rights violations.

One big agreed exception to the non-intervention principle was the Genocide Convention of 1948. But it was almost as if, with the signing of the Convention, the job was seen as done. Nothing much was done throughout the Cold War years to give practical force and effect even to the plain terms of the Genocide Convention itself, in situations where legal arguments about lack of provable intent and so on were simply not an issue. Even with the Cambodian situation, which the world did come to appreciate as a catastrophic genocidal situation, there was no great disposition to intervene to stop it; on the contrary, there was widespread international condemnation of Vietnam when it crossed the border to displace the Khmer Rouge. I do not suggest that Vietnamese motives were absolutely pure and entirely humanitarian, but their intervention had the desired result. But so little respect or regard was paid to the notion that this was some kind of larger international responsibility, that all the pressure was on the interveners rather than those perpetrating the horror to begin with.

Other relevant instruments emerged during this period, including the Universal Declaration itself, and the 1966 Conventions on Civil and Political and Economic, Social and Cultural Rights. But essentially, in terms of practical implementation and commitment, the world remained at the level of grandiloquent rhetoric, with non-interference in domestic affairs still heading the list of God-given commandments as far as international discourse was concerned.

With the arrival of the 1990s, the end of the Cold War and the new era of apparent cooperation between formerly warring parties, it seemed there was new hope for a new international system with reestablished basic roots and principles. The defence of Kuwait against the invasion of Iraq in 1991 was a classic example of the international system working as it was intended to in response to acts of interstate aggression: a hugely significant step forward in reestablishing the elements of the Charter as it was originally conceived.

However, euphoria about a rules-based system emerging, or reemerging, did not last long. The quintessential problem of the 1990s became the one we are dealing with today: intrastate conflict, civil war and violence perpetrated on a massive scale. With the breakup of various Cold War state structures (most obviously in Yugoslavia) and the removal of some superpower constraints, conscience-shocking situations repeatedly arose, but old habits of non-intervention died very hard. Even when situations cried out for some kind of response, and the international community did react through the UN, it was too often erratic, incomplete or counter-productive. Thus, we had the debacle of the intervention in Somalia in 1993, the pathetically inadequate response to the genocide in Rwanda in 1994, the lamentable failure to prevent murderous 'ethnic cleansing' in the Balkans (in particular in Srebrenica) in 1995, and the situation in Kosovo in 1999, when the international community did in fact intervene as it probably should have done, but did so without the authority of the Security Council in the face of a threatened veto by Russia.

All this generated very fierce debate about so-called humanitarian intervention: what are the circumstances in which it is appropriate for the international community to respond, through the UN or outside it, in these situations? The battle lines were drawn around, on the one hand, the claim of 'the right to intervene', as expressed by Bernard Kouchner among others, and on the other, claims equally strongly made about the primacy and continued resonance of the concept of national sovereignty, seen as a complete inhibitor to any such coercive intervention. The debate was indeed fierce and utterly unresolved in the UN or anywhere else. This led Kofi Annan to make an agitated plea to the General Assembly in 2000, which resonates to this day: 'If humanitarian intervention is indeed an unacceptable assault on sovereignty, how should we respond to a Rwanda, to a Sebrenica, to gross and systematic violations of human rights?' Kofi Annan's own initial solution to this problem was to say that in these situations, national sovereignty had to be weighed against individual sovereignty – but this formulation was seen as doing not much more than merely restating the basic dilemma, and was not seen as helpfully solving the critical issue, which was when did individual sovereignty claims take primacy over state sovereignty. How do you articulate a point where one overrides the other?

So what are the principles that should govern our responses, if and when these kinds of situations come along? The most substantial effort so far to identify them, and to lay the foundations for an international consensus around them, has been the work of the Canadian government-sponsored International Commission on Intervention and State Sovereignty, which I had the privilege of co-chairing with Mohamed Sahnoun, and which presented its report to the UN Secretary General at the end of 2001. The Commission made four main contributions to the international policy debate.

The first, and perhaps ultimately the politically most useful, was to invent a new way of talking about the whole issue of humanitarian intervention. We sought to turn the whole weary debate about the right to intervene on its head, and to recharacterize it not as an argument about any 'right' at all, but rather about a 'responsibility' – one to protect people at grave risk – with the relevant perspective being not that of the prospective interveners but, more appropriately, those needing support. This new language has been helpful already in taking some of the heat and emotion out of the policy debate, requiring the actors to change their lines, and think afresh about what are the real issues. Our hope – and so far our experience – is that entrenched opponents will find new ground on which to more constructively engage, just as proved to be the case between developers and environmentalists after the Brundtland Commission introduced the concept of sustainable development.

The second contribution of the Commission (perhaps most conceptually significant) was to come up with a new way of talking about sovereignty: we argued that its essence should now be seen not as control but as responsibility. The UN Charter's explicit language emphasizes the respect owed to state sovereignty in its traditional Westphalian sense, but actual state practice has evolved in the nearly sixty years since the Charter was signed: the new focus on human rights and, more recently, on human security, emphasizes the limits of sovereignty.

We spelt out the implications of that change by arguing that sovereignty implies responsibilities as well as rights: to be sovereign means both to be responsible to one's own citizens and to the wider international community through the UN. The starting point is that any state has the primary responsibility to protect the individuals within it. But that's not the finishing point: where the state fails in that responsibility, a secondary responsibility to protect falls on the international community acting through the UN.

The third contribution of the Commission was to make it clear that the responsibility to protect was about much more than intervention, and in particular military intervention. It extends to a whole continuum of obligations:

- *The responsibility to prevent:* to address both the root causes and direct causes of internal conflict and other man-made crises putting populations at risk.
- *The responsibility to react:* to respond to situations of compelling human need with appropriate measures, which may include coercive measures like sanctions and international prosecution, and in extreme cases military intervention.
- *The responsibility to rebuild:* to provide (particularly after military intervention) full assistance with recovery, reconstruction and reconciliation, addressing the causes of the harm the intervention was designed to halt or avert.

Of these three dimensions to the responsibility to protect, the Commission made very clear its view that prevention was the most important. But that said, the question of military action remains, for better or worse, the most prominent and controversial one in the debate. Whatever else it encompasses, the responsibility to protect implies above all else a responsibility to react

– where necessary coercively, and in extreme cases with military coercion – to situations of compelling need for human protection. So the fourth contribution of the Commission was to come up with guidelines – in terms of both legality and legitimacy – for when military action is appropriate.

The ICISS report was born at a very unpromising time: December 2001, very soon after the 9/11 trauma. The issue of intervention for human protection purposes, dominant for a decade, disappeared from public debate almost overnight, and remained on the margins. Nonetheless, the report started to have some significant impact almost from the outset. Kofi Annan immediately embraced the language of the responsibility to protect and said it was the key to bridging the divide that he saw in the international community. We also had a very positive response from the African Union: African countries have tended to be much less anxious about the concept of intervention in state sovereignty than others in the developing world community, mainly because it seems that Africans – within recent memory – have suffered far more from neglect by the international community than from its exuberant interference.

The idea started to develop that here was an emerging norm that ought to win the support of the wider international community. Although there was an enormous amount of continuing debate, there was a new language in that debate, and it was changing the conceptual framework. Then there came a big setback to this evolving process: the second Gulf war and the use of the responsibility to protect rationale (especially by Tony Blair) to justify the war when its other rationales dropped away. As the issue of weapons of mass destruction became harder and harder to argue, and the terrorist connection effectively became impossible to argue, the chosen ground then became Saddam's tyranny and his mistreatment of his own people, the Kurds and Shiites: this was a man who breached all known norms of human decency and deserved to be dealt with militarily for those human rights and human security reasons.

The conceptual problem about this justification is that, whatever its prima facie moral attractions, it simply did not satisfy all the very specific, detailed, demanding criteria for military intervention that the Commission spelled out, bearing in mind that war is always full of horror, and that the case for waging it has to be overwhelming, not least in it being clear that more good than harm will be done by pursuing it. The political problem was that it was perceived immediately in the developing world as just another example of how any acknowledgement of the legitimacy of intervention will breed its misuse. This was the kind of refrain one constantly heard: do not concede the point about the legitimacy of intervention for human protection purposes, or any coercive military intervention, because to do so will be to open the door to bad old habits.

Notwithstanding all that, the idea of the responsibility to protect has proved tenacious. The next stage of its evolution was the report of the High Level Panel, established by the Secretary General in 2004 to bring to him suggestions for fundamental reform of the UN system, and in particular reform of the way the world went about addressing current and future security concerns. The HLP squarely embraced the concept of the responsibility to protect, in more or less identical terms to those spelled out in the original Canadian Commission report, with unanimous consensus in the 16-person panel drawn from very highly experienced people from all around the world. I was pleasantly surprised to find it much less difficult than I had anticipated to persuade my colleagues on the panel as to the virtue of this approach. They saw that there was a problem, and that there was no better solution that anyone had articulated to the way it should be addressed.

The next critical stage in the history of this idea was in the report prepared by the Secretary General to go forward to member states in the context of the UN's sixtieth anniversary, 'In larger freedom'. Kofi Annan here picked up and completely embraced the language of the HLP's report, saying without ambiguity that member states should adopt this emerging norm: 'While I am well aware of the sensitivities involved in this issue, I strongly agree with this approach. I believe we must embrace the responsibility to protect and when necessary act on it.'

So that is almost where we now are. However, there has been one further development which is a little worrying. The idea has come a long way, has been endorsed, reiterated and repeated, and is now rather delicately poised: capable of rapid further evolution and entrenchment, but also at some risk of derailment. Kofi Annan's report is now being scrutinized in the General Assembly by the member states under the chairmanship of its president, who has been asked to prepare a 'draft outcomes statement' as a result of these consultations and deliberations, to go to member states and to form the basis of hopeful resolutions of the Millennium Summit in 2005.

I was in New York earlier this week at the UN and alarm bells were starting to ring. Especially within the G77 group of countries, some were really quite determined to derail the whole concept of the responsibility to protect, to remove the language from the proposed declaration and to restore the preeminence of the notion of national sovereignty, with no rules at all being articulated about what to do in situations of catastrophic internal human rights violations. The real problem is the passivity of many other states in the G77 group when confronted with a determined derailment exercise of this kind.

My plea today is to recognize that if some of those African and other voices are raised, it will be very difficult for the president of the General Assembly to be able to report back to member states and the Secretary General that there is not a sufficient degree of consensus around the notion of the responsibility to protect for it to survive in the draft. I suggest there is a particularly important role for the World Council of Churches here, if you accept the utility, relevance, timeliness and role of the responsibility to protect concept: to do some lobbying right now to try and turn round that situation in New York.

However, before I can ask you to do that, you have to believe in the concept. I have already emphasized that the responsibility to protect is not just about military intervention, but about an umbrella of responses, all the way from prevention to rebuilding – with prevention being the most important. But the issue that has generated most discussion and concern, and on which I will now focus, is when it is right to fight. If prevention has failed, if you are faced with a situation of likely or imminent atrocities, when is it right to move to the stage beyond sanctions, to forcible military action?

The ICISS report identified six criteria that have to be satisfied: a 'just cause' threshold, going to the seriousness of the violations occurring or anticipated; then four precautionary criteria, including 'last resort' and 'proportionality'; and finally a legality criterion, 'right authority'.

The HLP essentially picked up this content, but expressed it in a rather simpler way: a legality criterion has to be satisfied, then in addition five criteria of legitimacy. The criteria in question owe their primary intellectual origins to Christian just war theory, but it is important to appreciate that these criteria are meant to incorporate universal values and not just traditions in Christian theology. My own research, and that of both ICISS and the HLP, has turned up absolutely nothing inconsistent with these principles in the other major religious traditions.

So what are the criteria? First, as to legality, both ICISS and the HLP held the line very firmly and unanimously on the primacy of the UN Charter (though there was some intense internal argument on hard-case situations, returned to below): the only alternative to embracing its rules is international anarchy. Those rules set out the only circumstances in which military force can be used without the endorsement of the Security Council: self-defence, very narrowly defined to include only actual or imminent attack, and not applicable at all to purely internal threats. So the only legal justification for the use of military force is in the context of an explicit UN Security Council resolution under Chapter VII. Despite the critique of some 'realists' who say there are no rules anymore, that they have been abandoned in the turmoil of international power politics, ICISS and the HLP (and, not surprisingly, the UN Secretary General) have taken a totally different view, that there are international rules and they must be observed.

None of us should be naive about the dilemma that does sometimes arise in the real world. What if the Security Council fails to approve military action in a case crying out for it? What if a permanent member threatens to use the veto in a situation where some conscience-shocking, massive violations of human rights are occurring? The difficulty is that if you cede the right under those circumstances to go outside the Security Council, you do put at risk the viability of the whole rule-based system of international law, and that ultimately serves nobody's interests – not even that of the superpowers, who may not remain the sole superpowers forever. But if, on the other hand, you treat the requirement for Security Council authorization as absolute and absolutely unbreachable, you do of course face the prospect on some occasions of having to stand by while human beings are slaughtered on a massive scale. What do you do when confronted with this kind of dilemma?

ICISS remained firm, stating that you have to hold fast to the principle of the rule-based system and the Security Council being the sole determinant of these matters: the task is not to seek alternatives to the Security Council, but rather to make the Security Council work better and in a more principled way. But it also offered an essentially political answer: if the Security Council fails to act in conscience-shocking circumstances, but some other country or coalition does act, and if that action is perceived by the wider international community to be appropriately responsive to the need, and is successful in stopping the killing without any other major negative consequences, then the Security Council, and the whole UN system, will have a lot of explaining to do in terms of its own credibility and its longer-term viability. This is not as clear an answer as some would like, and there continues to be some hungering for another institutional solution, but I do not believe one can be found.

'Legality' is never the end of these matters. There is also the question of the reasonableness and morality of the action: it might be legally right, because the Security Council support is there, but is it morally and ethically right to take the course of action? This is where the five criteria of legitimacy come in:

1 *Seriousness of the threat.* In the particular context of internal threats, or so-called humanitarian intervention, the bar here should be set quite high, involving genocide or other large-scale killing, 'ethnic cleansing' or very serious violations of international humanitarian law, either actual or imminent.

2 *Proper purpose.* The primary purpose of the military action must be to halt or avert the threat in question, even if other motives or purposes might also be involved, as they may well need to be to mobilize sceptical domestic political constituencies.

3 *Last resort.* Has every non-military option for meeting the threat in question been explored, with reasonable grounds existing for believing that other lesser measures than military coercion will not succeed? That does not mean waiting chronologically while every single other option is actually explored; rather, it means being satisfied that if other options were in fact used, they would not be successful in meeting the threat.

4 *Proportionality.* The scale, duration and intensity of the proposed military action must be the minimum necessary to meet the threat in question.

5   *Balance of consequences.* Is there a reasonable chance of the military action actually succeeding in meeting the threat in question, with the consequences of the action not being likely to be worse the consequences of inaction? This criterion is always likely to generate particularly intense argument, but getting it right is of great importance, as events in Iraq have shown all too clearly.

It is important to appreciate that these five criteria of legitimacy are both enabling and restricting. Pacifist streams of thought will tend to focus on the first characterization, claiming that anything which gives encouragement to military action in any circumstances will be for that very reason problematic. On the other hand, a response one hears from Washington and elsewhere is that these criteria are too restrictive and if really applied, they would remove our capacity for free-ranging action of the kind sometimes necessary.

The real world in which we live demands a set of criteria that are both enabling and restricting, that enable the choice to be made in each case as to which is the appropriate way to go. There can be no push-button certainty about the results when you apply these criteria in any given situation. Reasonable men and women, and even reasonable members of the Security Council, may differ on occasion as to the relevance of these criteria to a particular situation. The only claim that ICISS made is that to have such criteria – hopefully, adopted formally as guidelines by the Security Council, supported by the General Assembly – will maximize the chances of consensus on the Security Council. When policy-makers are forced to address these criteria and respond publicly to questions about them, there is a better chance of obtaining a marriage of minds on this subject than has been the case in the past. Furthermore, there will be a much greater chance of maximizing support in the wider international community for whatever decision the Security Council takes if these criteria are seen to be systematically applied and applied in good faith. And, as a corollary, there will be less of a chance that the Security Council is bypassed by states taking action on their own.

There is obviously much to argue about and discuss on the language of these criteria, and on the whole concept of the responsibility to protect as it has evolved. I think the truth of the matter is that there is no competing model, no alternative conceptualization, no alternative refined policy discourse, which gets us closer to resolving these issues than the concept of the responsibility to protect. So my plea to this very influential organization is this: please recognize the utility of the concept and do your best to maintain the momentum of its evolution, not merely as a talking point in international discourse but as an actual accepted norm, and ultimately as an accepted and enforceable rule of international law.

The Ethics of Protection

Konrad Raiser

The topic of this seminar has a certain history in ecumenical discussion. It is recalled in the report to the 2003 meeting of the WCC Central Committee and there is no need to repeat this summary. What should be underlined, however, is the fact that we witness a remarkable shift of focus in the international debate with far-reaching implications. The debate began in response to the experience of the tragic conflicts both in Africa (Somalia and Rwanda) and in Europe (Bosnia, Kosovo, Chechnya). The immediate spark was provided by the report of the Panel on United Nations Peace Operations (Brahimi Report) and by the urgent pleas coming from the Secretary General of the UN for a new approach to the issue of 'humanitarian intervention'. The WCC in its 2001 study paper on 'The protection of endangered populations in situations of armed violence: toward an ecumenical ethical approach' expressed reservations regarding the very concept of humanitarian intervention and argued in favour of reshaping and clarifying the terms of the debate 'in a way that would emphasize the fundamental ethical issues at stake'. This led the WCC to focus on the 'protection of endangered populations' with special emphases on prevention and just peacemaking.

While discussions within the WCC were taking shape, the Canadian government took the initiative to form the International Commission on Intervention and State Sovereignty, which placed the responsibility to protect as a shared concern at the centre of the debate. What had been suggested in a tentative way in the WCC study, through the work of this Commission has become a fully developed framework for political and legal considerations. Indeed, in an impressive way the Commission has succeeded fundamentally to reshape the terms of the debate. This becomes evident in reading the report of the High Level Panel on Threats, Challenges and Change which was presented to the Secretary General in November 2004. Without much further argument it simply takes for granted the shift of perspective from the rights inherent in state sovereignty to the responsibility of states under the Charter of the United Nations:

> Whatever perceptions may have prevailed when the Westphalian system first gave rise to the notion of State sovereignty, today it clearly caries with it the obligation of a State to protect the welfare of its own people and meet it obligations to the wider international community ... What we seek to protect reflects what we value. The Charter of the United Nations seeks to protect all States, not because they are intrinsically good but because they are necessary to achieve the dignity, justice, worth and safety of their citizens. These are the values that are at the heart of any collective security system for the twenty-first century.

What we encounter here is more than a shift of terminology from rights to responsibilities, from intervention to protection, and from the interests of states to the concerns of citizens, of the people. At the centre of this shift stands a new interpretation of sovereignty which reflects the deepening of the concept of human rights and the progressive development of an international rule of law based on the universality of human rights. The ICISS report has successfully overcome the dilemma inherent in the Charter of the United Nations and which had for a long time blocked the efforts of the UN effectively to provide for the security of all peoples and to 'save succeeding generations from the scourge of war': the tension between the prohibition of intervention into the internal affairs of sovereign states (Article 2.7) and the affirmation of the universal validity of human rights and the recognition that the observance of human rights and fundamental freedoms for all is essential for international peace (Articles 1.3 and 55c). Neither the Charter nor the Universal Declaration on Human Rights provided the United Nations with appropriate instrumentalities and with the authority judicially to pursue violations of human rights. Only the Convention against Genocide of 1948 placed an obligation on the member states to prevent and to punish genocidal actions as a crime under international law.

Meanwhile, the Human Rights Pacts of 1966 and especially the optional protocol to the pact on civil and political rights, together with a series of further human rights instruments, have considerably extended the responsibilities of states and governments to observe and to make provisions for the implementation of human rights as the minimal requirements of a just and peaceful order of human society. In addition to this framework of human rights instruments, reference needs to be made to the conventions of international humanitarian law, in particular the Geneva Conventions and the additional protocols which establish rules under international law for parties engaged in conflict. Most recently the creation of the International Criminal Court has further strengthened the sense of obligation and accountability of states and of their leaders under the international rule of law. Even individuals can now be brought before a court of justice for crimes against humanity.

A similar development has taken place in the understanding of security. The primary security concern among the founders of the United Nations was state security. Since then, understanding of peace and security has undergone significant change. Thus, the report of the Palme Commission in 1982 introduced the notion of common security, emphasizing that the security of one nation cannot be defended at the expense of the security of others. The growing recognition that respect for human rights is a fundamental condition for a lasting peace has since then led to the introduction of the concept of human security. The reports of ICISS and the Commission on Human Security (2003) have given official recognition to this perspective. In the words of ICISS: 'Human security means the security of people – their physical safety, their economic and social well-being, respect for their dignity and worth as human beings, and the protection of their human rights and fundamental freedoms'. Lately, the HLP has acknowledged:

> The biggest security threats we face now, and in the decades ahead, go far beyond States waging aggressive war. They extend to poverty, infectious disease and environmental degradation; war and violence within States; the spread and possible use of nuclear, radiological, chemical and biological weapons; terrorism; and transnational organized crime. The threats are from non-State actors as well as States, and to human security as well as State security.

The agenda for peace and security, therefore, extends far beyond the traditional concern for the military means to defend state security. State security and human security have to be seen as interdependent.

By means of this development the responsibility to protect has been given a clear focus: what is at stake is the human security of all people everywhere. It is a truly universal responsibility. The Report of the Track on 'Human Security' as part of the Helsinki Process on Globalization and Democracy, issued under the title 'Empowering people at risk' (2005) declares:

States have obligations, legal and moral, to respect, protect and fulfil human rights and human security within and outside their territories ... Global interdependence has altered the meanings of state sovereignty. For the exercise and protection of human rights, sovereignty now accommodates transnational obligations – rooted in the Universal Declaration of Human Rights and manifested, for instance, in the jurisdiction of the International Criminal Court ... These trends signal the globalization of the responsibility to protect. And they mark the emergence of new forms of global governance, to advance human rights and human security more justly and more reliably through cooperation. This is the security diplomacy in the service of an obligation we all share – to empower people at risk.

The reports of both ICISS and the HLP point out that through the process of globalization the threats to human security have multiplied and many can no longer be met effectively through the efforts of individual states and governments acting alone. Nevertheless, the primary responsibility to protect the security of people rests with the respective government. In fact, the capacity of a government to provide for the human security of its citizens has to be considered as the fundamental source of its legitimacy internally and for the international recognition of its claim to sovereignty. Good governance in the sense of an accountable and democratic exercise of state power and authority has become a basic requirement for both the security of a state and the human security of its citizens. Since, however, the threats to human security – and by implication also to state security – extend beyond the borders of individual states and their capacity for responsible action, the responsibility to protect becomes an obligation for the international community as a whole. The threats of poverty, infectious disease and environmental degradation, as well as the threats of terrorism, the proliferation of small arms, of human trafficking and organized crime, require transnational cooperation within the framework of a collective security strategy as advocated by the HLP. In this perspective, development is to be considered as the indispensable foundation for a collective security system that takes prevention seriously:

It helps combat the poverty, infectious disease and environmental degradation that kill millions and threaten human security. It is vital in helping States prevent or reverse the erosion of State capacity, which is crucial for meeting almost every class of threat. And it is part of a long-term strategy for preventing civil war, and for addressing the environments in which both terrorism and organized crime flourish.

The recognition of the responsibility to protect not only shifts the focus from the traditional concern about state security to the human security of the citizens; even more specifically it aims at people at risk. Under the conditions of globalization the potential exposure to risk has dramatically increased for all people. In fact, today more than ever before, we are obliged to acknowledge that vulnerability is part of the basic human condition. All efforts to safeguard human security must reckon with this fundamental human exposure to risk. And more specifically, the condition of globalization and interdependence has implications for understanding the relationship between security and vulnerability. The recognition of mutual vulnerability can become the basis for cooperative security arrangements which recognize the legitimate security interests of the potential adversary, as was the case during the final stages of the Cold War. Also, concern for human security in the broader sense could draw strength from the acknowledgement of vulnerability. Contrary to common perception, dependency and vulnerability are not necessarily marks of weakness, but the decisive indicators for recognizing life in relationships. The open recognition of human vulnerability leads towards favouring cooperative solutions to security threats instead of seeking to defend positions of power and individual interest. Acknowledging mutual vulnerability can engender trust, which is the precondition for security.

For the ethics of protection, however, it is the perspective of people who are actually at risk, who have become victims and are at the mercy of powers beyond their control, which should serve as the decisive reference point. Of course, the legislation and social security programmes of governments have to address generalized risks to human security. Police and the forces of public order are responsible for maintaining a general climate of public security. Ethical concerns arise when this general framework for human security breaks down and specific people or groups of the population find themselves exposed to threats to their basic human rights and their human security which are not addressed by the competent authorities. Under normal conditions such conflicts will come before the courts of law for judgement and decision. If the threat to human security is inherent in the legal order of the society itself, democratic constitutions provide for the possibility of changing the government through elections and thus to influence the process of legislation. Recent experience in several countries shows that people's experience of deprivation at the hands of autocratic and corrupt governments can become a source of collective will-power that is able even to change constitutionally elected authorities. The primary resource for responding to the requirements of human security is the determination of the people themselves. Empowering the people to take responsibility for their own security, therefore, becomes a central criterion for the ethics of protection.

However, the more critical situation arises when we deal with people or populations at risk that have become the victims of armed conflict within their own country and find themselves without any effective protection – unarmed civilians, especially women, children, old people and refugees or internally displaced people. The same is true for minority communities that are being violently persecuted because of their ethnic, religious or national affiliation. In a situation of state failure the risk increases dramatically for entire populations. The universal validity of human rights and the entitlement to fundamental human security calls for measures of protection. The ethics of protection can draw inspiration from the biblical tradition, which makes the protection of the weak and vulnerable, in particular the poor and aliens, widows and orphans, a fundamental obligation under the law given by God (see Exodus 22:20–26; Isaiah 1:17). In the Hebrew Bible, God is confessed as the protector of the weak and the powerless. In Psalm 82 God confronts those who claim godlike power with the basic demands of an ethic of protection: 'Give justice to the weak and the orphan; maintain the right of the lowly and the destitute. Rescue the weak and the needy; deliver them from the hand of the wicked.' But where they fail in their responsibility, they are told: 'You shall die like mortals and fall like any prince.' The arrogance of power is not protected from the basic vulnerability of mortality.

The responsibility to protect must never pretend to provide total security for all. The ethics of protection can be compared to the ethics of the medical profession. Its primary objective is to protect life and to avoid additional risk and harm. But even the most advanced medical skill cannot protect people from dying eventually. Medical intervention may address the immediate cause of a given illness, but it cannot provide a guarantee against a possible relapse. Important, therefore, as the search may be for the root causes of a given conflict that threatens the human security of people, the ethics of protection primarily calls for a response to the immediate risk, even though it may only be a symptom of a deeper unresolved conflict. It is directed to the people who are at risk now and who need immediate protection, while the root causes may have to be addressed later. And yet the response to the immediate need must not cause additional harm or pose additional risk; and, being aware of the more basic causes of the conflict, it must not create conditions in which addressing the root causes is avoided or becomes impossible. There are therefore different levels of acting on the responsibility to protect. The WCC study paper focuses on the issues of prevention of violent conflict, the question of an eventual failure of prevention and the task of just peacemaking. ICISS speaks of the responsibility to prevent, to react and to rebuild. The HLP deals first with the challenge of prevention and only then considers the potential use of force and the tasks of peace enforcement, peacekeeping and post-conflict peace-building, following the steps outlined in the earlier agenda for peace. The analogy with the medical approach is relevant here again: prevention is the most important strategy for health security; but there are clear professional criteria for reaction when prevention has failed, and treatment after an intervention or operation is an integral part of the medical responsibility.

Prevention of acute threats to human security, therefore, has to be seen as the primary form of exercising the responsibility to protect. The traditional preoccupation with state security has led the discussion to focus too quickly and too much on ways to prevent situations of armed conflict which threaten both state security and human security. The more basic concern with human security broadens the understanding of the responsibility to prevent. The Millenium Declaration adopted by the leaders of UN member states in 2000 identifies many of the threats to human security which can become the cause of violent conflict within or between states. From this perspective, national governments and the international community share a common responsibility in the areas of human sustainable development, health, education, labour, trade, etc., where human security is at risk even before any open conflict emerges. In particular, the international community has a responsibility to strengthen the capacities of individual governments to respond effectively to such threats to human security. This raises fundamental questions about the policies pursued by the international financial institutions, which have contributed to a weakening of the capacity of many governments to prevent a deterioration of the conditions for the human security of their citizens. Furthermore, the responsibility to prevent extends beyond the actions of governments and intergovernmental institutions. It includes the business sector as much as the broader network of civil society organizations. They can make an indispensable contribution to building a 'culture of prevention', to empower people at risk, and to help public action focus on areas susceptible to becoming sources of conflict.

Prevention as the primary expression of the responsibility to protect involves further the whole spectrum of political, diplomatic and legal responses to situations of acute risk to human security. They become important in situations where the respective state authorities are either unable or unwilling to respond in effective ways. Reference here needs to be made to the provisions of Chapter VI of the Charter of the United Nations and in particular to the role of the International Court of Justice with regard to the settlement of disputes and conflicts. The Charter, however, limits the competence of the organs of the UN to disputes which can become a threat to world peace and international security. Under normal circumstances, therefore, the response to civil conflicts, even when they escalate into armed violence, remains outside the competence of the UN. However, new instruments of response have been created within the framework of international human rights institutions (e.g. the despatching of fact-finding missions or the appointment of special rapporteurs). They have become important means for the international community to fulfil its responsibility to prevent. In many situations election monitoring has become an effective way of preventing tensions from escalating into open and violent confrontation. The African Union has developed the instrument of peer review among its member states and their governments, which could help to prevent an escalation of threats to human security. Mention should also be made of various non-governmental organizations like the International Crisis Group, Amnesty International, Human Rights Watch, the International Commission of Jurists and also many of the religious organizations which play an increasingly important role in the areas of early warning and conflict analysis. Finally, the study document of the WCC has drawn attention to the link between post-conflict settlement and prevention of further conflict. This concerns in particular the responsibility to overcome impunity by bringing the perpetrators of human rights violations to justice and to include clear human rights provisions in any peace accord. Lack of structures of accountability in the settlement of conflicts and disputes all too often becomes the source of new confrontation. The conclusion of this discussion in the ICISS report deserves full support:

> Underlying all the specifics, what is necessary is for the international community to change its basic mindset from a 'culture of reaction' to that of a 'culture of prevention'. To create such a culture will mean, as the Secretary General reminds us, 'setting standards for accountability of member states and contributing to the establishing of prevention practices at the local, national, regional and global levels'. It is a task long overdue.

However, even with the best intentions on all sides, prevention often has failed and will continue to fail to remove acute risks to human security. The responsibility to protect then takes on the form of direct intervention or reaction. There is no need here to review all the political, economic and judicial measures which are at the disposal of governments, regional organizations like the EU, OSCE, AU, OAS, etc., and the international community represented through the UN. Often, a preventive response can turn into direct intervention simply by using more coercive means like the imposition of sanctions, the sending of unarmed observers or the stationing of peacekeeping military units. The principles of an ethic of protection make it necessary to take a fresh look at the instrument of sanctions and their intended or unintended consequences for the people most at risk. But even where a more 'robust' use of force under Chapter VII of the Charter of the UN or according to the emerging norms and criteria as spelled out by ICISS and the HLP may be considered necessary, the ethics of protection imposes clear limitations. Many of the recent studies of the issues involved turn to the classical criteria of the theory of just war, since they provide valid precautionary principles which could be used to spell out an ethic of protection. It should be recalled that the original intent of this doctrine was to limit and reduce the recourse to war as a legitimate means of resolving interstate conflict; unfortunately, it has more often been used precisely to provide moral legitimation for the decision to respond with military means to violent conflict either within or between states. Since the primary objective of an intervention should be the protection of people or populations at risk, the choice of the means of intervention and of the rules of engagement for the military units involved becomes of crucial importance. They need to focus on a defensive stance, avoid provocative actions and minimize the risk of escalation. As much as possible they should protect the civil infrastructure and the economic viability of the country or territory concerned, since these are of essential importance for the people to regain the mastery of their own security. Particular care must be taken not to damage or destroy places of symbolic importance for the religious, cultural or national identity of the people concerned. Protective actions must be directed most of all towards those who have no means of protecting themselves: refugees and displaced people, and among them especially women, children and old people.

Any intervention which follows the ethics of protection must be concerned to reestablish and strengthen legitimate authorities and the rule of law in the country concerned, so as to transfer the responsibility for protection to them as soon as possible. An intervention therefore has multiple components: military, political, administrative, judicial and humanitarian. Their responsibilities are distinct and should not be placed under military control. Even the military component follows a logic that is closer to the role of police; their task is not to 'win' and to liquidate an enemy, but rather to stop armed violence and to bring to justice those responsible for acts of violence. While military units may be equipped to assist in humanitarian relief and reconstruction, it is of utmost importance that the humanitarian mandate of relief agencies not be confused with military requirements or interests. In any event, the use of military units must be part of a political strategy to restore peace and justice and should never become an end in itself. In the case of failing or failed states the international community must be prepared to assume temporarily the responsibility for civil order, as has happened in Kampuchea, Kosovo and East Timor. The aim should be to empower those who are recognized as credible leaders in the community to rebuild a viable order. All this means that the levels and phases of prevention, reaction and rebuilding do not simply follow each other; they flow into each other and the priorities for post-conflict rebuilding need to be clearly in perspective right at the beginning of any intervention

These considerations regarding an ethic of protection should ultimately find expression in new norms to be incorporated into the framework of international law. The reports by ICISS and the HLP discuss in detail the options available under the present Charter of the United Nations. While this discussion goes beyond the limited purpose of this presentation, it would seem important to underline in conclusion that the new focus on the responsibility to protect makes increased demands on the accountability of the actors involved. Whose interests are being served in deciding about the ways and means of response to situations of extreme risk to human security? Since the responsibility to protect has to be considered as a shared responsibility of the international community as a whole, the multilateral authority given to the Security Council provides at least a minimum of accountability for decisions. However, the Charter and its provisions in Chapter VII – including Article 51 – were formulated with the primary interest of protecting state security. The broadening of focus with the introduction of the criterion of human security will have to lead to a critical review and eventual recasting of the respective provisions. In addition, the Security Council should be obliged to submit the evidence which might serve as a basis for deciding about a form of intervention to a neutral body not involved in executive and operational decisions. Transparency and accountability are essential elements in the ethics of protection.

A Few General Comments

Ernie Regehr

Gareth Evans' strong defence of the ethic of the responsibility to protect reminded me of the way in which Ramesh Thakur, one of the members of the Commission on Intervention and State Sovereignty, characterized the threefold political dilemma that presents itself to the international community in trying to respond to victims of crimes against humanity. If I recall his comment correctly, the dilemma runs as follows:

- If we simply accept the primacy of national sovereignty and make no collective move to help the victims of crimes against humanity, we (the international community collectively) become complicit in those crimes that occur behind the inviolable shield of sovereignty.
- If we accept that sovereignty is not absolute, but insist that the international community must always, without exception, follow prescribed legal procedure (i.e. Security Council approval) in overruling sovereignty and in intervening to protect victims of such crimes, then the international community is destined to face ongoing paralysis. In such circumstances legal procedure is effectively privileged over the protection of people.
- But if the requirements for strict legality are set aside in order to intervene in the internal affairs of states to protect victims, such intervention will lack the legitimacy needed to make it effective and consistent.

We understand and recognize that legality – laws and procedures and a system of accountability – is itself a fundamental source of protection for people, communities and nations. We do well, therefore, to honour legal requirements and procedures in the name of protecting people. But there is obviously an extraordinary cold-heartedness in insisting that process trumps safety when people are suffering in extreme conditions. At the same time, we cannot know the full extent of the consequences of actions which run roughshod over the law; that is, the carefully constructed restraints on the actions of the powerful, in the name of what is understood to be in the crisis the greater good.

The dilemmas will continue, but what we can expect, and what we in the WCC need to encourage, is the long, slow process of modifying international and institutional behaviour in ways that gradually shift the emphasis of responsible action toward a primary responsibility to people who are clearly in grave peril. We need to work toward the recognition that the safety of people trumps the prerogatives of states. And, in saying that, we of course also have to remind ourselves that state structures are themselves sources of protection of people. At the moment, however, there is little doubt that the prerogatives of states are privileged over the needs of the vulnerable. One cannot help but be struck at how muted the political pressure to intervene in Darfur has been. In the West, a relatively small, interested public has called for action, but there has not been the kind of broad public response that there was, for example, in opposition to the invasion of Iraq.

I take the lack of a massive outpouring on Darfur to be a failure that must be placed particularly at the feet of civil society and religious communities. It is a failure that will have consequences, for the way in which we will change the international community's response to people in peril will not be by rewriting laws or passing resolutions, but by changes in behaviour. Behaviour is precedent setting, and the precedents set in Iraq and Darfur are not promising. We obviously need to start building consistent responses to people in peril and in the presence of crisis. And it is the special responsibility of civil society, not least of which is the church, to challenge the international community to be responsive at least to extraordinary need.

There is a very broad consensus building in support of the very high threshold for military action articulated in the ICISS report and then repeated in the HLP report. It is obviously appropriate that the threshold for military intervention be high, but I worry that we are also constructing a very high threshold for emergency action of any kind – a great deal of terror and catastrophe can slip under that very high bar. We are in danger of creating an international norm that requires response once we have passed a certain bar, but which is sanguine about responding to very high levels of violence because it hasn't reached this extraordinary bar. We also seem to be implicitly requiring what some have called a 'spike effect'; that is to say that there needs to be a very sharp increase in violence and victimization of people in order to get the attention of people. For instance, in Kosovo, that spike of activity existed, whereas in southern Sudan there were very few spikes in the levels of calamity but, in the face of the cumulative calamity of decades of humanitarian crisis, the international community was left largely unmoved and unengaged even though the human disaster surpassed all other examples, such as Rwanda, Kosovo and Somalia.

Discussion of military intervention in response to humanitarian crises must also include recognition of the very real limits to force. Indeed, the responsibility to protect principle sets out very minimalist objectives for intervention. In the extraordinary cases of military intervention, the objective is not to solve the problem, and certainly not to deal with the root causes that have created the crisis. It is the minimalist objective of bringing some immediate measure of safety to people. The parallel in a case of domestic violence would be to call the police and social workers to restrain an abuser or remove the vulnerable and house them in a shelter. That certainly does not solve the problem, but it brings some short-term protection. And it is in effect expressing some faith in other community and support services that can be brought in to deal with the more fundamental conditions that need changing in order to bring longer-term security to the victims of abuse.

Recognition of the very limited utility of military force is based on the understanding that the responsibility to protect doctrine that includes intervention for humanitarian purposes is not a system for the attempted military engineering or repair of societies, or for creating new social structures that are going to solve the problems. Conditions for sustainable security must surely be built, but they will not be built by intervening military forces. The responsibility to protect doctrine is confined to the limited but difficult task of attending to the immediate security and safety of the vulnerable. Longer-term security must come from other peace-building efforts. In domestic situations, we understand that the police have very limited roles: they are not social workers or pastors.

We need to think increasingly of developing automated (i.e. consistent) responses to particular kinds of conditions. When rates of child mortality rise above certain levels, for example, then there must be structures and systems in place to trigger appropriate investigative responses automatically. As more is learned and understood, other programmatic responses should kick in. The objective should be to have in place a set of escalating responses to emerging crises. Civil society and churches have the means to act as monitors of such things as human rights abuses and deteriorating conditions relating to basic human needs, followed by the mobilization of NGO and governmental responses.

The Christian Responsibility to Protect

Hugo Slim

Christ Calls Us to Protect

Time and again in the gospels, Christ calls us to protect one another. He encourages us to show mercy and to rescue. He also calls us to speak the truth about violence and to thirst for justice and righteousness for others. Christ leaves us in no doubt that we are called to speak and to act in order to protect one another and that in matters of protection there are no limits around who we should protect. Even those we feel least close to are to be recognized and protected as our neighbours.

In calling us in this way, Christ also alerts us in his teaching and in his own suffering and death that to do this may often involve sacrifice – taking the way of the cross. Finally, of course, Christ makes it known to us that, like the sheep and the goats, we will be judged on how we love and protect one another.

Christ Calls for Responsible Authority

The Christian commitment to the victims of violence is clear. What of the Christian response to perpetrators and those with the power to stop them – to enemies and authorities? This picks up on the second major moral dynamic in the R2P approach. If the first is to reach out and protect the victims, the second is to call those in power to their own responsibilities. Here, too, the gospel is in accord with R2P.

Christ makes it clear that we should love our enemies. In other words, we should love those who persecute us and others. In this way, Christ leaves us in no doubt that we have enemies, but he calls us to love them with God and to call them to their responsibilities in that same love. And, just as enemies are to be called and challenged, so too are authorities. In all his dealings with the authorities of his day, Christ showed that God expects power to be used lovingly and responsibly in the interests of everyone, most especially the poor and weak.

Christ Calls Us Into Conflict

Christians understand that conflict and violence are integral to the world as it is and that following Christ often means moving further into conflict. Christ knows that he asks this of his followers and, as Christians, we know that we cannot avoid conflict. Here, too, R2P's third main moral insistence on the importance of intervention and international action finds much resonance with Christianity. Avoidance of conflict as we live the gospel is not possible. Gospel action often means moving deeper into a conflict rather than away from it.

Reflecting on Particular R2P Themes

Gospel resonance with these three key moral demands of the R2P approach – protection, responsibility and action – means that as a Christian I can agree deeply with the moral basis of the R2P document and with the presentations we have heard today. Other R2P themes also struck me as I listened and it may be worth reflecting on their Christian significance.

The Gospel and Sovereignty

R2P gives great emphasis to sovereignty and to primary state responsibility. In line with current international relations and human rights norms, it demands that states take lead responsibility for solving their own problems and determining their own just futures. This is essentially the hard doctrine of self-determination that people must find their own freedom.

This is a problematic doctrine much open to abuse – either by a perpetrating state which feels protected from outside interference, or by outside states who can feel relieved of responsibility and act neglectfully as a result. But, importantly, R2P argues for a mitigation of the harshest doctrine of sovereignty. Sovereignty and self-determination must be respected, but not at any price.

In his dealings with people, Christ placed a similar emphasis on the sovereignty of the individual and his or her self-determination. He never forced anyone to change, but rather called them to change or helped them directly when they asked for it. This gospel call to responsible personal sovereignty and assisted self-determination can be applied internationally by the church. In its advocacy, both loud and soft, the church can similarly call states to their responsibilities and call peoples to determine a just future of their own. But, equally, it can also help them practically when they ask for it. This makes the notions of the call on authorities, the challenge to violence, the requests of victims and the assistance of outsiders critical to any development of church doctrine on the protection of civilians.

The Gospel, Political Will and Effective Action

Christianity has much to say about volition, capacity and prudence, which are usually at the heart of international discussion of intervention. Much of the political debate about protection agonizes and disputes around what should be done, what can be done and what it is wise to do. Typically, different parties exaggerate or play down the feasibility of interventions as befits their interests. Quite rightly, a great part of this international discussion turns on what is practical, possible and prudent in a highly compromised political world.

Christians are especially mindful of sin and incapacity in their understanding of the world, constantly relying on grace, love and forgiveness in their own lives. We know how often we fail, avoid our responsibilities or face genuine difficulties in meeting them because of our own fallenness, the sins of others or the simple brokenness of the human world around us. The church must recognize this as true in the political realm as well and must not make absurdly idealistic demands of politicians, organizations and situations in its pain for the suffering of others and a sense that something must be done. It must be attentive to the prudential calculations of potential interveners and respectful of the hard choices, competing priorities and risks they usually face in political confrontation and the use of force.

Being realistic in this way need not mean being a bystander. In any political discussions around protecting and rescuing civilians, the church needs to be compassionate and encouraging in the face of genuine difficulties. It needs also to be practical in always trying to negotiate and reveal real possibilities for effective action. And it must also be uncompromising in unmasking denial, mistaken priorities or hidden interests in policy-making over people's lives.

In particular, when recommending action, the church should always be wary of the sword and scrutinize the resort to arms before they are taken up and as they are being used. The church needs always to be alert to the dangerous momentum that arms can develop – the tendency to breed a permissive and ingrained culture of violence once it is applied in a given context. As such, the church needs always to be alive and open to other ways of rescuing and protecting, while making clear demands for the careful limiting of force whenever it is applied as a means of protection.

In short, the church should actively and creatively argue for people's protection, but should not be surprised if mixed motives, lack of capacity, fear, carelessness, mistakes, discrimination and neglect continue to characterize human attempts to love and protect one another.

Christ and the Continuum

R2P is determined in seeing protection across a continuum that reaches well before and after an emergency response or rescue towards prevention and reconstruction. This continuum is easily embraced within the church's mission. Christ offers hope and comfort before, during and after the worst of times. In the gospel, he seeks to call people away from disaster before it happens, to be with them as they suffer and to remake lives anew after they have been shattered.

The church too must be present throughout the continuum of human suffering and renewal. It can join in R2P's concern for prevention by proclaiming a warning and empowering all concerned in the ways of love and goodness – both those at risk of suffering and those at risk of perpetrating. It can stand beside people in the moment of their catastrophe, eating and mixing with the victims of this world, speaking truth into a conflict with words of blessing to those who suffer and words of woe to those who make them suffer. It can recognize and challenge people's enemies while preaching the gospel of love, so risking suffering itself and enduring the way of the cross alongside others. And after the devastation, it can preach and practise healing, justice, redress and forgiveness – daring to share the unlikely news of the risen Christ.

Christ and Consequences

Not surprisingly, much R2P discussion and deliberation is about the consequences of international action or inaction. The way of the cross and the good news of the resurrection does not teach Christians to think particularly logically or lineally about actions and consequences. We do not expect to be able to predict what good or ill will come from particular actions or situations. Neither do Christians expect perfection in the means and events of this world. Instead, the gospel teaches us to live with continuing contradictions, ambiguity and imperfections.

Not surprisingly, therefore, the church can never expect to enjoy total satisfaction in any international response – whether it is the use of force or a major humanitarian operation to rescue and protect. Any such intervention will also have difficult and damaging consequences alongside the good it secures. The perfect option is not likely to present itself on earth.

The church will never be able to regard a forceful military intervention or massive humanitarian influx with sheer joy and relief. Each will bring shadows of its own. Military actions will mean new deaths as well as lives saved. All kinds of invasive international action can bring new humiliations as well as protection. An influx of international duty-bearers can bring real problems for self-determination and can paradoxically obscure the place and power of rights-holders in certain situations. Helping people is a difficult and often ambiguous business. Being helped can be complex too.

The Gospel, Risk and Vulnerability

Christians know that we cannot guarantee protection or peace in this world. We can only work and hope for them. Christ teaches us that although we are dearly loved and known by God, we can never truly live without risk, vulnerability and suffering in this world.

This Christian knowledge is perhaps the most difficult of all for the church to express amid the protection debate. In a real but difficult sense, protection and peace remain eschatological for Christians: they are things for which we long and hope. Knowing what we know about Christ's own death we cannot expect our world to be a different one to that in which God himself was unprotected, tortured and killed. Yet, knowing what we know about Christ's resurrection, we know that extraordinary things are possible here on earth and that it is our place to hope for them and to recognize and encourage them when they happen.

This gospel faith means that, as Christians, we cannot share the rationalist assumption and hope in the R2P approach that if only the world can get the criteria, the means, the international organizations and the public support in place then people will not perpetrate and suffer as they do. For Christians, human problems and solutions are not just about mechanics, but about suffering and love, faith and hope, death and resurrection.

This is perhaps a fundamental difference between the gospel and the rationalist aspiration of the R2P project. But there is a danger that, when voiced, this Christian view can be heard not as religious insight but as fatalism and inaction – which it is not. Christian realism in international relations needs to be understood by the church, but expressed carefully, compassionately and constructively. It should never stop the church from trying actively to protect people, but it inevitably does so in a different context – a different cosmology perhaps than the United Nations and the states who are its members.

A Reaction from Africa

M. K. Stephen

It is important for some of us church leaders from the South to add our voices, particularly in the light of our recent experiences. In the last two decades the continent of Africa has witnessed extreme forms of violence, armed conflicts, inter-ethnic armed confrontations, religious violence, 'ethnic cleansing' and in a few cases, genocide. These various forms of violence and conflict result in large-scale loss of life and property. Communities that once lived in peace have become virtual enemies.

Africa has had more than its fair share of wars and violent conflicts, and one wonders whether there is a reasonable basis for generalizing about the causes of these wars. Undoubtedly, each of the war-ridden countries has its sociological peculiarities, but it is also a fact that all African countries are artificial creations of European colonialism, and are similarly affected by the scourge of cultural pluralism, ethnic rivalry, material pauperization, and the congenital corruption of the ruling elite. In addition, all African countries are affected by a hostile international environment dominated by political blocs whose policies toward Africa are remarkable for their inconsistencies, incoherence and condescension. Thus, those of us from the South (particularly from Sub-Saharan Africa) constantly come face to face with the kinds of situations that often raise many issues requiring careful theological and ethical analysis.

Unfortunately, the speed at which these events occur and the ever changing political dynamics rob us of much needed time for proper reflection – reflection that could fashion a responsible ethical response that could affect the position of the leadership of the churches and political leadership of the state. For this reason, it has been difficult for the churches to act as salt in society and as light that can provide a way forward for various political institutions.

Thus, this discussion on the responsibility to protect is one of the major ways in which the World Council of Churches and other organizations can facilitate a careful examination of the major issues confronting our world today, so that they can be analysed on a theological, moral and ethical basis.

The subject remains a major concern for churches and similar institutions in Africa. The responsibility to protect is often seen as a shared responsibility and not the exclusive preserve of the state. The head of a family believes he has a responsibility to protect his family; similarly, the village or community head, and nothing is spared in the way of exercising this right. However, in modern societies, such responsibility belongs to the state, which is therefore expected to place very great emphasis on human protection. Where the state fails for some reason, each affected group within the state tends to take the law into its own hands, believing that it is only by this means that justice will be accomplished and human lives protected.

For Christians, however, who believe they are called to a ministry of just peacekeeping, this becomes a dilemma. How are they to understand the gospel imperatives, the command not to resist evil with evil (Matthew 5:39), to love our enemies (Luke 5:44; 6:27), those prophetic Old Testament passages warning us not to rely on force to defend ourselves against our enemies (Hosea 7:11; Isaiah 30:15–16), and other Old Testament passages expressing the vision of world peace (Isaiah 2:14; Micah 4:3–4)?

Some Christians believe that taking up arms in any form – even to protect endangered populations amid armed conflict – runs counter to biblical injunctions. However, there is some consensus among African theologians and church leaders that the theory of just peacemaking does not necessarily rule out the use of force as part of a comprehensive peacemaking strategy. This position is valued for its proactive nature and its overall intention to deaden the political urgency of war. It is also flexible in its practical prescriptions, as it recognizes the validity of diverse pathways to reconciliation. The pathways suggested by Stassen in the Religious Ethics Journal 26:2 (1998), 320, take on board the following:

1   Employing non-violent direct action.
2   Taking independent initiatives to reduce threat.
3   Using cooperative conflict resolution.
4   Acknowledging responsibility for conflict and injustice and seeking repentance and forgiveness.
5   Advancing democracy, human rights and religious liberty.
6   Fostering just and sustainable economic development.
7   Working with emerging cooperative forces in the international system.
8   Strengthening the United Nations and international efforts for cooperation and human rights.
9   Reducing offensive weapons and the weapons trade.
10   Encouraging grassroots peacemaking groups and voluntary associations.

In the light of recent experiences and the call by many Christians caught up in religious crises, the position of just peacemaking tends to be preferred because it allows the use of armed force in extreme situations. It is acknowledged, however, that the responsibility to protect does not guarantee total protection or security. The use of force should be applied only by those designated by the state to perform such functions and only for the purpose of bringing perpetrators to justice.

Where a nation's ability to maintain peace and order fails in the face of uncontrolled violence, it becomes necessary for the international community to act: first, by mobilizing domestic political opinion so as to be able to secure broad-based understanding of the domestic situation; second, by mobilizing international political will for action – military action as a last resort, or other forms of action that can guarantee human protection. Whatever action is taken, it must be in accordance with the doctrine of human protection operations established by the International Commission on Intervention and State Sovereignty.

There are still many within the church who believe that the best form of protection for society and its people is through the enthronement of economic justice by means of the promotion of communal values. The armed conflict in the Niger delta region of Nigeria, for example, derives basically from a perceived lack of economic justice: throughout the area there are manifestations of poverty and material deprivation. This is a negation of koinonia, which seeks to promote justice and righteousness.

The responsibility to protect must therefore embrace some core elements already identified, among them the responsibility to prevent. There ought to be mechanisms in place to assist states to identify the root causes of conflicts that threaten human populations and which usually pave the way for violence. Poverty, for instance, forces people to make decisions out of desperation; poverty accentuates existential fears and exposes people's vulnerability. No nation can enjoy its citizens' loyalty when basic human needs and human rights are not protected. It is important to identify and protect people's social and economic rights.

The prompt and immediate response by the international community to the compelling human need following the recent tsunami in South Asia is one example of global action to protect human life. The deployment of military personnel was solely for the purpose of saving lives. Actions such as these can only lead to reconciliation and the furtherance of world peace.

However, this example of military intervention is completely different to situations such as those in Liberia and Sierra Leone. While it can be a justified form of intervention in order to protect, the aftermath of military operations often poses serious challenges for reconstruction, recovery and reconciliation. More often than not, resources are easily found when armed intervention becomes necessary as a last resort, but they are very hard to come by for post-conflict reconstruction. Thus, it is important to remember that the responsibility to protect is best served by the responsibility to prevent.

Five Comments to the Session

Thierry Tardy

My first point is about the continuum of responses implied by the concept of the responsibility to protect. Gareth Evans has stressed that the responsibility to prevent is as important as the military intervention component of the concept. Conceptually, I accept that prevention is as important as military intervention. In policy terms, it should be as important. Yet, in practice, my feeling as an observer is that despite all the efforts to put the prevention issue at the forefront, it is still the military intervention component which seems to be the most important, the element that questions a state's policy the most, the element that puts them in front of their responsibilities much more than the prevention issue. Prevention failed in Rwanda in 1994 and in Srebrenica in 1995, but when we look at these two examples, implicitly what we deplore is the fact that there were no robust military interventions to stop the killings and the massive violations of human rights. In order for it to be accepted, the concept has to be presented in a holistic, comprehensive way. But again in practice, it is extremely difficult not to focus on the military issue underlined by the concept.

My second point is the following. When we examine the concept of the responsibility to protect we see three different issues:

1   *The purpose of a possible intervention, its objectives.* Here it is more or less clear that it has to be established on humanitarian grounds: it has to stop massive violations of human rights, to respond to conscience-shocking situations.

2   *The norm, the framework of a possible intervention, its legality.* This should come from a Security Council resolution, and its legitimacy should derive from the criteria that have to be met. Here again, it is more or less clear what we mean by this.

3   *The question of who is intervening, who is implementing the concept.* Who protects when a given state fails to protect its own people? This raises the question of who comprises the international community. One has to ask which of the states among the 191 member states of the UN are able (if not willing) to implement the concept. I guess there are not much more than four to six of them, and most of the time they come from the North and the West. It is not possible to look at the concept of the responsibility to protect without also looking at the policies of potential intervening states. If we talk about military interventions, then we have to talk about military capacities. Who has the ability to project forces and power? The US, UK, France and Italy; maybe Canada, Australia in East Timor – but not many more countries. Have they the political will to act, the propensity to act? I think there is a missing link in the report at this point. How can we enhance the political will of these states to implement the concept?

The third point is about the tension between what the responsibility to protect implies (i.e. the necessity to protect people who are threatened – that is, the liberal approach/agenda) and the necessity of states to serve more narrowly defined security interests. Those two sets of agendas or interests may coincide. I guess they are two sides of the same coin. But they may not coincide.

The responsibility to protect concept will only be implemented if these two sides do coincide: if the necessity to protect as an interest of the potential intervening state coincides with the necessity to serve more narrowly defined interests. This convergence is likely to be very rare. In Darfur, the convergence is not there yet. There is clearly a necessity to protect in Darfur: the concept needs to be implemented. But the broader strategic interests of the potential intervening state are not there: there are other interests at stake that may prevent implementation of the concept. That is the issue of mixed motives. To take other examples: the convergence was not there in Rwanda; it is not there in Chechnya; in Kosovo, maybe it was there, but unfortunately there was no legality to the operation; the EU–French operation in Bunia in the Democratic Republic of Congo in the summer of 2003 can be seen as close to an implementation of the concept, even if neither France nor the European Union invoked it. But there was a willingness to stop – to a certain extent – massive violations of human rights. However, here again, I guess some mixed motives explained the French intervention.

The fourth point concerns the importance of the norm and whether it constrains states if it is adopted. This is not a recent question. In a way, norms constrain states. They shape their national interests. They act as a framework, as a constraint integrated into decision-making processes. One cannot easily ignore them, especially in Western states, which are perhaps watched more than others. And it may actually help advocacy institutions to do their job when a norm is there: by pointing to the norm, they can put states in front of their responsibilities.

If some states are reluctant to have the norm adopted, they probably believe that such norms do play a role. On the other hand, whatever the norm says, the right of people to be protected is unlikely to create a duty to intervene. There might be a moral or legal duty, but I am more sceptical about the actual practical duty of potential intervening states to implement the norm when faced with conscience-shocking situations. Thus, the implementation of the norm may be extremely limited. It is very difficult to think of instances where such a norm or principle has been implemented. This leads us back to the constant tension between the liberal and realist paradigms.

Fifthly, there is the question of the manipulation of the norm. States might invoke it to pursue other interests. They may have a hidden agenda. It is a well-known risk. We partly saw that in Iraq, when the US only invoked humanitarian grounds after the operation, not prior to it. Whenever a norm is manipulated, it suffers a direct blow. Imagine the US invoking humanitarian grounds to strike at North Korea. How many people would believe in its stated motives?

When looking at conscience-shocking situations and the concept of the responsibility to protect, what is to be feared is more abstention, with a state's indifference rather than its self-interest manipulating the norm. The general risk with the norm lies more in its non-implementation – states refusing to intervene in a given state to stop the fighting or to protect the people, rather than states manipulating the norm to invade another country. (I admit that as far as the US is concerned, we can discuss that element. But let's set aside the US for now.) The likelihood that states would manipulate the norm to do something else is not that high. The risk lies more in their indifference than in their self-interest.

Notes on the Just War Tradition

Sturla J. Stålsett

The just war tradition is a body of ethical reflection on the justifiable use of force which aims at limiting the resort to force by clarifying when force may be used (jus ad bellum) and restraining damage done by military forces during war (jus in bello). In other words the tradition begins with a strong presumption against the use of force and establishes the conditions when this presumption may be overridden for the sake of preserving the kind of peace which protects human dignity and human rights.

The name is misleading, as it implies a licence to kill. It would better be called something like 'tradition on legitimate or justifiable use of coercive power in international affairs'. This brief presentation look at some key moments in the historical development of the main criteria of the just war tradition.

Thoughts on the moral restriction of warfare have pre-Christian origins. There are elements in both Plato and Aristotle that later developed into the tradition on the just war (iustum bellum). Aristotle was the first to use this concept. What is to be considered a just war evidently depends on the understanding of justice. For Plato, for instance, justice was that which rightfully 'becomes' or 'belongs to' a person. A just order could therefore be strongly hierarchical and stratified, as we know from his vision of the ideal society. Based on Plato's understanding of justice it became possible for Aristotle to argue that it could even be considered just to wage a war aimed at forcing certain people into slavery, since this was considered to be their destiny, that which rightfully became them. They would be 'natural slaves'. In the sixteenth century such reasoning was used by Juan de Sepulveda in defence of the Spanish war against the indigenous peoples of the New World.

The concept of justice has often been linked to a determined understanding of natural law, but the specific content of this understanding has varied. For Plato, seeking a stable peace was a great good. The possibility of reconciliation with the enemy after a war had to be kept open. The Roman thinker Cicero gave the concept of just war a more juridical interpretation. Warfare could only be just if the enemy was guilty. The purpose of the war had to be taking back stolen goods, be it property or rights. Based on this reasoning, Cicero developed several criteria for a just war, two of which have had lasting significance: (1) warfare must have a just cause; and (2) only the emperor had the right authority to go to war.

Ambrose was the first Christian theologian to introduce this concept, but it was really only when Augustine further developed his teacher's ideas that a distinct Christian doctrine of the just war was developed. The problem of how to relate to warfare as Christians had of course become urgent in a different matter when Emperor Constantine I made Christianity the religion of the Roman Empire. To Augustine, the issue became even more urgent because of what he saw as the threat from the 'barbarians'. How could a more permissive Christian attitude to participating in war be developed without directly contradicting the Sermon on the Mount? The answer to this was found both in turning ethics 'inwards' by placing primary emphasis on personal attitudes, and by relating to the tradition of the just war. The attitude of the Christian should be determined by the greatest Christian virtues: love (caritas) and justice. Going to war has to be grounded in love, and can therefore only happen with the recta intentio (right intention) – in Augustine's view, to restore peace, and with a right or just cause, that the enemy has violated justice. Where justice is violated there is a need for punishment and retribution. Only in that way can justice be upheld, according to Augustine. A war that was aimed at taking revenge for injustice could be a just war, but it had to be conducted in a rightful manner. Only a political authority (the emperor) could decide to go to war (auctoritas principis) and only soldiers could wage war. Furthermore, the classic rules for warfare had to be upheld.

Thomas Aquinas took up Augustine's three main conditions for going to war (ius ad bellum): just cause, right intention and right authority. But he gave them a twist in the direction of consequential ethics, which gradually opened the way for offensive wars if these are considered to promote a good. Here, the teleological bent of Aristotelian ethics clearly comes through. When Aquinas introduced the distinction between the intended result of an action (e.g. defending oneself) and its unintended side-effects (e.g. killing one or more other persons), and showed less interest in the actual way in which war was conducted (the jus in bello), the doctrine of the just war could begin to be used to justify aggressive wars, crusades and even brutal coercive conversion to Christianity. During the Middle Ages such wars (even under the leadership of the pope) were at times justified by the aim to promote the good (i.e. the will of God). The just war clearly became holy war, too.

This classic doctrine on the just war, iustum bellum, was well known to Martin Luther and the other reformers. It is therefore highly possible that it is this tradition that is meant in Article XVI of the Augsburg Confession, where it says that Christians are permitted to (liceat) conduct or participate in war according to what is right or just (iure bellare). On the basis of his teaching about the two reigns or regimes of the secular and the spiritual, Luther could accept the teaching on just war, but in comparison to contemporary Catholic theologians he restricted some of its criteria. He rejected any ethical legitimacy for holy wars or crusades: no one should wage war in the name of Christ. He also rejected aggressive wars: only defensive wars could be just (Wer Krieg anfähet, der ist unrecht). In this, the emerging state system and its emphasis on territorial borders was an important new development. It was only by defending its territory with the purpose of upholding law and justice that the authority could wage a just war. Thus Luther made the requirements for justifiable warfare more strict. The criteria were also gradually turned in a juridical direction.

The doctrine of just war was further discussed and developed by the Spanish Catholic theologians Fransisco Vitoria (1493–1546) and Fransisco Suarez (1548–1617) of the Salamanca school, in the context of the Spanish conquest of Las Americas. The Dutch scholar Hugo Grotius (1583–1645) made an important advance in a juridical direction with his famous De jure belli ac Pacis. Later developments can be summarized by means of two criteria. First, any warfare has to be last resort. All peaceful means must have failed before war can be a justifiable option. Secondly, the proportionality criterion, requiring that the predictable costs and negative consequences of the war should not be greater than the value of what is being defended.

In spite of differences and variations, there is enough common ground in the history of the concept for it to be seen as a tradition on the justifiable use of coercive force, with the following criteria:

1   *Jus ad bellum.* Whether lethal force may be used is governed by the following criteria:
- Just cause
- Legitimate authority
- Right intention (objective/subjective)

- Probability of success
- Proportionality
- Last resort

2   *Jus in bello*. This is a restraint on armed combat between contending parties. It imposes the following moral standards for the conduct of armed combat:

- Discrimination or non-combatant immunity
- Proportionality
- Respect for international and humanitarian law

These criteria have an important role in both the ICISS report and the High Level Panel report. In our study document 'Vulnerability and security' (Church of Norway), we also made use of these criteria for assessing the possibility of humanitarian intervention. Although there will and should be continued critical debate on the content and applicability of these criteria, their relevance for the ethical and political challenges of our day seems clear.

REFERENCES

Stålsett, Sturla J. 1999. 'Med rett til å intervenere?' Kirke og kultur 104(5/6): 481–97.
Stålsett, Sturla J. 2004. 'Med rett til å angripe? Etisk vurdering av forkjøpsangrep og preventiv krigføring.' Pacem 7(1).
Walzer, Michael. 2000. Just and Unjust Wars: A Moral Argument with Historical Illustrations. 3rd edn. New York: Basic Books.
Yoder, John Howard. 1996. When War is Unjust: Being Honest in Just-War Thinking. 2nd edn. Maryknoll, NY: Orbis.

WEB RESOURCES

'A More Secure World: Our Shared Responsibility.' The Secretary-General's High-Level Panel on Threats, Challenges, and Change. United Nations, 2004. www.un.org/secureworld/.
'The Responsibility to Protect.' Report of the International Commission on Intervention and State Sovereignty. www.iciss.ca/pdf/Commission-Report.pdf.
Stålsett, Sturla J., Raag Rolfsen, Karin Dokken, and Hans Morten Haugen. 2002. 'Vulnerability and Security: Current Challenges in Security Policy from an Ethical and Theological Perspective.' Expanded version of the Norwegian 'Sårbarhet og sikkerhet' (2000). Oslo: Church of Norway. www.kirken.no/engelsk/VULNERABIL.doc.

Christianity and War: The Pacifist View

Arnold Neufeldt-Fast

In recent years, the awareness of past abuses of just war theory and practice, the greatly increased destructiveness of war, and the desire to be faithful to the witness of the gospel accounts of Jesus Christ have helped make Christian pacifism an attractive option for many Christians of non-pacifist traditions.

At the same time, however, there are significant factors that have made pacifism difficult for non-pacifist Christians: 'the concern to liberate, defend or preserve the neighbour from oppression, evil and death – using the sword if necessary – out of love for the neighbour, renders pacifism difficult for non-pacifist Christians'[1]. It is precisely the affliction of the other in situations of overwhelming evil that also makes the non-pacifist approach attractive and tempting to Christian pacifists concerned with justice. Those of both traditions wish to follow Jesus faithfully, but the pacifist position raises suspicion if the desire for faithfulness is understood more as purity than as responsibility.

In this regard the joint response from the perspective of the Historic Peace Churches to the WCC document 'The protection of endangered populations in situations of armed violence: toward an ecumenical approach' begins with a confession of complicity:

> We have often failed to live up to our commitment to the Spirit of Jesus Christ. We have often been silent and failed to act on behalf of those who are suffering the scourge of injustice and violence. We do not always know exactly what constitutes justice – or peace – in any given situation; we lack wisdom in addressing the complex issues of our time.[2]

The responsibility to protect also provides a specific challenge to Christians who espouse a pacifist approach to violent conflict. Does a consistent Christian pacifist approach – which places faithfulness above efficacy – take seriously the Christian responsibility for the protection of endangered populations in situations where armed violence is a reality? What experience or wisdom do the Historic Peace Churches bring to this question?

It has become abundantly clear that in our present deliberations we are dealing with very difficult and perplexing questions. These questions demand that we as churches respond with our own best theological and ethical wisdom; that is, as churches, so as not to simply repeat what other NGOs or governmental agencies could say just as well or better. This is the kind of service which the community of churches owes the world.

Though it has been persuasively argued that the church was largely a peace church in the first three centuries of the Christian movement[3], the term 'Historic Peace Churches' (HPC) is of recent origin. It is a label that refers collectively to the Mennonites, the Society of Friends (Quakers) and the Church of the Brethren. These three groups originated separately in the sixteenth, seventeenth and eighteenth centuries, respectively, and had only occasional contact with each other before the twentieth century. However, on account of the challenges growing out of the two world wars – including support for conscientious objectors and alternatives to military service, war-sufferers' relief, peace witness and the like[4] – more common endeavours were undertaken together. In the last forty years further joint thought and cooperation was stimulated through peace studies programmes in the Peace Church colleges and seminaries.

The World Council of Churches has occasionally called on the HPC to share with the community of churches their witness, resources and experience in peacemaking and disarmament.[5] Not infrequently, ecumenical interest in the HPC has been limited to their unique social-ethical position; that is, insofar as 'they bring out an aspect of the Christian faith which no other denomination represents, the complete absence of which would result in a serious impoverishment of Protestantism'[6]. Yet the import and validity of the peace ethic represented by the HPC can only be properly understood and evaluated as part of a coherent web of specific theological convictions, especially regarding the nature and significance of Christ and that of the church.[7] Indeed, the HPC invite and encourage the notion that orthodoxy consists not only in believing rightly but also in obeying rightly. Yet the HPC want not only to be interesting on one point (as a sort of sectarian oddity or a prophetic exception), but also to be taken seriously as a theological approach to dilemmas of our age. The appeal is to classical catholic Christian convictions properly understood.

I have been asked to present the pacifist view to Christianity and war. I must note at the outset that there is not one but a variety of religious pacifisms: John Howard Yoder counts 28 types![8] A pluralism exists even within the HPC,[9] due largely to variations in theological assumptions, ethical principles and procedures, but also to differences in historical location and experience. Nonetheless a set of components can be identified which the various HPC models have in common. For the purpose of brevity this common position reflected in the joint response has been variously called 'evangelical pacifism' (Duane Friesen)[10] or 'principled pacifism' (J. Denny Weaver).[11] Correspondingly, Jesus did not simply preach prohibitions, but rather active, transforming initiatives to make peace. This pacifism is Christian or evangelical not because it makes sense or has 'practical' application; it is a moral and theological commitment to non-violence which rests on the conviction that the rejection of violence was intrinsic to who Jesus was, and that overcoming violence and working for a sustainable reconciliation is at the heart of Christian belief and mission. (It is important to note that 'pacifism' has different etymological origins to 'passivism'. The term 'pacifist' comes from the Latin phrase pax facere, to make peace.) With John H. Yoder and Dietrich Bonhoeffer, pacifism is a 'discipleship-pacifism' – a commitment to peacemaking and non-violence as a way of life in all relationships based on loyalty to Jesus Christ and desire to witness to the coming of God's kingdom. This is a different pacifism to the 'rule-and-exception' ethics pacifism.

Following the line of discipleship-pacifism, I want to present a particular type of pacifism grounded in fundamental notions about Christ (christology) and the nature of the church (ecclesiology), and framed by the specific Christian hope in the Lordship of Christ (eschatology).

Christian Pacifism and Christology

First, a coherent Christian pacifism builds on the assumption that Jesus Christ is a norm not only for reflecting on the nature of God and God's activity in history, but also as providing the model and norm for what it means to be fully human.

Many Christians define Christ in ways that make him irrelevant to politics. Mainline Christian social ethics has often sought guidance from common sense or the nature of things – that is, we measure what is 'fitting', 'adequate', 'relevant' or 'effective' – with the intention to be 'realistic' and 'responsible'. Epistemologically, these slogans point to a 'theology of the natural', assuming that 'it is by studying the realities around us, not by hearing a proclamation from God, that we discern the right'.[12] Implicitly or explicitly, it is argued that Jesus is irrelevant for social ethics. The stakes in the argument are high: if the sources or content of Christian ethics are discernible via natural wisdom, then we must ask if there is such a thing as a Christian at all.

John H. Yoder's *Politics of Jesus* – a classic reference for Christian pacifism – presents three basic theses: (1) that the New Testament consistently testifies that Jesus renounced violence and coercive power; (2) that the example of Jesus is directly relevant and normatively binding for the Christian community; and (3) that faithfulness to the example of Jesus is a political choice and not a withdrawal from the realm of politics. Christologically defined faithfulness is repeatedly characterized in the New Testament as self-emptying, where coercive power is relinquished, dominion is replaced by servanthood, and hostility is absorbed through forgiveness. It is in this respect alone that the New Testament exhorts us to be like Jesus. Understanding the example of Jesus as norm entails the rejection of all forms of violence and seeks to create peace and bring about reconciliation between human beings.

The example of Jesus offers a third way between the alternatives of the use of violent force and passive resignation to evil. Duane Friesen writes: 'A follower of Jesus is committed to a pilgrimage of seeking concrete initiatives within the culture where we live that can creatively transform conditions of injustice and violence into occasions of justice and peace.'[14] Friesen goes on to say that we need a christology that can provide a vivid picture of a Christ who is not disembodied from culture, but who is concrete enough to provide leverage for assessing how we should engage with the particularities of culture. In short, Christians need a christology that integrally links Christ to politics.

This type of christocentirc pacifism is informed by a particular strategy of reading the Bible. It suggests the Bible wants to be read directionally; that is, we follow its narrative logic and see where the story points, rather than attempt some form of synthesis of various contrasting moments. Following this strategy, the cross is revealed as the decisive revelation of the way that God is in the world, and this result supersedes any sanctions for war which one might draw from the Old Testament read in isolation. That is, the cross becomes the hermeneutical key, the canon within the canon, the lens through which the whole canonical story is to be read.[15] Read in this way, peace or shalom (wholeness or salvation in all spheres of life) serves as the integrative concept to describe God's redemptive activity in history and to describe the witness and mission of the church as well.

The HPC are also beginning to listen to the challenge of the wider ecumenical church to explore how a trinitarian framework might better inform its traditionally christocentric approach – linking faithful and patient discipleship, for example, with the impatient resilience of the Spirit of God groaning within us and fighting for redemption wherever death and sin continue their reign.[16]

Christian Pacifism and Ecclesiology

Second, a coherent Christian pacifism is based on an understanding of the church as a calling to live among the nations in a way that reflects this politics of Jesus. The HPC document emphasizes a view of the church as the new alternative society which seeks to express in its life the reality of God's shalom as revealed in Jesus: it is a community where the dividing walls of hostility are broken down and there is neither Jew nor Greek, slave nor free, man nor woman. The church should be the space in which God's project of shalom or peace takes shape. Being the church – that is, maintaining the integrity of the churches' own life and witness – is not a retreat from social issues to private piety. Rather, it is a responsibility to be a light to all the peoples of the world, not to meet violence with violence and thereby challenge the illusionary power of the world's death-systems; it is to be a transnational community whose loyalties are defined not primarily by nation, race or ethnicity but rather by Jesus Christ and his mission.[17]

Especially since the Second World War, the HPC have gradually evolved from traditions emphasizing non-resistance and non-participation in war towards active non-violent peacemaking, which also involves active participation in the relief of suffering, building the institutions of peace and working to remove the causes of war.[18]

Christian Pacifism and Christian Hope (Eschatology)

Third, a coherent Christian pacifism employs an eschatology of trust in Christ 'the slain Lamb' as the Lord of history. Faith is the attitude of trust in the victory over evil by the God revealed in the life, teachings, death and resurrection of Jesus; it is the 'willingness to accept the apparently ineffective path of obedience, trusting in God for the results'.[19] Non-resistance and active peacemaking are right in the deepest sense, insofar as they anticipate the coming peaceful kingdom, the triumph of the Lamb that was slain. The responsibility for bringing about victory is not ours, but God's alone. Yet if Jesus is Lord, then the *way* of Jesus reveals the 'grain of the universe' (Yoder); then the universe does 'bend toward justice"(as Martin Luther King was fond of saying); then faithful, non-violent action must also be more effective in the long run than injustice and war. In the end, a coherent Christian pacifism does not need to choose between being faithful and being responsible. The shape of the world presented by scripture enables us to break through traditional no-win dichotomies rendered by conventional wisdom (for example, utility versus duty). Again, Yoder argues that if Jesus Christ is Lord, then obedience to his rule cannot be dysfunctional, cannot be imprudent generally, though it may appear to be so in the short range:

> When it *seems* to me that my unjust deed is indispensable to prevent some much greater evil deed being done by another, I have narrowed my scope of time, or of space, or of global variety, or of history. I have ruled some people out of my Golden Rule, or have skewed the coefficients in my utility calculus.[20]

Yoder's writings have consistently shown that we should be clear that the commitment to secure justice through violent force is also an eschatology, a competing vision of how best to 'secure' the future. The Bienenberg Statement recognizes that both those who claim to secure the future through armed force and those who trust ultimately in God's victory over evil through the way of the cross must guard against exaggerated claims. Neither the pacifist nor non-pacifist positions can guarantee success:

> Ultimately, a Christian vision of life is based on the conviction that in the life, death and resurrection of Jesus Christ we have a vision of the kingdom of God. In Christ we have a revelation of the way God's sovereign power works in history, a vision of the non-violent cross as the way in which God's victory over evil is accomplished. This is the foundation for our work as Christians.

> Ultimately, our work as peacemakers is not based on our ability to be successful, but is invested in means of action grounded in our trust in the way of Jesus, our calling to be the Body of Christ, and the guidance of the Holy Spirit. May we truly 'embody' that vision, and repent of all arrogant trust in our own schemes to make history come out right.

Conclusion

It is important not to overlook the fact that the larger debate between Christian pacifism and just war theory – focusing typically on the question if it is ever right to fight a war – has not only diverted attention, but also served to neglect the positive task and obligation of committing the energies of both (especially the HPC side) toward the prevention of war and the development of war-preventing practices. I would suggest that a just war theory should not be based on an argument that during times of war or because of the fallenness of the world the way of Jesus is no longer relevant; it too must be based on the presumption of minimizing non-violence and injustice:

'either it serves the purpose of reducing violence and seeking justice under Christ's lordship, or it serves some idolatrous loyalty such as rationalizing a ware that we have an urge to make'.[21] Both Christian pacifists and just war theorists should urge their governments to adopt policies that are as non-violent as possible and as active in taking peacemaking initiatives as possible. Clearly, non-Christians cannot be expected to take this route because of Christian faith. But if we believe that the gospel reveals God's will, 'we must seek to persuade them to do peacemaking based on the ethics they do acknowledge'.[22]

NOTES

1. 'Summary Statement' of the Douglaston Consultation on the Apostolic Faith and the Church's Peace Witness', sponsored by the Commission on Faith and Order of the National Council of Churches of Christ in the USA, October 1991. See Marlin E. Miller and Barbara Nelson Gingerich, eds, The Church's Peace Witness (Grand Rapids, MI: Eerdmans, 1994), pp. 208–15. For a recent critique in this direction, see Michael Haspel, Friedensethik (Neukirchen: Neukirchner Verlag, 2003).
2. 'Just peacemaking: toward an ecumenical ethical approach from the perspective of the historic peace churches', in Fernando Enns, Scott Holland and Ann K. Riggs, eds, Seeking Cultures of Peace: A Peace Church Conversation (Telford, PA: Cascadia Publishing, 2004), pp. 232–43.
3. For a brief review of recent scholarship, see David G. Hunter, 'The Christian Church and the Roman Army in the First Three Centuries', in Marlin Miller and Barbara Nelson Gingerich, eds, The Church's Peace Witness (Grand Rapids, MI: Eerdmans, 1994), pp. 161–81.
4. See D. F. Durnbaugh, ed., On Earth Peace: Discussions on War/Peace Issues between Friends, Mennonites, Brethren and European Churches, 1935–1975 (Elgin, IL: Brethren, 1978). See also the entry for Historic Peace Churches at: www.wcc-coe.org/wcc/who/dictionary-article8.html.
5. See Fernando Enns, Friedenskirche in der ÷kumene: Mennonitische Wurzeln einer Ethik der Gewaltfreiheit (G˘ttingen: Vandenhoeck & Ruprecht, 2003).
6. Otto Piper, Protestantism in an Ecumenical Age (Philadelphia: Fortress, 1965), p. 170.
7. See Enns, Friedenskirche in der ÷kumene.
8. John Howard Yoder, Nevertheless: Varieties and Shortcomings of Religious Pacifism (Scottdale, PA: Herald Press, 1992).
9. See J. Richard Burkholder and Barbara Nelson Gingerich, eds, Mennonite Peace Theology: A Panorama of Types (Akron, PA: Mennonite Central Committee Peace Office, 1991).
10. Duane Friesen, 'Peacemaking as an Ethical Category: The Convergence of Pacifism and Just War', in T. Whitmore, ed., Ethics in the Nuclear Age: Strategy, Religious Studies, and the Churches (Dallas: Southern Methodist University Press, 1989).
11. J. Denny Weaver, 'Response', in Ivan Kauffman, ed., Just Policing: Mennonite–Catholic Theological Colloquium (Scottdale, PA: Herald Press, 2004).
12. John Howard Yoder, The Politics of Jesus (Grand Rapids, MI: Eerdmans, 1994), pp. 8ff.; see also Yoder's essay 'Peace Without Eschatology?' in M. G. Cartwright, ed., Royal Priesthood: Essays Ecclesiological and Ecumenical (Grand Rapids, MI: Eerdmans, 1994), p. 162: 'The error here is not in affirming that there is a real Christian responsibility to and for the social order; it is rather in the (generally unexamined and unavowed) presuppositions that result in that responsibility's being defined from within the given order alone rather than from the gospel as it infringes upon the situation. Thus the sinful situation itself becomes the norm, and there can be no such thing as Christian ethics derived in the light of revelation.'
13. Yoder, Politics of Jesus, p. 131.
14. Duane K. Friesen, 'The DOV: A Historic Peace Church Perspective', Ecumenical Review (July 2003).
15. See the comments on Yoder by Richard B. Hays, The Moral Vision of the New Testament (San Francisco: Harper, 1996), p. 250.
16. In another direction, John D. Rempel argues that the mainstream of the HPC has accepted two major correctives: first, their need for a theology of creation in order to live responsibly in society; second, the

realization that their model of the church is not a pure deduction from the apostolic age, but (like that of others) shaped by the conditions under which it arose. See 'The Unity of the Church and the Christian Peace Witness': www.peacetheology.org/papers/rempel.html.

17. For a more thorough account of the relationship between Christian pacifism and ecclesiology, see Enns, *Friedenskirche in der ÷kumene*, and Yoder in Cartwright, *Royal Priesthood*.
18. See the various contributions in C. Sampson and J.-P. Lederach, eds, *From the Ground Up: Mennonite Contributions to International Peacemaking* (Oxford: Oxford University Press, 2003).
19. Yoder in Cartwright, *Royal Priesthood*, p. 152.
20. John Howard Yoder, *The Priestly Kingdom* (Notre Dame, IN: University of Notre Dame Press, 1984), p. 38.
21. Glen H. Stassen and David P. Gushee, *Kingdom Ethics: Finding Jesus in Contemporary Context* (Downers Grove, IL: Intervarsity Press, 2003), p. 165.
22. Ibid., p. 169.

Orthodox Christian Positions on War and Peace

Grant White

There is no single Orthodox Christian position on war. Unlike the Catholic tradition, the Orthodox tradition does not contain the kind of sustained reflection on the use of force that resulted in the celebrated just war doctrine of Augustine and his followers in the Latin West. Therefore, when one asks an Orthodox Christian what the Orthodox position on the use of force is, she or he is likely to point to one or another strand in the broad (or, to use a more theological term, catholic) tradition of Orthodoxy, rather than make a categorical statement about the entire tradition. However, this recognition of the multifaceted character of the tradition on this point ought not to be used by the Orthodox today as an excuse for inaction in the face of suffering of incomprehensible proportions. Instead, the very catholicity of the Orthodox tradition must act as a goad to the Orthodox to take positions on the pressing humanitarian crises of today, particularly the issue of the responsibility to protect those facing or experiencing genocide. What follows is by no means a thorough reflection on this subject, but I hope it will be a first step toward critical reflection on these life-or-death issues in the light of Orthodox tradition.

In their refusal to be monolithic, the Orthodox churches of the twenty-first century are of course taking up the 'patristic mind' (to use a phrase often utilized by Georges Florovsky). For the patristic tradition in which Orthodox views on war and the use of force are rooted is itself not of one mind about the use of force. The pre- and post-Constantinian centuries alike saw within the ranks of the church both witnesses to a pacifist position and the presence of Christians in the army of the state, even in positions of authority. It can be argued, however, that the preponderant view of the pre-Constantinian church was pacifist. Embracing the example of Christ, who did not fight against those who arrested, tortured and executed him, it appears that the early Christian communities taught their members also to avoid the use of force, even against enemies. Thus martyrdom became an expression of non-violent discipleship.

That form of non-violent discipleship continues in the Byzantine church, but came to be located not in the local parishes, but in the monasteries of the Eastern Christian world. We have examples of non-violent resistance in the fifth-century collection of monastic sayings entitled the *Apophthegmata Patrum,* where we read of Abba Moses and his companions:

> One day, when the brethren were sitting beside him, he said to them, 'Look, the barbarians are coming to Scetis today; get up and flee.' They said to him, 'Abba, won't you flee too?' He said to them, 'As for me, I have been waiting for this day for many years, that the word of the Lord Christ may be fulfilled which says, "All who take the sword will perish by the sword"' [Matthew 26:52]. They said to him, 'We will not flee either, but we will die with you.' He said to them, 'That is nothing to do with me; let everyone decide for himself whether he stops or not.' Now there were seven brothers there and he said to them, 'Look, the barbarians are drawing near to the door.' Then they came in and slew them. But one fled and hid under the cover of a pile of rope and he saw seven crowns descending and crowning them.[1]

Here we see a kind of individualization of the burden of pacifism, even an unwillingness to impose it on others. In addition, the earlier Christian situating of their response to violence in the context of following Christ who suffered, is present here.

However, this pacifist tradition was not limited to monastics. In Orthodoxy there developed a lay pacifism centred on the 'passion-bearer', a person who voluntarily gave himself or herself up to a violent death rather than retaliate with force. The emblematic examples of the passion-bearer are the eleventh-century Kievan princes Boris and Gleb, who chose not to resist their brother's murderous intent toward them when they learned of his plans to kill them in order to seize their father's throne.

Even as a pacifist strain continued, there was also recognition in the post-Constantinian church of the necessity of going to war, particularly for defensive reasons. However, unlike in Latin Christianity, where the carefully reasoned just war theory made it possible for Christians to participate in certain kinds of war with a clean conscience, in the Byzantine church, war was understood as always involving the soldier in sin, for which repentance had to be made. Further, the ancient canons make clear that the clergy and monastics are never to participate in war. Thus, even as there develops a 'justifiable war' doctrine, there is no sense here that war is ever 'just'. Further, there develops the view that, while the clergy and monks are absolutely prohibited from waging war, even laity who do so are subject to penance for their participation. This nuanced view therefore allows for war to be waged, but also retains the pre-Constantinian view of war as sinful. Canon 7 of the Council of Chalcedon (ad 451) states:

> Those who have entered the clergy or have been tonsured into the monastic state may no longer serve in the army or accept any civil charge; otherwise those who have dared do so, and who have not repented and returned to their prior occupation for the love of God, shall be anathemized.[2]

Three canons of St Basil (d. 373) are pertinent here as well:

> He that kills another with a sword, or hurls an axe at his own wife and kills her, is guilty of wilful murder; not he who throws a stone at a dog, and undesignedly kills a man, or who corrects one with a rod, or scourge, in order to reform him, or who kills a man in his own defence, when he only designed to hurt him. But the man, or woman, is a murderer that gives a philtrum, if the man that takes it die upon it; so are they who take medicines to procure abortion; and so are they who kill on the highway, and rapparees.[3]

Even more specifically, Canon 13 of St Basil says: 'Our fathers did not think that killing in war was murder; yet I think it advisable for such to have been guilty of it to forbear communion three years'.[4] Finally, Canon 43 adds this directive: 'That he who gives a mortal wound to another is a murderer, whether he were the first aggressor, or did it in his own defence'.[5] These canons are still in force in the Orthodox churches, and so provide the foundation for Orthodox reflection today on the participation of Orthodox Christians in war.

To summarize, there are in Orthodox tradition different views on the use of force and on participation in war. There is a strong pacifist stance that is certainly an inheritance from the pre-Constantinian church. Far from being simply a relic, however, this tradition continued to develop within Orthodoxy, finding expression not only in monasticism and in the ranks of the clergy, but also in the lives of the so-called passion-bearers. The name itself indicates the central identification of a non-violent response to aggression with Christ's voluntary assumption of suffering and non-retaliation in the face of his torture and execution. This pacifist tradition has been researched and analysed by the American Orthodox scholar (and military chaplain) Alexander F. C. Webster.[6]

Coexisting with this pacifist tradition is another perspective which also has roots in the pre-Constantinian church, and which developed in the context of the life of the church of the Byzantine Empire. The so-called justifiable war tradition acknowledges the occasional necessity of war (especially for defensive purposes), and of the necessity of the participation of Christians in the armed forces of a state. At the same time, this tradition also recognizes the evil of war, and requires penance of any Orthodox responsible for killing another human being. There is no question here of a just war, much less any kind whatsoever of holy war. Rather, war is seen as the evil it is, and the occasion for great sin.[7]

What do these two traditions have to say to Orthodox churches confronted with the issue of intervening militarily in humanitarian crises? I have to make full disclosure at this point and state that I am a member of the Orthodox Peace Fellowship of the Protection of the Mother of God. In my case, this association means that I find attractive the pacifist tradition within Orthodoxy. At the same time, it is very important to take seriously the critique of pacifism made by those who see such a stance often being taken at the expense of others.[8] That is, anyone wishing to embrace the pacifist position still has to take into account the possibility that others may well suffer because of one's refusal to participate in war.

It seems to me that for Orthodox churches in the case of intervention in humanitarian crises, the resources of the justifiable war tradition make such intervention not only possible, but even necessary if one interprets intervention in this context as a defensive measure. It seems that the pacifist position also affords the resources for justifying intervention, but in a very different mode. If in the former tradition the intervention is military, in the latter tradition intervention on behalf of innocent, suffering others takes on the character of passion-bearing, an individual effort to give oneself for nothing less than the salvation of another. This is a more radical approach, perhaps, but one totally in keeping with Orthodox tradition.

NOTES

1. Moses 10. In Benedicta Ward, trans., *Sayings of the Desert Fathers: The Alphabetical Collection* (London: A. R. Mowbray, 1975), pp. 118–19.
2. ET in Hildo Bos and Jim Forest, eds, *'For the Peace from Above': An Orthodox Resource Book on War, Peace and Nationalism* (Syndesmos, 1999), p. 41.
3. St Basil the Great, First Canonical Epistle, Canon 8. ET in Bos and Forest, *For the Peace from Above*, p. 45.
4. Ibid.
5. Ibid.
6. Alexander F. C. Webster, *The Pacifist Option: The Moral Argument Against War in Eastern Orthodox Theology* (San Francisco: International Scholars Publications, 1998).
7. Ibid., pp. 86–9.
8. Ibid., p. 262.

Defining the Responsibility to Prevent

Cornelio Sommaruga

In what follows, I shall draw from my participation on the Panel on UN Peace Operations (Brahimi Panel) in 2000, the International Commission on Intervention and State Sovereignty (ICISS) in 2001, and my 13-year presidency of the International Committee of the Red Cross.
I reject the term 'humanitarian intervention', as well as the right to intervene, for three reasons:

1   It necessarily focuses attention on the claims, rights and prerogatives of the potentially intervening states, much more than on the needs of the potential beneficiaries.
2   By focusing narrowly on the act of intervention, the traditional language does not take into account the need for prior preventive effort or subsequent assistance, both of which are often neglected in practice.
3   The familiar (traditional) language neglects sovereignty, jumping directly to intervention.

This brings me to affirm (with ICISS) that the responsibility of a sovereign state is first and foremost to protect its people (its national citizens) from violence and other grave harm. It is the most basic and fundamental of all responsibilities that sovereignty imposes on its authorities. If a state cannot or will not protect its people from such harm, then coercive intervention for human protection purposes, including ultimately military intervention, by others in the international community may be warranted in extreme cases.

The shift in the terms of the debate from humanitarian intervention to the responsibility to protect involves a change of perspective, reversing the perceptions inherent in the traditional language. The responsibility to protect implies an evaluation of the issues from the point of view of those seeking or needing support, rather than those who may be considering intervention. Responsibility to protect refocuses attention on the duty to protect communities from mass killing, women from systematic rape and children from starvation. The responsibility to protect underlines the fact that primary responsibility rests with the state and it is only if the state is unable or unwilling to fulfil this responsibility (or is itself the perpetrator) that it becomes the responsibility of the international community. In the language of the responsibility to protect, one can detect a concept that bridges the divide between intervention and sovereignty, whereas the right to intervene is confrontational.

Responsibility to protect also means responsibility to prevent and responsibility to rebuild, in addition to the responsibility to react. Prevention and reconstruction (not simply material rebuilding, but reconstruction of the whole of society and its functioning) were also a preoccupation of the Brahimi Panel. The conclusions of both reports (ICISS and Brahimi) are not very different. They underline the need for the involvement of civil society in both prevention of conflict (peacemaking) and post-conflict rebuilding (peace-building). There is a real need to close the gap between rhetoric and financial and political support for prevention. A major problem has been the limited commitment in real terms to development assistance. The shortfall revealed by the mid-term review of the UN Millennium Goals is particularly acute.

Human security should be the centre of attention for long-term conflict prevention. The ICISS report stresses the need to address root causes: insecurity in all its facets has to be removed in order to avoid the kind of desperation that is so often the cause of violence. The world lacks clear commitment to human security. Such security encompasses not only the nation-state and its defence, but also individual citizens, their human dignity and their worth as human beings. This is the legitimate concern of ordinary people in their daily lives. Human security also has to address the enormous amounts of national wealth and human resources diverted into armaments and armed forces, while countries fail to protect their citizens from the chronic insecurities of absolute poverty, hunger, thirst, disease, inadequate shelter, crime, unemployment, social conflict, environmental hazards, small arms and landmines. When rape is used as an instrument of war, when thousands are killed by floods resulting from a ravaged countryside, and when citizens are killed by their own security forces, it is plainly inadequate to think purely in terms of national or territorial security. The recent tsunami, for example, has shown how millions of people of different races, cultures, clans, religions, nationalities and languages can be hit at the same time by a single catastrophic event. Human security, embracing such diverse circumstances, calls for an urgent, determined and integrated approach to coping with the real problems of today.

There is growing insecurity among indigenous peoples everywhere: their very existence as distinct societies and cultures is often endangered. For example, at the occasion of a journey to Australia, I have been particularly impressed by the aborigines question, that while well recognized, seems to be very slow in being globally approached. In all these situations people are not only affected by all sort of discriminations, but also by government agricultural policies pushing poor peasants out of business to become itinerant agricultural laborers. The very existence as distinct societies and cultures is often endangered.

There is gender insecurity: violence directed at women and children, particularly by the military– including peacekeepers and humanitarian field personnel – is a sad reality. Such insecurity affects whole families. The expansion of the global sex industry, for example, accompanied by the trafficking in industrialized countries of women and children from developing countries, constitutes violence against women and a double discrimination: gender-based and racial.

Spiritual and human values should be at the centre of politics, for politics implies ethics. All political systems provide moral instruction, indirectly through legislation and directly via civil teaching. A nation's law reflects its underlying moral norms; a nation reflects its constitutional mores. It is essential that education should insist on human values and individual responsibility, as well as the constant need to assess the credibility of the mass of information.

After the attacks on the US in September 2001, the Human Security Network issued the following statement:

> These terrorist attacks are a further, horrifying indication of the pervasiveness of threats to people's safety, rights and lives. As the international community faces the implications of these tragic events, we must recognize that innovative approaches are needed to address growing sources of global insecurity, remedy its symptoms and prevent the recurrence of threats that affect the daily lives of millions of people.

This statement made the threat to people – the risk to individuals – the central issue. The Human Security Network is an association of some twenty like-minded countries, founded in 1999 on the initiative of Norway and Canada. Its statement was not a call to arms, nor a call for retaliation or revenge. It was much more: a call for responsibility. A responsibility to prevent.

It is the responsibility of every citizen in the world to be engaged in the dynamics of human security. This participation in the political life of our countries is essential, for it contributes to the clarification and development of norms and integrated activities. Let us recall in this context the policy conclusions of the UN Commission on Human Security in 2003, co-chaired by Sadako Ogata and Amartya Sen:

1　*Protecting people in violent conflict.* This recalls the fundamental norms of international humanitarian law, with an appeal to do more to disseminate the basic principles in the Geneva Conventions.

2　*Protecting people from the proliferation of arms.* This does not only refer to weapons of mass destruction – of a strategic and tactical nature – but also to small and light arms (including landmines) and their transfer.

3　*Supporting the security of people on the move.* This reveals the weakness of international legal instruments pertaining to migrant populations.

4　*Establishing human security transition funds for post-conflict situations.* Here the Ogata/Sen Commission joins the Brahimi Panel and ICISS in underlying the importance of rebuilding war-torn societies in order to consolidate peace. The signing of peace agreements is not enough: peace has to enter the spirits and hearts of people through a dynamic of reconciliation, forgiveness and justice; the availability of financial means is an indispensable tool for political and physical reconstruction.

5　*Encouraging fair trade and markets to benefit the extreme poor.* The whole problematic of the international trading system is here addressed.

6　*Working to provide minimum living standards everywhere.* This is a crucial field: the fight against widespread, acute poverty that leaves so many people in desperation. Honest dialogue is required for multilateral solutions: no single country can act as policeman or benefactor for the entire world.

7　*According higher priority to ensuring universal access to basic health care.* Pandemic diseases such as tuberculosis, poliomyelitis and HIV/AIDS are an absolute priority.

8　*Developing an efficient and equitable global system for patent rights.* The emphasis here must be on equitable.

9　*Empowering all people with universal basic education.* This is a fundamental human right, so obvious that it requires no comment.

10　*Clarifying the need for a global human identity, while respecting the freedom of individuals to have diverse identities and affiliations.* Human security becomes human solidarity: humanitas, human values, enhancing our common humanity.

The responsibility to prevent asks us to respond to the recent statement of Robert McNamara: 'We human beings killed 160 million other human beings in the twentieth century. Is that what we want in this century?'

The Imperatives of Prevention

Kjell-Åke Nordquist

The notion of a responsibility to protect has been a key idea in the discussion about possible reformation of the United Nations, and it has brought about a debate on the meaning both of sovereignty and international justice.

This essay is not about protection, however, but about the responsibility to *prevent*. There are some interesting similarities and differences between these concepts, which merit development. This dynamic relationship can be developed by the churches, as well as by the international community at large, to find a new basis for the protection of peace and human rights.

It is often said that prevention is better than cure. It is also the case in international politics. As the debate before the UN summit in September 2005 has shown, reaching an understanding about the meaning and utility of a responsibility to protect is quite a difficult thing. Would there be any relevance for political action in discussing the responsibility to prevent, which seems even further away? Wouldn't it simply be too idealistic, too much like wishful thinking?

'Protection' is here seen in terms of measures taken to ward off direct or indirect threats or threatening situations. The ICISS report argues that states need to shift from conventional thinking (i.e. in terms of justification of intervention) to a responsibility to protect, where the basic idea is that responsibility lies with governments to protect their own people, as well as other peoples subject to other governments. The root of this responsibility is the concept of sovereignty: any government recognized as sovereign is at the same time assuming a protective role vis-à-vis its population. Sovereignty and responsibility are then two sides of the same coin, of being a legitimate government.

When a government fails to live up to this responsibility it may be necessary for other governments to intervene against its will, due to existing or imminent threats to a group or whole population. Such a failure can come for instance from a protracted civil war, an external invasion, an epidemic, a predatory dictator or rebel leaders. Seen in this way, protection is a reactive initiative, based on an actual or perceived threat, direct or indirect. To protect, then, is in its most simple form to stop a negative development and reduce or eliminate its impact on a group, community or whole population.

Prevention, on the other hand, is a different thing. It means here – briefly and ideally – to change conditions so that a negative development does not even begin. Prevention is future-oriented and therefore partially imaginative. It is based on the fact that we know that certain conditions breed injustice, poverty and human rights violations. To prevent is then to create a changed or totally new situation with the help of a combination of imagination – of what could happen if preventive measures were not taken – and experiences about what it is possible to do by reforming societies.[1]

As a short summary: prevention is a proactive and preemptive initiative built on a combination of imagination and a grounded experience of social change in order to establish conditions that make violence and human rights violations less likely to happen; protection is here seen basically as a reaction to the (near-in-time) outbreak of such violations.

From the above observation it is not hard to see that there is much in common between traditional power politics *(realpolitik)* in international relations and the protection idea. Borders, for instance, are in traditional thinking created for the purposes of control and protection. Without borders it was unclear who was to be taxed and who was therefore to be protected. The point today is that there is a responsibility for governments to protect both their own and other countries' populations if necessary, an understanding of protection that goes beyond the traditionally limited and inward-oriented view. And, as mentioned above, the duty is not only to protect oneself; other populations that suffer are also within one's sphere of responsibility.

As a consequence of the above argument, protection is linked to just war theory in the sense that it deals with the conditions for external action – war/intervention – when there is broken order or injustice in another state. The most important difference, however, between traditional just war theory and thinking about the responsibility to protect is a move from conditions in which it is right (or justifiable) to intervene, to conditions in which it is a moral obligation. This is the purpose of bringing 'responsibility to protect' into the discourse of international organizations such as the United Nations.

The reasons for intervention in both approaches are the restoration of peace and justice and the elimination of major threats to local and global communities. This is what should be protected in both traditions. The scope of responsible actors has increased, but how far does the responsibility stretch? On the whole, just war theory is weak on the issue of what should be protected, while the R2P thinking of the ICISS report and elsewhere follows the same line as the examples given above, albeit in a more developed and thorough way.

If we accept the difference between prevention and protection, we see that the idea of protection is an approach within the realm of 'action and reaction'. The common problems for a responsibility both to protect and to prevent are then twofold: (1) What should be prevented/protected? (2) Which means are justifiable for these tasks?

General and Specific Prevention

In order to undertake structural as well as social and political reforms – which is what preventive action is about – and thereby address areas of vulnerability, a consistent policy in the international community is necessary. A framework for this policy is what the international community is now debating. In a world based on the UN Charter's principle of prohibition of illegitimate use of violence, the responsibility to protect becomes a 'last defence', since it addresses the last phase in a violent spiral of actions. If there is widespread or global agreement, then we can justify intervention against the will of targeted governments that do not protect the fundamental interests (human rights) of their people. That is the idea. And the reason is not an interest in intervention, but an interest in protecting people.

The responsibility to prevent, however, leads our thinking one step further: which spirals of violence – direct and indirect – can we identify today? We need to keep in mind the nature of international challenges. Let's consider one possible categorization of such challenges:

General and specific prevention

	General	Specific
Long term	Structural injustices; human security issues	Eradication of HIV/AIDS and child soldiering
Short term	Preventive security deployment; maintain peace and security in post-conflict areas	Explicit security threats (e.g. terrorism) eliminated

While many leaders and scholars recognize the differences in the nature of the problems indicated above, it is nevertheless the linkage between the short term and long term that seems to dominate the debate. Short-term measures (e.g. against terrorism) are debated against the view that they will not solve the problem. And long-term change (e.g. climate change) is not short-term enough to motivate strong action in the same place, even if the likelihood of catastrophic effects within a time period are as high as that for terrorist acts.

To combine the seemingly contradictory perspectives of time and level of action is a challenging intellectual task. The churches have always dealt with long perspectives and their relevance for a short life, and vice versa. I have found few 'languages' as useful for expressing the dynamics and contradictions of time dimensions as those of religions.

Violence and Its Justification

Prevention is often thought of as non-violent. However, prevention can be very harmful. Sanctions, for instance, taken against states are intended to harm; not necessarily to kill, but to harm, in order to cause action. This is true also for the newly developed idea of targeted sanctions. The introduction of targeted sanctions is an adaptation by the international community to the same reality that has prompted rethinking of just war theory into a responsibility theory. The fact that there are leaders of states who do not act responsibly toward their own populations (but rather the opposite) requires other methods on the part of the international community. The traditional thinking about sanctions assumed that responsible leaders would change their policies when they realized their people were suffering. However, irresponsible and sometimes predatory leaders who don't care about their populations can only be influenced from outside – it seems – through a specific targeting of them as individuals.

The line between prevention and protection cannot be placed effectively between violence and non-violence. Protection could well happen without violence, and prevention might need violent action in order to work. The difference between prevention and protection is a matter of the type and timing of action, not of the degree of violence. This means that we need a comprehensive set of criteria, both for the right of prevention and of protection – *a jus* ad for both situations. In the same way, we need a jus in for both prevention and protection. As of now, the international discussion is in reality limited to *jus ad bellum* and the case of protection.

Jus ad and jus in

	Protection	Prevention
Jus ad	Gross human rights violations or threat of such	If necessary, imposed reforms for more justice within states; gross injustice should never be tolerated even for short periods
Jus in	Defending a human dignity principle (i.e. 'least harm to those that are protected')	A preferential treatment for those that suffer from human rights violations; trust-based approaches preferred to threat-based ones

The right to go into protective measures – *jus ad* – has been developed by ICISS and will not be repeated here.

The table above indicates that prevention may require imposition and rapid reaction to short-term violations of human rights. This requires an international commitment to upholding fundamental values. It means systematically addressing crises that are normally quelled by force, but which in a longer perspective threaten peace and stability both within and between states. It is like a zero-tolerance approach to intransigent violators.

The ICISS report in a way equates sovereignty with responsibility. A state that is unable to fulfill its responsibility to protect its population has lost its (legitimate claim to have) sovereignty in the eyes of the international community. This argument presupposes that sovereignty is something given to a state by others (directly by states normally, but sometimes indirectly by states through an international organization such as the UN). It cannot be taken, only given. A territory and its population can claim to be sovereign, but it is not a God-given right. The final word lies with states outside the territory in question.

Human Dignity

In helping to develop a redefined approach to international relations between states and nations, churches need to look to their specific contribution to human life and reflection in order to find a concept and a reality that projects their fundamental beliefs.

One possible point of departure is the concept of human dignity. As an answer to the question 'what should be defended?' churches can start with human dignity, as a principle from which the construction of states, international relations, and human rights and duties could be developed. An ethical and theological contribution to the idea of a responsibility to prevent and protect may have as its foundation the principle of human dignity. As long as sovereignty, intervention, protection and prevention are effective tools for maintaining and strengthening human dignity, they could very well be legitimate instruments. However, it is as important to remember who is the composer as much as who is 'playing the instrument'.

For prevention – and protection as well – this could mean the following way of thinking. We noted above that protection is basically a reaction to events, while prevention is a kind of preemptive measure.

Action-reaction or preemption?

	Action-reaction	*Preemptive initiatives*
State interest-based	Just war thinking	Preventive diplomacy
Rights-based	Responsibility to protect	Targeted actions against violence (direct/structural); responsibility to prevent

One important reason for states not to get involved in preventive action – not even in situations of evident humanitarian crises – is the lack of visible connection between action and outcome, the need to have one's interests unhurt, and (still) a lack of operational alternatives: what is the best way to act?

Global warming, long-term environmental change, the new wave of terrorism and fundamental shifts of global action from one part of the world to another – all such developments have prepared people and leaders for the need to take action as a response to seemingly long-term processes. A combination of protection and preventive action taken within a framework of identified roles for various actors would not be an entirely strange kind of political act under such circumstances. The building of such a framework is a task for states and communities as a whole. Churches can and should be a part of it. Further thinking is needed on what should be protected and how.

NOTE

1. This does not imply acting out of the blue. Social reform, for instance, is something many societies are familiar with in one way or another, mostly for other purposes than avoiding social conflict and its probable long-term consequence, armed confrontation.

Ethical Perspectives on State Failure

Yury Ryabykh

This subject can be understood in two different ways. First, it presupposes sustained reflection on the actions that should be undertaken if national authorities fail – by churches, civil society, states and international organizations. Second, it can mean research into the conditions under which national authorities may be defined as having failed. Such definition of failure is most important, as it provokes divergences. When the notion of a failed state first appeared in analyses of contemporary international relations it was applied to poor and weak states in which authorities were largely decorative and not in control. Since then the notion has evolved. It is often applied today to 'strong' states that are supposed to have problems with human rights. The evaluation of the quantity and quality of these violations is often problematic because it is made in different contextual backgrounds. The challenge for the ecumenical movement is to find ways to harmonize ethical approaches to this evaluation and to define its theological and ethical foundations.

Evaluations depend on the perception of the responsibility of a state to protect. If it has such a responsibility to protect, then a state faces a kind of dilemma: protection of a specific person or protection of all persons in society. In today's world the majority of conflicts are civilian, not interstate. Very often they are motivated by different identities: social, economic, national and religious. How can a state protect all its citizens if some minority among them is a menace? A state may have adequate means to eliminate all threats of separatism and terrorism, but still has to protect individual citizens.

One ethical perspective from which states can be evaluated uses the ethical binarism of victims–persecutors. This way of thinking is very deeply rooted in the mentality of Christianity, which perhaps unconsciously retains memories of persecution during the Roman Empire. There is also the historic memory of persecution in Europe after the French Revolution and in Central and Eastern Europe after the communist revolution in Russia. In addition, of course, we have the examples of peoples of other faiths – Jews, Armenians, Indian communities and others – who have also suffered dreadful persecution in different parts of the world. Sometimes it is very clear who is guilty of violating human rights and it is easy to identify the 'good guys' and the 'bad guys'. For example, when the International Convention against Genocide was adopted in 1948, everybody remembered the genocide organized by the Nazis. And if today we define genocide as systematic, continuous and massive human rights violations, such criteria are derived from the experience of the Second World War.

However, in today's conflicts it is often very difficult to differentiate between persecutors and victims. In conflict resolution, use of the binary victims–persecutors is sometimes misleading: while in some circumstances one side are the victims, in others they are the persecutors. This was clearly the case in Kosovo: when the Albanians grew stronger in the region, they began to oppress the Serbian minority. Thus, when a situation is described in terms of oppression or violation, we cannot simply strengthen the weaker side so that it too becomes oppressive. It is necessary to consider both sides as victims of conflict.

The best approach is to develop the theories and practices of conflict transformation. The experience of the Life and Peace Institute is precious in this regard. The results of conflict transformation theories can be evaluated from the point of view of Orthodox theology, which prefers to speak of transfiguration rather than transformation. A transfiguration approach helps to deal with those in conflict as they are, without the aim of suppressing one or other of them. It concentrates on changing the mentalities and even the convictions of those in conflict, so as to change their mutual relations. Thus, if the transformation approach stresses the reconfiguration of given structures and agents, transfiguration deals with agents as human beings who have to be changed.

Another ethical perspective concerns the duty of a state to protect human dignity and human life. Protection of life in general demands the development of theological and ethical thought about human life and human dignity. The understanding of these notions influences a state's implementation of its responsibility to protect. Man was created by God in his image and after his likeness. Gregory the Theologian says that through this way of creation every human being has 'the stream of invisible divinity'. The value of human life is also based on christology. The embodiment of the Word of God restored the union of God with man by means of the union of divine and human natures in the person of Jesus Christ. This Christian belief leads to the ethical affirmation of the value of every human being because he or she has the God image in his or her nature. If this view is implemented in the responsibility to protect, than the state has to provide a basic level of security for everybody in society. This is not something new: a secular version of it was elaborated by Thomas Hobbes.

However, Christianity does not end with this affirmation. The Holy Fathers (e.g. Gregory of Nice) understood the likeness of God as a task to be fulfilled: acquiring the likeness is the task of every person in this life. In Orthodox tradition this process is called theothis. There is no personality in its full meaning if a person does not strive to realize the divine likeness and instead chooses the way of sin. According to the apostle Paul, the way of sin is death. So the duty of a state is not only to protect individuals, but also to contribute towards their transfiguration by creating the right conditions.

Theological Reflections on Vulnerability, Sovereignty and the Responsibility to Protect

Sturla J. Stålsett

How should the international community respond when national authorities fail to comply with their responsibility to protect their fellow citizens? The Report of the International Commission on Intervention and State Sovereignty (R2P) represents a new conceptual framework for dealing with this difficult political and ethical question in international affairs. This framework is now gradually becoming official UN policy. It has been recommended for endorsement by the UN Secretary General and is adopted in the High Level Panel's report 'A more secure world: our shared responsibility':

> We endorse the emerging norm that there is a collective international responsibility to protect, exercisable by the Security Council authorizing military intervention as a last resort, in the event of genocide and other large-scale killing, ethnic cleansing or serious violations of international humanitarian law which sovereign governments have proved powerless or unwilling to prevent.

What should be the churches' response to this development?

Theology and Power

I have chosen a theological framework for my contribution. My theology is basically shaped by two sources. First, being born in Norway, I was baptized into the Church of Norway and raised in the Lutheran tradition. My theological studies in Oslo were coloured by the Scandinavian version of Lutheran theology, with its clear emphasis on the theology of creation. Since my particular interest from early on was the interface between Christian faith and political praxis, issues related to the use of power were constantly at the forefront of discussions during my student days. The famous (or infamous) Lutheran two kingdom doctrine inevitably had a lasting impact, even when I find it necessary to distance myself from it.

The second source for my theological work is Latin American liberation theology, particularly the christology of Salvadoran Jesuit Jon Sobrino, which became the topic of my doctoral dissertation. His emphasis on following Jesus in a contemporary political praxis for the liberation of the poor strongly influenced my theology.

There is a considerable degree of tension between these two sources. I have found this tension to be fruitful. As I hope will become clear, it can also work well when we try to get a theological grip on the issue before us: how to respond when national authorities fail.

The overall theme of our reflection belongs in some sense to the inner core of all theology. It is the issue of power: the power of God, our power or the lack of it, and not least our neighbour's powerlessness. Creation and salvation bear witness to God's power. Human beings' astonishing lust and capacity for power, for abusing power for their own benefit, are expressions of sin. The wages of sin is death, as Paul teaches us (Romans 6:23). Today, we can add that the wages of sin is the death of millions of human beings created in God's image, and destined through Christ for a life of abundance and joy. It was the self-interested abuse of power disguised as concern for national security, as the interests of the state, and even as a defence of religious truth, that in the end crucified Jesus of Nazareth. Likewise today, this self-serving power crushes the children of God of all cultures and creeds when national authorities fail or neglect their responsibility, and when the international community and churches look the other way. Theology has every reason to be critical of power, not least its own complicity with power.

Yet there is another side to power. Power is inevitably present in all human interrelationships and endeavours (including the churches and their theology) and is not in itself corrupt. It can also be an expression of compassion, of care, of love. Every human being will at some stage, in some relations, in some contexts, exert power over others. God created us as profoundly relational beings born into interdependence. We are from the outset embedded in structures of power: power that we are dependent on; power that we suffer under; power that we are given as other persons are dependent on us. Responsibility is only a meaningful word for one who has some degree of power to respond – respond to the call, the need, of the other person. Hence, there is a need for a constructive theology of power. With all the risks this entails, theology should portray a responsible and hence legitimate use of power, in order to prevent its abuse. What is the theological basis of the use of power that is necessary in order to disarm the assassin? What justification should be given to the power that protects victims and helps them restore their right, freedom and dignity?

For the Sake of Others?

In a completely different historical and social context, the possibility of a theologically legitimate use of power is what Martin Luther sets out to explore in his treatise on 'secular' or 'worldly' authority, *Von Weltlicher Oberkeit* (1523). He aims to provide theological guidance for respecting and responsibly carrying 'the Sword' (i.e. potentially coercive power). It should always be used 'for the sake of others, so that evil may be prevented and justice upheld'. It should be 'devoted wholly to the service of others' and for 'the preservation, protection and peace of others'. The Christian ideal of turning the other cheek, of peaceful non-resistance, is a principle that can and should be validly applied on one's own behalf, Luther holds. But it is not a Christian virtue to 'turn the cheek of the other person', so to speak. That would equal a cynical turning away from the appeal of a fellow human being in need. It would be to neglect the suffering of the other and give license to injustice and violence:

> If someone wanted to have the world ruled according to the Gospel, and to abolish all secular law and the Sword, … what do you imagine the effect would be? He would let loose the wild animals from their bonds and chains, and let them maul and tear everyone to pieces, saying all the while that really they are just fine, tame, gentle, little things. But my *wounds* would tell me different. (*Von Weltlicher Oberkeit;* emphasis added)

Of course, much could be said about certain aspects of Luther's argument in this treatise. It definitely has elements and implications that we cannot apply today. But his main point – that any legitimacy of power is dependent on its use for the 'preservation, protection and peace of others' – is of lasting relevance, not least for theological reflection on the responsibility to protect when national authorities fail.

There is a turn from self-interest to other-interest here that is as deeply Christian as it is typically Lutheran. The interesting thing about it is the way it is related to the exercise of political power. This move is not self-evident. Among Luther's contemporaries we find a certain Niccoló Machiavelli

(1469–1527), by some held to be the father of modern political theory. He was not the first, but surely one of the most explicit and consistent, to hold that the ability to pursue self-interest above all was decisive in both acquiring and successfully maintaining political power. The so-called Political Realism school in international relations stands clearly in this tradition in its emphasis on 'national interest' as the basic value for and key to understanding the actions of states and state leaders. In the words of Hans J. Morgenthau:

> The main signpost that helps political realism to find its way through the landscape of international politics is the concept of interest defined in terms of power … We assume that statesmen think and act in terms of interest defined as power.

It is in this line of thought that the concept of state sovereignty, a cornerstone in the post-Westphalian international order up to this day, becomes so central.

Reconceptualizing Sovereignty

In my view we see a similar move – from self-interest to other-interest – in the ICISS report, particularly in its discussion of the concept of sovereignty, moving from seeing it primarily as a matter of control (i.e. control of arms, people and territory) to a matter of responsibility:

> There is no transfer or dilution of state sovereignty. But there is a necessary recharacterization involved: from sovereignty as control to sovereignty as responsibility in both internal functions and external duties. (R2P, para. 2.14)

In this understanding then,

> sovereignty implies a dual responsibility, externally – to respect the sovereignty of other states, and internally, to respect the dignity and basic rights of all the people within the state. (R2P, para. 1.35)

This recharacterization of state sovereignty is of major importance. It can be seen as something of a breakthrough, solving a dilemma that had appeared much earlier, but particularly urgent during the last few decades. After the end of the Cold War, the reality of state sovereignty changed in several of its aspects. Globalization has put nation-states under pressure. More importantly, the spread and escalation of internal violent conflicts and the devastating humanitarian catastrophes related to them, raised the question of whether it really was true that national self-interest was the best guiding principle in international society, and whether it was correct to give such absolute priority to state sovereignty.

In a speech at the University of Bordeaux in April 1991, former UN Secretary General Javier Pérez de Cuéllar pointed to what he held to be 'probably an irresistible shift in public attitudes towards the belief that the defence of the oppressed in the name of morality should prevail over frontiers and legal documents' (quoted in Himes 1994: 91). Perez de Cuéllar was soon to make this 'irresistible shift' bear upon the basic principle of non-interference in interstate affairs. Later that year, before leaving office, he said:

> It is now increasingly felt that the principle of non-interference within the essential domestic jurisdiction of states cannot be regarded as a protective barrier behind which human rights could be massively or systematically violated with impunity. (UN Doc. A/46/1, Ramsbotham and Woodhouse 1996: 84)

This irresistible shift can in my view today be rephrased as a shift from a primary concern with state security to human security, or even from the sovereignty of nations to what could be seen as the sovereignty of the human person/body. I think this shift is theologically warranted. But before giving my reasons for this, we need to look at what is actually implied in such a shift.

The dilemma is of course that such an understanding seems directly to undermine perhaps the most basic principle in the state-system created after the Westphalian peace accords of the seventeenth century: the principle of non-intervention. This is a strong counter-argument, indeed. The international principle of non-intervention is indirectly confirmed in UN Charter Article 2(7). Two UN General Assembly resolutions state the prohibition on intervention more explicitly: 'Declaration on the Inadmissibility of Intervention in the Domestic Affairs of States and Protection of Their Independence and Sovereignty' (GA Res. 2131 (XX), 1965), and 'Declaration on Principles of International Law concerning Friendly Relations and Cooperation among States in accordance with the Charter of the United Nations' (GA Res. 2625 (XXV), 1970): 'No state or group of states has the right to intervene, directly or indirectly, for any reason whatever, in the internal affairs of another' (see Semb 1992: 9). There is no doubt then, that 'an intervention in the traditional language of international law is an illegal action' (Kaysen and Kaysen 1993: 7).

Non-intervention has thus served as an ordering principle in interstate affairs for several centuries, and is firmly rooted in international law and practice. Although it has frequently been violated, especially by the strong states, it has guaranteed predictability and stability in a system that for the lack of one supreme authority may be regarded as anarch(ist)ic in principle. It has contributed to limiting the use of force and reducing the risk of war between states (Himes 1994: 95).

The non-intervention principle has also served, at least to some extent, to protect smaller and weaker states against the stronger. For this reason, national sovereignty continues to be a highly appreciated value, not least in many former colonies in the Third World. Sovereignty stands for self-determination and independence. The UN Charter Article 2(2) states as one of the purposes of the UN:

> to develop friendly relations among nations based on respect for the principle of equal rights and self-determination of peoples, and to take other appropriate measures to strengthen universal peace.

Of particular relevance for the actual world situation, it should be added, is the fact that it is a principle that respects and protects plurality: it respects cultural differences between states, cultures and societies.

Thus, there are reasons to uphold the principle of non-intervention. In the global South some would clearly see a psychological linkage between intervention and colonialism which works against the concept of humanitarian intervention (Gamba 1993: 118). One should not be surprised, therefore, when voices from the South, as well as from the Muslim world, representing regions where interventions have been concentrated in recent years, appear to be sceptical with regard to the real intentions and motives of intervening states. They pose a legitimate concern: are we witnessing a return of neocolonialism in the name of human rights?

It is this Gordian knot that the ICISS report cuts through by its recharacterization of national sovereignty and its reformulation of the whole debate on humanitarian intervention. If it is framed as a 'right to intervene', the irresistible shift would inevitably conflict with the non-intervention principle. But by affirming the primary responsibility of national authorities for the basic well-being and human rights of their citizens – their responsibility to protect – it is possible to uphold the value of state sovereignty and the non-intervention principle, and yet at the same time indicate their limits.

What the ICISS report proposes is a move from absolute to conditioned sovereignty. It is based on the observation that the dilemma before us is not just between state sovereignty and the dignity of human beings. It is actually a dilemma within the principle of sovereignty or non-intervention itself, since one principal condition in the normative foundation of non-intervention is self-determination. Sovereignty is not only something which regulates the interstate relationship; it is also based on an intrastate or domestic relationship, the relationship between the government and the population in a given state (Semb 1992: 23ff.). In this respect, the state's right to sovereignty depends on its government's legitimacy in the eyes of its population. In other words, a government that does not respect the rights of all its citizens is in fact jeopardizing its own right to sovereignty. The rights of human beings are above the rights of states.[1]

My Wounds Would Tell Me Different

Theologically speaking, this reflects the flip side of the argument in Luther's treatise on the secular authority. When it is said that the Sword should always be used 'for the sake of others, so that evil may be prevented and justice upheld' (cf. Romans 13), it is implied that any use of power that is *not* used for the sake of others, or any authority that does *not* prevent evil, is not legitimate, and should consequently not be obeyed.

This reasoning can be strengthened if we consider the phrase in Luther's argument above. In fact it is a detail that can easily be overlooked. He uses the image of someone letting loose wild animals from their bonds and chains, and letting them maul and tear everyone to pieces, while claiming that the beasts are just fine, tame, gentle, little things. Then Luther adds a small comment: 'But my wounds would tell me different', he says. This comment may seem simple and obvious, but I think it opens up an immensely important space for theological and ethical reflection. It points towards an epistemology based on the sensibility and vulnerability of the human body. The deceit will be uncovered, and truth can be known, through the experience of wounds. In this case, Luther refers to his own wounds, but they should be seen as closely related to the wounds of others. And, not least, they should be seen as referring to the wounds of the crucified Christ, which reveal God's own vulnerability and its saving significance. I take this small comment as an opportunity to outline what can be called a theology and an ethics of vulnerability. Reflection on human vulnerability in view of the vulnerability of God displayed on the cross can be a way of bridging these different views in the ecumenical movement. There is a lot of common ground here.

The 'Vulnerability and security' study document from the Church of Norway (Stålsett et al. 2002)[2] has its origin in a continuous discussion and struggle with the dilemmas concerning 'intervention vs. sovereignty' in the context of the Committee on International Affairs of our church. In the document we seek to shed new light on this dilemma by moving beyond the traditional language of 'realist vs. idealist' approaches by proposing a reflection on the phenomenon of human vulnerability as an entrance to a different understanding of security.

In short, the position that we developed is one that sees vulnerability not as the opposite of security, but as a *precondition* for ethical behaviour and hence for common well-being and safety. Vulnerability is not only an inescapable fact of human life; more importantly, it is also what makes it possible for us to relate responsibly, ethically – that is, humanely – to other human beings. It is by recognizing our own vulnerability that it is possible for us to see the vulnerability of other human beings as a call to us. Moral behaviour is unthinkable without some level of empathy. Empathy rests on sensibility. Corporeal sensibility is what makes us able to receive and give; it is a precondition for community. To put it in somewhat 'elevated' terms, only the vulnerable is able to love – and to be loved. Hence, vulnerability should not be removed for the sake of security; vulnerability is what should be protected.

Theologically, this position draws from various sources. The *teologia crucis* – theology of the cross – in various versions from Luther via Bonhoeffer to Sobrino is of course central here. Luther's statement about what he learns from his wounds is deeply connected to his nineteenth and twentieth Heidelberg theses on recognizing God *sub specie contrarii*, in an opposite form, in the crucified Christ. True theology rests on this ability, Luther claims, and it can recognize the victory of the love of God in what the world only can perceive as a scandalous defeat. The victorious, glorious God is revealed in the vulnerable, wounded Christ on the cross.

Arnold Neufeldt-Fast stated that the cross holds the status of a canon within the Historic Peace Churches. It is *the* hermeneutical key for interpreting the Christian message. The cross is the decisive way in which God is in the world. Grant White's description of the ascetic pacifist trajectory in Orthodox theology (particularly the Russian kenotic tradition, seeing the interconnection between *kenosis* and *theosis*, self-emptying as a way to perfection) would seem to provide strong theological resources for a renewed concept of vulnerability.

Similarly, from the viewpoint of liberation theology, Jon Sobrino argues that God is mysteriously present, and present for the salvation of the world, in and through contemporary crosses (; cf.). The victims in our history, whom Sobrino daringly calls the crucified peoples, are thus given a key role in Christian faith and praxis. In my opinion, one of the most important changes in the development of Christian theology in the last century was this conversion to the victimized other, which happened in political theology emerging after the Holocaust, feminist theology, black theology and a plurality of other contextual liberation theologies. Ecumenical theology has certainly been influenced by this. Taken as a whole, this is what I have called a 'victimological turn' in theology. In view of the cross, all Christian theology should be formulated from the perspective of victims, for their liberation and salvation – or, we can say, for their protection. For, as Sobrino is eager to point out, the crucified peoples are to be *taken down* from their crosses. Their very presence cries out for mercy, for liberation, for justice.

The Responsibility to Protect: Cautions and Challenges to the Churches

It is of course a short step from such a theology to ethical and political action. In my view it must lead to the political consequence that we cannot give absolute value to the principle of non-intervention when national authorities fail to hinder, or even themselves actively cause, human catastrophes. The criteria that the R2P document proposes for assessing if such a situation is emerging are applications of the main insights from the so-called (wrongly) just war tradition. These criteria are helpful up to a certain point, as we also argue in the 'Vulnerability and security' study. Nevertheless this is a difficult step, fraught with risks and temptations. While having argued that the position taken in R2P regarding the failure of national authorities can and should be theologically endorsed, it is clearly also necessary to be extremely cautious. It may be a slippery slope.

In this regard, I am particularly concerned about one passage in the R2P document, namely paragraph 4.21, on the possibility of anticipatory military action:

> What we do make clear, however, is that military action can be legitimate as an anticipatory measure in response to clear evidence of likely large-scale killing. Without this possibility of anticipatory action, the international community would be placed in the morally untenable position of being required to wait until genocide begins, before being able to take action to stop it.

The concern is of course that allowing military action as an anticipatory measure may open the door to the logic of preventive/preemptive warfare.

Gareth Evans responded to this concern. He thinks it will not be problematic in principle (remember Rwanda) – only in practice. How do you convince the international community that such a situation is occurring, that it requires collective anticipatory action? I am not quite convinced that this would be sufficient. Anticipatory action could and should be short of actual military action. Although in reality there will be limit-cases and exceptions, I think it is important to maintain that armed action can only be an armed response to an actual outbreak of violence, and not to a perceived threat. That does not mean that military deployment, preparation and threat should be used before a genocidal process eventually starts.

What should be the role of churches when national authorities fail? I believe the churches have a prophetic role to play in the issue of human vulnerability. The memento vulnerabilis ('remember that you are vulnerable'), that to be vulnerable is to be human and to be invulnerable (if that were an option) is to be inhuman, is a critical discourse in a modern and postmodern culture in which weakness is something to be hidden or overcome.

Standing by, struggling with victims, is an absolute priority for a church as the community founded on fellowship with and faith in the crucified one. Standing with the victim is an act of mercy that implies standing up for justice. 'Compassion is an unstable emotion', Susan Sontag reminds us. 'It needs to be translated into action, or it whithers' (Sontag 2003: 101). Hence, believing that God raised the crucified one for the salvation of the world means also pointing to the strength, the force, even the power of vulnerability. This is an evangelical, missionary task.

When authorities fail (and they often do) how do we know that there is time for reaction? We know it when the situation is 'conscience-shocking', as repeatedly stated in R2P.[3] Yet conscience is as we know also something relative and unstable. Therefore churches, together with other religions and all people of good will, should work for the nourishment of the conscience, so that it can know when to be shocked. It is also commonly held that these new developments in international relations demand a change of 'mindset from a culture of reaction to a culture of prevention' (R2P 3.42). It is an important evangelical and missionary task, as well as an interreligious task, to contribute to this change in mindset.

We must also introduce an element that has been largely absent in our discussions, but should not be absent from any WCC statement on the issue: the gender perspective. There is without doubt a link between gender and violence. Men wage war. Women are the main protectors in crises, yet they seldom use violence. What are the protective skills and strategies of women – not least in poor nations and regions – that we should pay attention to and learn from?

I see in the R2P approach a balanced and necessary reformulation of the basic and valuable principles of state sovereignty and non-intervention in interstate relationships. When national authorities fail to protect their citizens from conscience-shocking genocide and mass death, there is a derived international responsibility to come to the rescue of these peoples. Although this move from national self-interest to international other-interest is not without dilemmas and risks, I hold that churches should support it and follow its implementation critically, always struggling to adopt the perspective of those primarily concerned, the victims. It is a huge task for churches today to counter the tempting illusion (present both in economic neoliberalism and political realism) that self-interest is ultimately beneficial.

REFERENCES

Gamba, Virginia. 1993. 'Justified Intervention? A View from the South.' In Emerging Norms of Justified Intervention, edited by A.-M. S. Burley and C. Kaysen. Cambridge, MA: Committee on International

Security, American Academy of Arts and Sciences, 115–25.

Himes, Kenneth R. 1994. The Morality of Humanitarian Intervention. Theological Studies 55.

Kaysen, Laura W. Reed and Carl Kaysen. 1993. Emerging Norms of Justified Intervention. Cambridge, MA: Committee on International Security Studies, American Academy of Arts and Sciences.

Ramsbotham, Oliver and Tom Woodhouse. 1996. Humanitarian Intervention in Contemporary Conflict: A Reconceptualization. Cambridge: Polity Press.

Semb, Anne-Julie. 1992. The Normative Foundation of the Principle of Non-Intervention. Oslo: PRIO.

Sobrino, Jon. 1994. Jesus the Liberator: A Historical-Theological Reading of Jesus of Nazareth. Translated by P. Burns and F. McDonagh. Tunbridge Wells: Burns & Oates.

Sobrino, Jon. 2001. Christ the Liberator: A View from the Victims. Maryknoll, NY: Orbis.

Sontag, Susan. 2003. Regarding the Pain of Others. New York: Farrar Straus & Giroux.

Stålsett, Sturla J. 2003. The Crucified and the Crucified: A Study in the Liberation Christology of Jon Sobrino. Vol. 127, Studies in the Intercultural History of Christianity. Bern: Peter Lang.

Stålsett, Sturla J., Raag Rolfsen, Karin Dokken and Hans Morten Haugen. 2002. 'Vulnerability and security: current challenges in security policy from an ethical and theological perspective.' Expanded version of the Norwegian 'Sårbarhet og sikkerhet' (2000) edn. Oslo: Church of Norway Council on Ecumenical and International Relations.

NOTES

1. Semb concludes that the principle of non-intervention applies to states 'only insofar as the government serves as an instrument of the popular will' (: 32). The problem this leaves us with, however, is the lack of objective criteria with which to judge the domestic legitimacy of a government.
2. See www.kirken.no/engelsk/VULNERABIL.doc.
3. The phrase is used seven times: pp. xiii, 33 (twice), 55 (twice), 70 and 74.

Ethical Remarks on the Criteria for Intervention

Jean-Luc Blondel

The ICISS report presented in 2001 aims at proposing criteria for legitimate international intervention in cases of grave violations of human rights in the territory of a sovereign state.

Let me start with four ethical remarks from a Christian reformed point of view:

1   For Christians (and possibly for all religions), national sovereignty is not an ultimate goal. Jesus Christ is the only universal sovereign. The faith should therefore limit adherence or obedience to national values and authorities. Faith goes beyond boundaries. Concern for the other comes before the promotion of one's own interests.

2   God is the creator of all human beings. For God, there are no enemies. Jesus Christ died for all. All human beings (who all experience vulnerability in one way or another) need protection. Thus, expressed in a positive dimension, the 'golden rule' is: like Christ, what can I do for this person, for this population?

3   When we criticize political authorities as churches we must demonstrate modesty: there are splits within the same confessions in different countries, and among churches and religions. Within churches there are pro-war and pro-peace people. Throughout history, churches and religious leaders have not always been signs of peace. Our task still is to be signs of peace, open to and fostering dialogue and reconciliation. In the fire of war, to pour water, not oil.

4   The issue of (military) intervention indicates how difficult it is to translate Christian principles into politics. The kingdom of God is not yet fully realized, to say the least.

General Observations on Criteria for Intervention

The criteria presented by the report on the responsibility to protect (repeated by the High Level Panel on Threats, Challenges and Change) reflect and modernize the classical concept of the just war. The proposed criteria are to be used in case of failure: when prevention has failed, when a 'just peace' (including respect for human rights) has not been achieved. In this sense, they are not normal. They only try to limit an intervention, to alleviate suffering, following the imperative 'do no (additional) harm', or 'act as normal (that is, with decency and respect) in an abnormal situation'.

Criteria represent guidance for reflection and decision. They do not replace the need for analysis, the weighing of interests and motivating (political) will. They do not give carte blanche to authorities. Indeed, in abnormal situations, there are no good criteria, but only a tragic search for approximate solutions to unsolvable problems. Whatever the criteria, they must be applied coherently and sustainably. Similar criteria must be followed in similar situations, with no double standards, no 'good for you, but not for me'.

In many circumstances, states (individually or collectively) are in an untenable position: if they act (e.g. military intervention) they will be accused of interference and abuse; if they do not, of cowardice or criminal passivity. The (ideal) positive intervention is always at the delicate and ever-changing middle ground between excessive restraint (non-assistance to persons in danger) and abuse of power for interested reasons. It has to be noted that, at least in democratic countries, populations, parliaments and the media can exert influence or pressurize a government. We cannot blame a government for not acting if its population does not mobilize and shows no concern; there are shared responsibilities.

As I work for the ICRC, I should also add a few words on international humanitarian law (IHL) and humanitarian action:

1   IHL only deals with *jus in bello*. Whatever the reasons for going to war (*jus ad bellum*), IHL must be observed in any armed conflict. IHL is about protection. Humanitarian action is a tool for implementing IHL. IHL has sometimes been thought of as too minimal (notably because it does not condemn war); however, the reality shows that this minimum is often already a maximum: warriors do not even respect minimal rules of distinction (spare civilians) and proportionality of the means engaged to wage attacks.

2   States have a key responsibility to respect IHL ('to respect and to ensure respect', as Article 1 common to all four Geneva Conventions states). In the majority of contemporary (internal) conflicts, however, most violations do not come from states, but from armed opposition groups whose 'political' motivation is too often mixed with a criminal striving for material goods and resources.

3   IHL and humanitarian action are generally not sufficient to restore peace, but countries or regions that have observed IHL rules might be closer to dialogue and reconciliation: less hatred, less desire for retaliation and revenge, facilitate the process of peace.

4   IHL is the legal expression of a fair balance between (legitimate) state security and respect for human dignity. Therefore, IHL does not tolerate exceptions (as human rights law does in certain circumstances). It knows the importance and probably the constant need for the convergence of interests. There is a lesson to be learned from other fields: an enterprise will most certainly work if it allies enlightened (political, economic) interests with (more generous) approaches to the protection of human dignity and human rights.

Further Developing the Criteria for Intervention

Roger Williamson

The remarks by Gareth Evans in the public session of this seminar, drawing on the report of the International Commission on Intervention and State Sovereignty, provided a valuable introduction to the cogent approach of the Commission. It is worth recalling that the issues which we face are not new or unique, although each generation faces them in new forms. The Christian church has a long tradition of addressing issues of war and peace. It has a sophisticated apparatus to apply, namely the just war tradition. It also has the ethical challenge of the pacifist tradition, which is closer to the original practice of Jesus and the early church.

I am not personally a pacifist, but it is incontestable that active non-violence is closer to the historical Jesus and that in our century the non-violence movements of Gandhi, the US Civil Rights Movement led by Martin Luther King, and movements in countries as far apart as the Philippines and the German Democratic Republic proved effective in achieving positive change in oppressive circumstances. I am also convinced that just war theory provides a valuable framework both for Christian reflection and dialogue with people of other faiths and holders of secular power. I am not aware, however, that its application has ever actually prevented a war.

At another level, however, it has to be said that the just war tradition is just a set of criteria, albeit a sophisticated one. It is valuable to Christian faith communities and individuals, as well as secular politicians and decision-makers. It is open to abuse as well as use. It is often cited by politicians to justify war rather than to rule out almost all war. Finally, it also has to be said that most of the data to be used in the application of the just war criteria are of the nature of prudential judgements, of political analysis – for example, the criterion of last resort requires a judgement that all other means of successfully resolving a conflict have been exhausted.

It is worth beginning with some reflections on the nation-state. I think it is correct to assert that the mainstream Christian tradition is a positive but critical evaluation of the state. Henry Chadwick, reflecting on St Augustine, spoke of a 'positive evaluation of government as a providential instrument of order – if not getting one to heaven, at least hedging the road to hell'.[1] The state's monopoly of legitimate violence (or armed force) has been called by Helmut Gollwitzer a 'precious step of progress in civilization'.[2] St Paul said that civil authority was to be obeyed, as it was not a 'terror to good behaviour' (Romans 13:3). However, we are all too aware of many situations where the state is exactly that; or where there is civil war; or where state authority has failed or is collapsing.

It is perhaps inevitable that one's thoughts turn to the witness and writings of Dietrich Bonhoeffer, 60 years after his death. His statement that 'anyone who does not cry out for the Jews should not sing Gregorian chant' underlines the ethical duty to prevent massive violations of human rights.

There are two cases of cross-border intervention in recent history which can arguably be justified on moral grounds, even if the case in international law was problematic. Tanzania's troops helped with the removal of Idi Amin's government, and the Vietnamese army removed Pol Pot's appalling regime in Kampuchea/Cambodia. It has always stuck me as strange that it would be morally legitimate for a Rwandan, for example, to use force to attempt to overthrow his country's genocidal government in 1994, but wrong for someone born a few miles away in Uganda to do so.

New Elements in our Current Context

Having stressed the continuity in our discussion, it is perhaps worth reflecting on the difference in our current situation.

1   We still live in a world of nation-states, but sovereignty is no longer seen as absolute. The state has duties and obligations of protection which it has to fulfil in order for its authority to be recognized by the international community.
2   As a result of the Second World War, largely because of a heightened awareness of human rights, the sense of responsibility encapsulated in the phrase 'never again' has become a stronger element in the politics of responsibility. The conviction 'never again world war and Holocaust' led to the founding of the UN 'to save succeeding generations from the scourge of war' and 'to reaffirm faith in fundamental human rights' and the acceptance of the Universal Declaration of Human Rights.[3] There are differences of scale, of course, but in our times it is widely felt to be unacceptable that the UN and its member states could not or did not stop the Rwandan genocide, or succeed in protecting those in a UN 'safe haven' at Srebrenica, or act effectively at an early point in the Darfur crisis.
3   Most wars and situations of massive violations of human rights are within countries. The issue of how, effectively, to protect internally displaced populations within countries has again been raised recently with the case of Darfur. Given that it is harder for people to cross internationally recognized boundaries and to become refugees or asylum seekers, and that even the 1951 Refugee Convention is being called into question, it is essential to develop more robust mechanisms to defend the displaced in a country – even without the consent of the government of the territory.

The Responsibility to Protect: Hints of a Theology

I would suggest that the concept of self-defence has to be central to the debate. Under Article 51 of the UN Charter, the state has a right of self-defence in event of being attacked. The state is also responsible for the defence of its people. In extreme circumstances, such as military occupation, tyranny or genocide, a people is unable to exercise that right effectively. The international community's responsibility to protect requires that conditions are created in which reasonably good government can be restored or created. A biblical image is that of the Good Samaritan ensuring that the victim can 'stand on his/her own two feet' or 'look after themselves'. In a way this is an application of Bonhoeffer's concept (developed in his *Ethics*) of *Stellvertretung* or standing in for others in a representative capacity, with the international community assuming responsibility until a reasonably good government can take over.

What Are We Talking About? Intervention and State Sovereignty

Are there situations in which war should be waged by or in the name of the international community, even to the point of overthrowing a government which has become intolerable?

In brief, I would comment that I find the work of the International Commission on Intervention and State Sovereignty and that of the Secretary General's High Level Panel very instructive. The report is set within the intellectual framework of the just war tradition, which includes criteria relating both to the decision to use military force and on the conduct of war.[4] Both dimensions are important – whether to go to war and also how the war is conducted. The Commission outlined an interlocking set of six criteria for military intervention for human protection purposes:

- The just cause threshold, which is set deliberately high, rules out most claims to the use of military force.
- Four precautionary principles: right intention, last resort, proportional means, and reasonable prospects of success.
- The final criterion concerns right authority.

In addition, the Commission outlines operational principles as a modern-day application of the criteria for how war is to be waged.

The just cause threshold

In the view of the Commission, military intervention for human protection purposes must be seen as an exceptional and extraordinary measure. To be justified, there has to be serious danger of irreparable harm occurring to human beings, or being imminently likely to occur, of the following kind:

A: large-scale loss of life, actual or apprehended, with genocidal intent or not, which is the product either of deliberate state action, or state neglect or inability to act, or a failed state situation; or

B: large-scale 'ethnic cleansing', actual or apprehended, forced expulsion, acts of terror or rape.

This criterion is deliberately drawn to be very restrictive. Military intervention must be exceptional, both for conceptual and practical political reasons. If intervention is to occur when it is necessary, it cannot be called for too often. The anticipatory dimension is also important, since it should not be necessary to wait until genocide has occurred in order to act. As described, this threshold could have been applied in the cases of Bosnia, Rwanda and Kosovo, as well as the state collapse and civil war situation of Somalia. No definition of 'large scale' is ventured by the Commission. That is intended to be a case-by-case judgement by the international community. It would not, however, require military intervention by the international community every time human rights violations are reliably registered.

Right intention

'The primary purpose of the intervention, whatever other motives intervening states may have, must be to halt or avert human suffering.' While complete purity of motive is seldom present in state behaviour, this criterion can be safeguarded in a number of ways. Collective or multilateral intervention is more likely to be disinterested than single-country intervention. The positive response of the people on whose behalf the intervention is made is essential – if the action is genuine and disinterested, it is more likely to be welcomed by the suffering population. The response of other countries in the region is also likely to be indicative.

Last resort

'Military intervention can only be justified when every non-military option for the prevention or peaceful resolution of the crisis has been explored, with reasonable grounds for believing lesser measures would not have succeeded.' This application of the traditional last resort criterion makes it clear that the use of military force is an extreme measure. It is not primarily a temporal criterion requiring that every other measure must have been tried and exhausted first before recourse to military power. A judgement must be made that all reasonable alternatives have been exhausted.

Proportional means
'The scale, duration and intensity of the planned military intervention should be the minimum necessary to secure the defined human protection objective.' The military action taken has to be in line with the stated purpose and the magnitude of the original provocation. The impact on the political system of the country targeted should be limited to what is essential to accomplish the purpose of the intervention.

Reasonable prospects
'There must be a reasonable chance of success in halting or averting the suffering which has justified the intervention, with the consequences of action not likely to be worse than the consequences of inaction.' This is a standard precautionary principle of the just war theory. It has the effect however of ruling out military intervention against the major powers – to take one example, it effectively rules out external military intervention on behalf of the people of Chechnya.

Right authority
'There is no better or more appropriate body than the United Nations Security Council to authorize military intervention for human protection purposes. The task is not to find alternatives to the Security Council as a source of authority, but to make the Security Council work better than it has.' The most difficult question relating to this criterion is what happens if the Security Council is unable to authorize the necessary action, as was the case with Kosovo. If the conclusion is reached that only the Security Council of the United Nations can legitimately authorize the use of force, the international community could again find itself unable to act even when confronted with genocide (another Rwanda) or threatened mass 'ethnic cleansing' (another Kosovo). In the context of the debate about the desirability or necessity of military action against Iraq, UK Prime Minister Tony Blair has termed this the issue of 'unreasonable veto'. Within the UN framework, there are two other possible routes: the Uniting for Peace[5] procedure or action within the area of jurisdiction of regional and/or sub-regional organizations acting under Chapter VIII of the Charter (especially Article 52) – as the West African states have done (e.g. in Liberia in the early 1990s and in Sierra Leone in 1997).

Three Further Issues
I think the work of ICISS takes us considerably further, but three different issues immediately occur.

1 Test case: Africa
If the work of the Commission were to be accepted internationally, it should provide the basis for an intervention to stop a recurrence, for example, of the Rwandan genocide. There remain issues of capacity and consistency. Will major industrialized countries really be prepared, in the foreseeable future, for example to make available troops in large numbers and possibly for a long period, to bring peace to a country like the Democratic Republic of Congo? It is clearly advantageous if African solutions are found to African problems, but is delegation of responsibility for peace and security in Africa to the African Union and regional bodies not in danger of being an abdication of responsibility?

2 Too high or too low?
There are also serious issues below the threshold of genocide or massive violations of human rights. I have some sympathy with arguments which suggest that consistent application of criteria will either

include too many cases and become unworkably interventionist, or that setting the bar too high will mean that only the most flagrant cases will be addressed and other serious cases will be allowed to continue because of rigorous application of a set of criteria which exclude almost all cases.

3 Consistency and pragmatism

A proper understanding of human rights regards all lives as equal. The Rwandan genocide was a massive crime, and the international community did far too little to support and augment the understaffed UN Mission of Romeo Dallaire. It would be perverse, however, to argue that failure in the large things should be used as a reason for not doing smaller things. For example, the British deployment in Sierra Leone helped to stabilize that country – in my view, it would be wrong to use the argument 'we didn't intervene in Rwanda, so it would be inconsistent to help Sierra Leone'.

Liberal Interventionism: The Blair Doctrine and Relevant Cases[6]

British Prime Minister Tony Blair has both elaborated a doctrine of intervention and put it into practice. At the time of the Kosovo crisis, he outlined five key tests (broadly applying the just war criteria) for intervention:

> First, are we sure of our case? War is an imperfect instrument for righting humanitarian distress, but armed force is sometimes the only means of dealing with dictators. Second, have we exhausted all diplomatic options? We should always give peace every chance, as we have in the case of Kosovo. Third, on the basis of a practical assessment of the situation, are there military operations we can sensibly and prudently undertake? Fourth, are we prepared for the long term? In the past we talked too much of exit strategies. But having made a commitment we cannot simply walk away once the fight is over; better to stay with moderate numbers of troops than return for repeat performances with large numbers. And finally, do we have national interests involved? The expulsion of ethnic Albanians from Kosovo demanded the notice of the rest of the world. But it does make a difference that this is taking place in such a combustible part of Europe. I am not suggesting that these are absolute tests. But they are the kind of issues we need to think about in deciding in the future when and whether we will intervene.[7]

This is a cogent presentation of the case for what has been called liberal interventionism. Blair has engaged in five distinct military actions, a significant departure for the head of a traditionally 'dove-ish' party. These are: air strikes against Iraq (1998); the Kosovo war (1999); sending British troops to Sierra Leone (2000); and the two post 9/11 wars – the removal of the Taliban in Afghanistan and the Iraq war.[8]

Deployment of British troops in Sierra Leone helped stabilize the country until UN troops could be deployed and legitimate government be restored. To me, the case is positive. After the war against the Taliban, the UN chaired talks in Bonn, leading to the agreement of December 2001 and democratic elections. There are still significant problems for the government. Kosovo and Iraq are more complex. The Kosovo action was under NATO auspices, as it was clear that the Security Council would not support military action. The war against Saddam Hussein's government was conducted by a coalition led by the US. In both these cases, there are significant, but different, problems. If one judges that the wars were on balance necessary, the issue of authorization is key. One of the issues which has to be addressed in the discussions emanating from the High Level Panel's report is what can be done to avoid a situation in which wars are being conducted in the name of the international community, without the specific endorsement of the UN Security Council. If one opposes the wars, the issue is even more acute: what can be done to prevent NATO, 'coalitions of the willing' or anyone else conducting such wars? The issues are highly charged and contentious. Blair used a number of justifications for the military action – weapons of mass destruction, the character of Saddam Hussein's government, failure to comply with previous UN resolutions (678, 687 and 1441) – as providing the legal basis for use of armed force. Internationally and nationally, these arguments have been challenged. For those operating within the just war framework, an assessment would centre on such criteria as last resort, legitimate authority and reasonable chance of success (in terms of the character of government in Iraq and the long-term stability of the country, not just military victory).

For opponents of military force, there are also questions. In a case like Kosovo, could the population have been protected adequately from Milosevic, given his record of 'ethnic cleansing'? In the Iraq case, would the continuation of weapons inspections, sanctions and pressure have resolved the crisis?

If one accepts the ICISS criteria and reserves military intervention for cases such as genocide or massive levels of human rights violations, one still has to develop effective policies for less grave situations.

The UN Secretary General's High Level Panel

The response of the UN Secretary General's High Level Panel is instructive. It accepts the basic approach of the ICISS report. Referring to the 'successive humanitarian disasters in Somalia, Bosnia and Herzegovina, Rwanda, Kosovo and now Darfur, Sudan', it refers to the emerging norm of the 'responsibility to protect'.[9] It is significant that Iraq is not on the list. The HLP concludes:

> We endorse the emerging norm that there is a collective international responsibility to protect, exercisable by the Security Council authorizing military intervention as a last resort, in the event of genocide and other large-scale killing, ethnic cleansing or serious violations of international law which sovereign governments have proved powerless or unwilling to prevent.[10]

The HLP produces a set of criteria compatible with those of ICISS:

In considering whether to authorize or endorse the use of military force, the Security Council should always address – whatever other considerations it may take into account – at least the following five basic criteria of legitimacy:

a) *Seriousness of threat.* Is the threatened harm to state or human security of a kind, and sufficiently clear and serious, to justify prima facie the use of military force? In the case of internal threats, does it involve genocide and other large-scale killing, ethnic cleansing or serious violations of international humanitarian law, actual or imminently apprehended?

b) *Proper purpose.* Is it clear that the primary purpose of the proposed military action is to halt or avert the threat in question, whatever other purposes or motives may be involved?

c) *Last resort.* Has every non-military option for meeting the threat in question been explored, with reasonable grounds for believing that other measures will not succeed?

d) *Proportional means.* Are the scale, duration and intensity of the proposed military action the minimum necessary to meet the threat in question?

e) *Balance of consequences.* Is there a reasonable chance of the military action being successful in meeting the threat in question, with the consequences of action not likely to be worse than the consequences of inaction?[11]

Earlier, I quoted Helmut Gollwitzer's statement on the importance of the state's monopoly of legitimate force. The efforts of the HLP are to seek to ensure that the equivalent at world level resides with the UN Security Council. It seeks to counter sins of omission (failure to prevent genocide in Rwanda) and sins of commission (the temptation to wage war without explicit Security Council endorsement). It presents a more comprehensive package than ICISS. In short, it seeks to reassert rule-based multilateralism and provide the basis for consistent and effective peacekeeping. Whether it will be accepted – particularly by the USA, given that it also addresses UN Security Council reform – remains to be seen.

It was noted above that Iraq was not discussed by the HLP in the context of humanitarian disasters and the responsibility to protect. Whatever one's judgement on the Iraq issue, it has clearly been damaging for the reputation of the UN that two of the five permanent members of the Security Council (in a coalition with other countries) felt that it was necessary to fight a war without its explicit authorization.[12] It has also been argued that Iraq presented a qualitatively new kind of threat. The HLP addresses this issue without specific reference to Iraq (therefore in a forward-looking, not backward-looking manner) thus:

> In the world of the twenty-first century, the international community does have to be concerned about nightmare scenarios combining terrorism, weapons of mass destruction and irresponsible states, and much more besides, which may conceivably justify the use of force, not just reactively but preventively and before a latent threat becomes imminent.[13]

The HLP concludes that preventive use of military force, under Article 51, can be authorized by the Security Council under Chapter VII of the UN Charter and that Article 51 does not need to be updated.

> For those impatient with such a response, the answer must be that, in a world full of perceived potential threats, the risk to the global order and the norm of non-intervention on which it continues to be based is simply too great for the legality of unilateral preventive action, as distinct from collectively endorsed action, to be accepted. Allowing one so to act is to allow all.
>
> We do not favour the rewriting or reinterpretation of Article 51.[14]

It reaches two more important conclusions:

> The Security Council is fully empowered under Chapter VII of the Charter of the United Nations to address the full range of security threats with which states are concerned. The task is not to find alternatives to the Security Council as a source of authority but to make the Council work better than it has.[15]

The HLP also warns:

> The Council may well need to be prepared to be much more proactive on these issues, taking more decisive action earlier, than it has in the past.[16]

The Role of the Military in Humanitarian Operations[17]
It must be stressed that the use of the military and potentially of armed force is not restricted to the cases of intervention addressed above. There is also the issue of how the military can and should be used in humanitarian operations.

Humanitarian specialists criticize the major powers for their reluctance or refusal to use even part of their military force for human protection purposes in the multilateral context of the United Nations. Humanitarian agencies stress their specialist qualifications in the delivery of humanitarian assistance, but require from the military a robust exercise of military force to secure the environment in which aid can be delivered. Politicians are often reluctant to provide such a mandate. The military can be frustrated by what is seen as a purist insistence by humanitarian agencies that they should be the ones delivering aid. If the military are there in force and have spare capacity, why should they not be used? Particularly in insecure environments, however, humanitarian agencies point to the added danger created by confusing the military and humanitarian roles. This can lead to the humanitarian agencies becoming military targets. Certain forms of delivery by the military of humanitarian resources are seen by humanitarian specialists as inefficient or even counter-productive; dropping food parcels from aeroplanes is a case in point. In cases where a military mission is not under UN control, the civilian–military interface is complex. Humanitarian agencies often need and benefit from military logistics (e.g. for food convoys). The military–civilian interface is a field where further clarification is necessary: between the United Nations and member-states; between military forces and humanitarian agencies at international and national level; and between governments and non-governmental organizations. It is also essential to clarify the issues both in principle and on a case-by-case basis (e.g. through memoranda of understanding).

Key Elements for Protection of Civilians[18]
The United Nations has been engaged in recent years in a systematic effort to improve the protection of civilians in armed conflict. This work is being carried forward through an international consultation process led by the Office for the Coordination of Humanitarian Affairs (OCHA). There is no shortage of 'lessons learnt' as a result of humanitarian activities, but there is a long way to go in translating this learning into protection in actual conflicts.

Through such measures as UN Security Council Resolutions 1265 (1999) and 1296 (2000), and the *Aide Memoire on Protection of Civilians in Armed Conflict*, the developing understanding of necessary measures has been elaborated. Key elements of the strategy include:

- Facilitation of safe and unimpeded access to vulnerable populations.
- Maintenance of the humanitarian and civilian character of camps for refugees and internally displaced persons.
- Ending impunity for those responsible for serious violations of international humanitarian, human rights and criminal law.
- Building confidence and enhancing stability through the promotion of truth and reconciliation.
- Strengthening the capacity of local police and judicial systems to enforce law and order.
- Achieving disarmament, demobilization, reintegration and rehabilitation of former combatants.
- Facilitating a secure environment for vulnerable populations and humanitarian personnel.
- Addressing the problems of small arms and landmines.
- Ensuring that security and peacekeeping forces are appropriately trained for the protection of civilians.
- Addressing the specific needs of women for assistance and protection.
- Addressing the specific needs of children for assistance and protection.
- Ensuring the safety and security of humanitarian and associated personnel.
- Addressing the impact of national natural resource exploitation on the protection of civilians (e.g. in situations where the revenue is used to fuel conflict).
- Minimizing unintended adverse consequences of sanctions on the civilian population.[19]

Recent statements by Under Secretary General Jan Egeland[20] to the UN Security Council have highlighted such issues as:

- Ensuring humanitarian access
- Security of humanitarian personnel
- Better protection of women and children in war[21]
- Refugees and internally displaced persons
- Disarmament, demobilization, reintegration and rehabilitation (DDRR)
- Compliance and an end to impunity
- Addressing 'forgotten emergencies'

Clearly, in most of these issues, properly defined and carried out military deployment can be a valuable element. Traditional humanitarian workers stress the need for civilian direction of policy and, wherever possible, well-defined mandates under UN auspices.

Peacekeeping and Peace Enforcement: An Increasingly Blurred Distinction?

The HLP has an instructive section on peace enforcement and peacekeeping capability.[22] This stresses that even though there is conceptual clarity between peacekeeping missions (Chapter VI operations) and peace enforcement missions (Chapter VII operations), there is an increasing recognition that missions which begin with the consent of the conflict parties can go sour and require a more robust mandate. There is a warning that more peacekeepers are likely to be needed if efforts to end several longstanding wars in Africa are successful.

Conclusions

1 The work of the International Commission on Intervention and State Sovereignty and its subsequent development by the High Level Panel provide cogent applications of the just war theory for our times. Their criteria for intervention uphold state sovereignty – properly understood – but reserve the right of the international community, sanctioned by the UN Security Council, to use military force in extremis.

2 Article 51 on self-defence does not require revision; rather than seeking other authority than the Security Council, member states should make the Security Council work more effectively.

3 Below the high threshold of major violations of human rights, there can be occasions when intervention is required – the case of Sierra Leone and some of the interventions of ECOWAS can be mentioned. These too should be internationally agreed.

4 There can be a military element in protecting and enabling humanitarian access, but the 'militarization of humanitarianism' carries dangers.

5 Peacekeeping and peace enforcement require robust mandates and a readiness by developed countries to deploy equipment and personnel. It is desirable, where possible, for regional solutions to be found (e.g. African solutions for African problems), but this can also require military support from developed countries.

It will be of great interest to see how the community of nations responds to the challenge of the UN Secretary General in his report 'In larger freedom'. I concur almost fully with this statement:

> The task is not to find alternatives to the Security Council as a source of authority but to make it work better. When considering whether to authorize or endorse the use of military force, the Council should come to a common view on how to weigh the seriousness of the

threat; the proper purpose of the proposed military action; whether means short of the use of force might plausibly succeed in stopping the threat; whether the military option is proportional to the threat at hand; and whether there is a reasonable chance of success. By undertaking to make the case for military action in this way, the Council would add transparency to its deliberations and make its decisions more likely to be respected, by both governments and world public opinion. I would therefore recommend that the Security Council adopt a resolution setting out these principles and expressing its intention to be guided by them when deciding whether to authorize or mandate the use of force.[23]

That would only be a first step, however; consistency of action – especially when it required deployment of significant numbers of ground troops in a 'far-away country of which we know little' – is the real test of commitment.

It is indeed true, as the Archbishop of Canterbury has reminded us, that 'moral vision is harder to convert into reality than we would like'. In his sermon in St Paul's Cathedral, London, after the Iraq war he said:

> Those who defended the action in Iraq rightly reminded us that while we talk, people are suffering appallingly; while we try to keep our hands clean, atrocity and oppression reign unchecked. Whatever the different judgements about the decision to go to war, we have to recognize the moral seriousness of those who carry out the decision.

> But as we look at a still uncertain and dangerous landscape, as we recall the soldiers and civilians killed since the direct military campaign ended, as we think of the UN personnel and the relief workers who have died, we have to acknowledge that moral vision is harder to convert into reality than we would like. We never know in advance quite what price will have to be paid in human lives, civilian and military, local and foreign, young and old.[24]

In my view, it is hard to argue that the criteria of last resort, legitimate authority and proportionality were met. Detailed accounts suggest that the decision-making was profoundly flawed. However, having taken the action, it is now necessary to work against the adverse consequences and to seek to ensure that Iraq is stabilized and that a functioning state is established.

The agenda of protection is far wider than this one issue, however, and requires a readiness to use the entire range of techniques, including use of military hardware and personnel to protect humanitarian space. The protection agenda should not be reduced to discussion of war-fighting. To paraphrase Gustavo Gutierrez, at the end of his book on *Liberation Theology*, one genuine act of solidarity with the vulnerable, those in need of protection, with or without the threat or use of proportionate force, is worth any amount of abstract theology. Balancing careful ethical reflection, we should recall such figures as Archbishop Oscar Romero and the six Jesuits murdered in El Salvador for an authentic witness on how to exercise the responsibility to protect. That is the authentic *imitatio Christi* – recalling Romero's words – *pauper vivens* – *imago Dei* – the poor person living is the image of God. Jon Sobrino, friend and colleague of the six community members who were killed, spoke in a reflection on the spiritual 'Were you there when they crucified my Lord?' of the first need of the church to be there where people are suffering. It is from this presence that the first steps of a praxis open up. He speaks too of the poor as those who are close to death – I would add, unnecessary death. With Bonhoeffer, I believe that the shedding of blood always involves guilt, but there can be situations in which that guilt must be accepted, for the greater guilt is to stand by and watch others being killed. Rather than 'taking down the crucified peoples from the cross', the task is to prevent them being crucified. A theology which does not prevent the unnecessary suffering of others, or seeks to explain and spiritualize it, is the worst misuse of religion. Helder Camara has rightly warned of the 'spiral of violence': the criterion of the last resort must be taken with great seriousness, as violence has a way of breeding violence. I do not believe that it can be totally ruled out. Faith should motivate the defence of life.

NOTES

1. H. Chadwick, *Augustine* (Oxford: Oxford University Press, 1986), p. 100.
2. 'Das staatliche Gewaltsmonopol ist ein kostbarer zivilisatorischer Fortschritt ...'. H. Gollwitzer, 'Zum Problem der Gewalt in der christlich Ethik', in *Forderungen der Freiheit* (Munich: C. Kaiser, 1976), pp. 126–46.
3. UN Charter, Preamble.
4. The following summary of the ICISS report is taken almost verbatim from my Wilton Park report: Roger Williamson, 'The Responsibility to Protect: The International Duty to Defend the Vulnerable', WPP 700. Available at www.wiltonpark.org.uk/web/papers/pdfs/WPP-WP700.pdf.
5. The Uniting for Peace procedure is described in more detail in the ICISS report, p. 53: 'The practical difficulty ... is to contemplate the unlikelihood, in any but very exceptional case [*sic*], of a two-thirds majority, as required under the Uniting for Peace procedure, being able to be put together in a political environment in which there has been either no majority on the Security Council, or a veto imposed or threatened by one or more of the permanent members – although Kosovo and Rwanda might just conceivably have been such cases.'
6. I have taken this case study for two reasons: I am familiar with the material and because it is instructive.
7. Tony Blair, 'Doctrine of the International Community', 22 April 1999, speech to the Economic Club of Chicago. Available at www.globalpolicy.org/globaliz/politics/blair.htm.
8. For a detailed study, see John Kampfner, *Blair's Wars* (London: Free Press, 2003). For a critical view, see two important articles by Rober Skidelsky, 'The American Contract', *Prospect* (July 2003), pp. 30–5 and 'The Just War Tradition', *Prospect* (December 2004), pp. 28–33.
9. Para. 201, p. 65.
10. Para. 203, p. 66.
11. Para. 207, p. 67.
12. The argument in support of military action centres on authorization deriving from UNSCR 1441 and earlier resolutions, which were being contravened by Iraq.
13. HLP para. 194, p. 64.
14. Paras. 191, 192, p. 63.
15. Para. 198, p. 65.
16. Para. 194, p. 64.
17. Also drawn from Roger Williamson, *The Responsibility to Protect*.
18. Also drawn from ibid.
19. These themes are explained more fully in the *Aide Memoire* and other documentation available on the OCHA website at www.reliefweb.int/ocha_ol/civilians/.
20. See his presentations in June and December 2004, also on the OCHA website.
21. Reference must be made here to UNSCR 1325
22. HLP, pp. 67–9.
23. Report of the Secretary General, 'In larger freedom: towards development, security and human rights for all', A/59/2005, 21 March 2005, at www.un.org/largerfreedom/.
24. Rowan Williams, 'Moral vision is harder to convert into reality than we would like', *The Times*, 11 October 2003.

International Response to Human Rights Violations
With Particular Reference to Palestinian Refugees

Jeff Handmaker

Violations of human rights and humanitarian law, particularly when systematically carried out by a state with no regard to their consequences, demand that the international community not simply take notice, but take action. Proportionate and 'effective'[1] responses from the international community arise, due in large part to an emerging international legal principle of the responsibility to protect, which forms part and parcel of state responsibility. The responsibility to protect is principally a duty to ensure that mechanisms are in place to prevent violations from taking place[2] and secondly a duty of states, acting in their individual or – ideally – collective capacities, to intervene in order to protect civilians from potential or further violations. With the creation of the United Nations in 1945, this has involved the establishment of multiple international authorities to fulfil these collective roles, in order, as the UN Charter provides, 'to save succeeding generations from the scourge of war [and] … promote social progress and better standards of life in larger freedom'.

When international authorities fail in their responsibility to protect, states, regional bodies (such as the EU) and indeed civil society continue to have important roles to play in ensuring that international law is promoted as a determining framework to protect human security and resolve conflicts. States, indeed, have legally binding obligations to hold other states to account to prevent violations of international humanitarian law.

John Dugard has stressed that a state's defiance of the international community can pose a threat not only to the 'international legal order', but also to the international order itself.[3] The challenges are how to hold states to account using mechanisms provided by international law. In this regard especially it is important to remember that 'urgent' situations demand equivalent responses, though at the same time ensuring that the focus remains on the protection of human security.

This essay outlines various responses available to states to respond to violations of human rights and humanitarian law, when international authorities fail. It describes the responses that civil society can take using various mechanisms for interacting with states and/or supranational organizations. It illustrates these responses by reference to one of the most intractable humanitarian crises: Palestinian refugees.

State Responses to Violations of Human Rights and IHL

Marco Sassoli speaks of the responsibility of states towards violations of international humanitarian law as formed by 'traditional' and 'new' layers of international law. The 'traditional' layer of international law refers to the desire for 'coexistence and cooperation' between states, referring only to situations in which states *violate* humanitarian law. A 'new' layer of international law refers to the 'law of the community of six billion human beings' in which individual violators are increasingly being held accountable through various ad hoc or permanent legal mechanisms. According to Sassoli, there is an interaction between these two layers, namely that while states desire to curb the belligerent behaviour of other states, such actions are 'irrelevant' unless there are also laws to protect the victims of war and those who wage it.[4]

There are indeed several possible interventions available to states to exercise pressure on an alleged violating or belligerent state in order to prevent or halt violations of international humanitarian law. Umesh Palwankar has produced a useful overview of possible state responses, in order of severity, from state protests to collective, armed intervention.[5]

Exercising diplomatic pressure through protests and denunciation

States can challenge the violations of states by way of stepped-up phases of diplomatic pressure, beginning with protests. Such official protests are directed either towards the ambassador and other diplomatic representatives of the alleged violating state, or directly to the government of the alleged violating state via one's own diplomatic representatives. In order to be effective, Palwankar argues that such protests be 'vigorous and continuous'.

A further level of diplomatic pressure is public denunciation of another state, preferably by more than one state and ideally through an influential, supranational organization such as the Council of the European Union or the Security Council of the United Nations. An example of such denunciations occurred on 20 December 1990, when the USA called on the UN Security Council to denounce Israel's deportation of Palestinian civilians from territories occupied by Israel and to 'comply fully' with the provisions of the Fourth Geneva Convention.[6]

Diplomatic pressure can be exercised by states directly or through 'intermediary' states, particularly when it is alleged that they are jointly responsible for violations taking place, for example by providing arms, training and other equipment to a belligerent state.

Calling states to account through fact-finding missions

Palwankar refers to international fact-finding commissions as a further means of exerting pressure against alleged violating states. Such mechanisms operate under the auspices of the United Nations and regional political organizations, which have established various committees and special rapporteurs to gather information about a particular issue and report back to the organization on recommended measures that could be taken against an alleged violating state.

Such commissions draw their legitimacy from a state (or group of states), who must declare their acceptance of the competence of that body and their desire to approach it, even if the alleged violating state itself has not declared its acceptance. However, such a body's effectiveness – not to mention its legitimacy – is obviously enhanced if the state under investigation accepts its competence or, minimally, does not block its operation. Such diplomacy in the establishment of a fact-finding commission can itself be a means of inducing a state to take steps to suppress continued violations of international humanitarian law, as a refusal to accept such a commission could be 'publicly regretted' by states.

Matters can also be referred to international tribunals, notably the International Court of Justice, which has the capacity to issue binding decisions concerning disputes between states, provided both states explicitly accept its jurisdiction. The ICJ also has the authority to receive requests from the United Nations to issue an advisory opinion on the application of international law to a given situation.

Holding states to account through retortion and reprisals

If 'diplomatic' measures prove to have little or no effect against a state's violations of international humanitarian law, then more aggressive options become available, though most such options still fall short of armed intervention. Palwankar explains, by reference to various examples, that states have authority to respond by way of acts of retortion or reprisals. Acts of retortion are designed to leverage external political pressure against an alleged violating state. Such measures, though 'unfriendly', are intrinsically lawful, provided they are carried out in direct response to an act of state that may also simply be unfriendly (and lawful), or internationally unlawful. State reprisals, on the other hand, are counter-measures and thus by definition unlawful acts, though considered to be exceptionally justified in light of prior unlawful acts committed by a belligerent state to which they are directed.

Acts of retortion

A state that is believed to be violating international humanitarian law can face expulsion of its diplomats and/or severance of diplomatic relations with other states. Such measures are exercised as temporary, though forceful responses. For example, the USA expelled Iranian diplomats and severed its diplomatic relations with the government of Iran when American diplomats were taken hostage in Tehran in the 1970s.

Further steps include halting ongoing negotiations on bilateral or multilateral agreements with a violating state, or refusing to ratify agreements already signed with a violating state. Such measures often concern trading agreements that provide for preferential terms of trade and can therefore be a substantial means of exercising combined political and economic pressure against a belligerent state.

A final act of retortion, which can have a particularly devastating impact on a country's civilian population, and must therefore be carefully thought through, involves reducing or suspending official development assistance to a belligerent state, either by a single state or through a development organization such as the European Union.

Reprisals

When a state refuses to comply with the will of the international community and continues to violate international humanitarian law with impunity, further counter-measures can be taken by individual or groups of states against a belligerent state. As with the above, most of these measures do not involve armed intervention, though they may well aim to reduce the military capacity of the belligerent state concerned.

Trade restrictions, bans on direct and/or indirect investment in a belligerent state and the freezing of capital held by nationals of a belligerent state are steps beyond state acts of retortion that aim to do more than simply remove trading privileges, but to place direct pressure on a belligerent state's economy. In order to be most effective, such restrictions should focus directly on the mechanisms of state repression, in particular the banning of military and other state security equipment. However, long-term efforts often demand broader trading restrictions. Such restrictions are intended as a means of punishing a belligerent state by way of economic sanctions and potentially a much broader official boycott.

Further measures, as part of a broader official boycott, include the suspension of transport and other agreements (e.g. sports, cultural and scientific agreements of cooperation). For example, the government of France in 1985 (later followed by the United Kingdom, the Netherlands and eventually the USA) banned all new investment in the Republic of South Africa in response to the apartheid regime's increasingly violent repression of the country's majority black nationals. Similar measures have been exercised against the governments of Uganda and Rhodesia and more recently Iraq and Zimbabwe.

A final measure of last resort that states can exercise against a belligerent state are armed interventions. Such measures must satisfy a range of minimum requirements, discussed by others, not least the High Level Panel. In principle, armed measures must only be carried out under the auspices of the United Nations Security Council in reference to Chapter VI or VII of the UN

Charter or, by way of delegation from the Security Council, in the context of regional security agreements such as NATO.

Responses to Violations from Civil Society

When both states and international authorities fail in their responsibility to protect, civil society organizations often present the last hope for ending a violent and/or repressive regime or to prevent mass violations of human rights. In this context, it is important to emphasize that civil society exercises a tertiary role in the responsibility to protect, with the primary purpose of its interventions to urge states to take action.

Civil society is a complex term, variously represented by affected individuals, collective groupings such as social movements, trade unions, non-governmental organizations and others, such as church and other faith-based networks. In this context, they play a critical, complementary role to states. While the state responsibility to protect is defined by the rights states grant to individuals, which Bas de-Gaay Fortman refers to as 'downstream rights',[7] civil society (particularly the grassroots) can also assert certain freedoms and entitlements, referred to by De Gaay Fortman as 'upstream rights'. In a practical sense, such a relationship between the individual and the state is characterized by the mixed roles that civil society plays. This involves a frequently complicated process of reconciling, on the one hand, their support to states (when they take progressive action) and, on the other hand, maintaining a critical distance and preserving their independence.

This complex process of claiming rights is deserving of our attention on the responsibility to protect. Individuals, both on their own and through collective mechanisms, are increasingly holding states to account. This is achieved through advocacy and in particular direct and indirect claims through an ever-growing array of national, regional and international mechanisms.

Direct human rights claims

The first level of claims against belligerent states is always the national courts and political systems of the belligerent state itself. For reasons that are not always so obvious, efforts to hold states to account through such official mechanisms can prove to be a frustrating, expensive and even fruitless exercise. Nevertheless, it is important that they be pursued, as it may indeed be a requirement for pursuing international claims (i.e. exhausting local remedies). As such, national mechanisms must be measured against international standards, including impartiality, independence, fairness and due process.

Diplomatic efforts through third-party states are a further means of pursuing direct claims, though they can also prove to be a frustrating exercise. However, if matched with equivalent efforts by states themselves to hold belligerent states to account (as discussed above), they can be effective. In addition to such efforts as described above, a third-party state can offer consular protection (political asylum), yet they are particularly urged to do so in the context of UN guidelines on the protection of human rights defenders.[8]

Further direct human rights claims can be made through regional political mechanisms, notably the European Court of Human Rights, which through Protocol 11 allows individuals the right to make claims directly against a member state to the European Convention on Human Rights. Less direct mechanisms exist for individuals to lodge claims in the Inter-American Human Rights Court and the African Commission on Human and People's Rights.

Indirect human rights claims

Indirect human rights claims that civil society can invoke come essentially in two main forms: civil claims and universal jurisdiction for international crimes. They are 'indirect' in the sense that a state is not per se the subject of the action, but rather individuals who may have been acting as representatives of a violating state. Both types of claims invoke national courts in a third country; in other words, it is not necessary that a country in which a claim is being sought have a direct connection with the subject of the litigation. Neither of these claims comes easily; indeed, both involve a high level of legal expertise, with the inevitable associated costs.

Civil claims: suing in a third country court

A good example of third-country civil claims is the USA, which passed a law in 1789 allowing foreign nationals to make a legal claim for damages against any individual – regardless of their nationality – provided the claim involved a violation of the 'law of nations' or any treaty that the USA was obliged to enforce. The law, known as the Alien Tort Claims Act (ATCA), was later amended by the 1991 Torture Victim Protection Act to specifically include torture as a basis for making a claim against an individual.

The United Kingdom and other countries have similar possibilities for making civil claims, although the law is not very 'tested' in this particular area, not least because it is very cumbersome to overcome the many legal obstacles, including *forum non conveniens*[10] and sovereign immunity.[11]

Criminal claims: prosecuting in a third country court (universal jurisdiction)[12]

International criminal law as a unique juridical concept emerged roughly during the last half-century, through the development of humanitarian law and human rights principles that sought to challenge impunity by prosecuting those individually responsible for perpetrating human rights violations. Universal jurisdiction is essentially an instrument of international criminal law that allows states to exercise national jurisdiction over individuals in respect of certain international crimes that are deemed to be of concern to all humanity, without regard to the nationality of the accused, the victim, or the location where the alleged crime took place.

Universal jurisdiction draws essentially from two sources: international humanitarian law and more recent developments in international human rights law and case law jurisprudence. The universal jurisdiction principle also draws on a range of other international conventions, including the Convention against Torture[13] and jurisprudence arising out of the various ad hoc tribunals created in the last century.[14]

A notable example in which the universal jurisdiction principle was invoked occurred when a Spanish judge requested the extradition of Pinochet for international crimes committed against Spanish citizens. The House of Lords in the UK, which considered the Spanish government's extradition request, determined that there was no immunity for torture – international crimes, it declared, were not the functions of a head of state. While the extradition/prosecution ultimately did not take place in either the UK or Spain, it is important to note that efforts to seek justice against Pinochet had a cumulative impact. Chile recently revoked Pinochet's immunity.

Other human rights advocacy strategies[15]

There are many other human rights advocacy strategies that civil society organizations can follow in seeking to hold authoritarian regimes to account. Bringing about change in a country that persistently refuses to abide by international law (such as South Africa during apartheid) is not an easy task, but it is by no means impossible. As veteran Dutch human rights advocate Adri Nieuwhof has noted,[16] bringing about this change rests on four fundamental principles: (1) a situation of deep crisis; (2) diplomatic pressure; (3) economic pressure; and (4) well organized civic structures. These principles present a framework for future action on the part of civil society and are worth examining more closely.

Interpreting the crisis

While it might be possible to argue that a situation of deep crisis exists, misinformation abounds in interpreting a given crisis. The media obviously play a central role in this. Both television and print media are prone to bias and misreporting.[17] The challenge to civil society in interpreting the crisis is to reflect the 'facts on the ground', which some organizations manage more successfully than others.

Increasing diplomatic pressure

Diplomatic pressure exercised by individual states rarely goes far enough. Furthermore, the permanent members of the Security Council have frequently obstructed it from taking direct, principled action – notably on the responsibility to protect.

Supported by the language of international law (notably by judgements of the International Court of Justice in advisory opinions), civil society organizations can equip themselves effectively to lobby their governments to take an uncompromising stance, insisting that international law be respected and implemented and warning a belligerent state that a failure to do so may well mean further diplomatic and possibly economic isolation. Civil society may also insist that its government's commitment to respect human rights be backed up by concrete actions. When things look bleak, it is important to remember that a strategic campaign can have long-term, cumulative consequences (as with Pinochet).

Stepping up economic pressure

There is a growing view among civil society organizations that the only realistic way to address state impunity and to stimulate a tougher line on the part of the international community is through citizen actions: divestment and consumer boycotts, as a prelude to economic sanctions.[18]

It is not always easy to determine when and which actions intended to isolate a country economically will prove most effective. It is essential in any event that there be clear political backing by the groups affected by international law violations. For example, during the anti-apartheid movement, several members of the ANC explicitly called for sanctions against South Africa. While initially the ANC was not unanimous in its position on the issue, it later determined boycotts and sanctions to be the correct policy once it became evident that boycott actions were having a positive impact in gaining the attention of powerful states. Alternatively, solidarity organizations might take direction from broad-based civil society groupings.

Supporting and activating civic structures

The final factor outlined by Nieuwhof is a complex one in the context of Palestine. Well-organized civic structures can be particularly effective in taking collective action, which is a principal reason why efforts are taken by authoritarian governments to weaken such structures.[19] Abroad, exiled groups often face numerous obstacles in finding safe refuge and exile communities are often deeply fragmented.

Consequently, there is a great need to support and develop civic structures, both in the country itself and abroad. Here, donors play a key role. However, there ought not to be complete reliance on donors. For example, as the anti-apartheid movement illustrated, some of the most successful and enduring civic efforts were based on principles of volunteerism.

Responsibility to Protect in the Context of the Palestinian Refugee Crisis

There has long been a reluctance on the part of the international community to take action on the issue of Palestinians generally and Palestinian refugees specifically. Some organizations –

quite outrageously – have called Palestinian refugees an 'extremist issue', while it is very clearly an issue that goes to the heart of the Palestinian struggle for self-determination and thus forms a 'core issue' in the Palestinian–Israeli conflict. Reluctance by organizations to address the Palestinian refugee issue therefore ranges from intimidation at its complexity to more perplexing concerns that to even acknowledge the issue would involve criticism of Israel's role in generating the forced displacement of several million people; and that such criticism may somehow be deemed anti-Semitic. The charge of anti-Semitism has indeed prevented a more open discussion on the underlying causes of the conflict in general.[20].Consequently, Palestinian refugees rarely feature on the 'radar screen' of human rights or peace discussions concerning Palestine and Israel.

Background to the crisis
Palestinian refugees form the largest single group of forcibly displaced persons in the world. Estimated at 5 million,[21] approximately a third of them live in refugee camps in the Israeli Occupied Territories of the Gaza Strip and West Bank, as well as Jordan, Syria and Lebanon, assisted by the UN Relief and Works Agency. The remainder live as part of host societies, although not all have been granted citizenship in these countries. Large numbers of Palestinian refugees live in Iraq and Egypt, while smaller numbers reside in Europe, the USA and elsewhere. The conditions of their reception vary greatly from country to country.

The Palestinian refugee crisis, well-documented by organizations such as Badil, arose in essentially three phases, the first two of which involved 'high-intensity' conflicts between Israel and neighbouring states, and the last of which involved a long-drawn out 'low intensity' (but no less devastating) conflict from the time of Israel's occupation of the West Bank and Gaza Strip territories in 1967 until the present day.

First phase: Arab–Israeli war of 1948
The first phase of the Palestinian crisis began in 1948, following British withdrawal from the Palestine Mandate territory and Israel's unilateral declaration of independence. Hundreds of thousands of Palestinians were expelled or forcibly displaced in the first Arab–Israeli war that followed and over 530 Arab villages and cities were destroyed and/or depopulated of Palestinians. Palestinians refer to this event as the *nakba* or catastrophe.

Second phase: Arab–Israeli wars of 1967 and 1973
The second Arab–Israeli war that took place in 1967 resulted in Israel's occupation of the Gaza Strip, West Bank, Golan Heights and the Sinai Peninsula. Although Israel later withdrew from Sinai after a peace agreement with Egypt, it maintained its occupation of the other territories, notwithstanding explicit demands from international authorities (notably Security Council Resolution 242 of 1967) to withdraw. Additional forced displacement and a tightening of Israel's control in the occupied territories were caused by a further war in 1973.

Israeli reprisals against Palestinians marked Israel's policy of collective punishment, a policy that has persisted up to the present day. Despite numerous UN Security Council and General Assembly Resolutions calling for Israel's withdrawal from these occupied territories, Israel has refused to accept that it is an occupying power and consequently also does not accept that it is bound by the Fourth Geneva Convention on the Protection of Civilians. This has had devastating consequences for the protection needs of Palestinian refugees, notably the Israeli government's transfer of Israelis to occupied territories as part of its settlements policy. Such transfers are expressly forbidden by international law under the Fourth Geneva Convention.[22]

Third phase: Israeli occupation, 1967–present
Israel's settlement policy, which began in earnest from the 1970s, has involved further expropriation of Palestinian land, forced displacement, denial of services and a massive increase in Israel's military presence in the occupied territories, as documented by organizations such as B'tselem[23] and Al-Haq.[24] Israel's closure policy, following the first and second uprisings or intifadas, and reinforced by further restrictive policies such as administrative detention, has greatly tightened controls on movement and led to countless documented violations of human rights and humanitarian law.

In 2002 Israel tightened its control over the occupied territories even more by beginning construction of a wall, mostly inside the so-called 'green line', or line of armistice following the 1967 war. Numerous protests and legal cases determined that the wall was illegal by its construction inside occupied Palestinian territory. However, Israel has mostly disregarded these efforts, even referring to a subsequent advisory opinion of the International Court of Justice as 'irrelevant'.

International legal responses to the Palestinian refugee crisis
There is no issue that has received more attention from the international community, and especially the United Nations, than the conflict in Israel/Palestine. Beginning with the UN Partition Plan in 1947, the UN has consistently sought to uphold international law as the context in which the conflict ought to be resolved and in which refugees are to be protected, but sadly, with only marginal success.[25]

Recognizing the responsibility to protect: creation of UN agencies to assist and protect Palestinian refugees
The UN recognized its responsibility to protect Palestinian refugees back in 1948, with the simultaneous creation of the UN Relief and Works Agency (UNRWA) and UN Conciliation Commission on Palestine in 1948. The UNCCP was given a protection mandate, intended to resolve the forced displacement of Palestinian refugees as a consequence of the first Arab–Israeli war. The creation of these two institutions was to ensure, respectively, assistance to and protection of Palestinian refugees. The mandates of these institutions were reinforced by UN General Assembly Resolution 194 of 1948, which in addition to other provisions provided that:

> refugees wishing to return to their homes and live at peace with their neighbours should be permitted to do so at the earliest practicable date, and that compensation should be paid for the property of those choosing not to return and for loss of or damage to property which, under principles of international law or in equity, should be made good by the governments or authorities responsible.[26]

Unfortunately, the UNCCP only carried out active operations for a few years and was able to fulfil just a small aspect of its mandate, namely the registration of Palestinian homes and property confiscated and/or destroyed as a consequence of the 1948 war. The ceasing of operations by UNCCP effectively left Palestinians unprotected. The UN Refugees Convention of 1951[27] unfortunately did not resolve this problem; indeed, Palestinians were implicitly excluded from its provisions through the Convention's Article 1D.

Following the second Arab–Israeli war, the UN Security Council passed Resolution 242 in 1967. In this key resolution, which emphasized the responsibility to protect vulnerable populations, the Security Council called for both 'withdrawal of Israeli armed forces from territories occupied in the recent conflict' and 'achieving a just settlement of the refugee problem'. However, neither of these demands was recognized by Israel.

Revisiting the responsibility to protect: UNHCR's clarification of article 1D
Growing concern over the protection needs of Palestinian refugees led the UNHCR to revise its position on Palestinian refugees in the context of the 1951 Refugees Convention. In a 2002 Note on International Protection, the UNHCR clarified article 1D.[29] While the Note confirmed that 1D was clearly aimed at Palestinians assisted by UNRWA and that the intention of the Convention was to avoid 'overlapping competencies', it also stressed that the intention of the Article was to ensure 'the continuity of protection and assistance of Palestinian refugees as necessary'. The Note confirmed that 1D affected both Palestinians displaced in 1948 (referring to UN General Assembly Resolution 194) and those displaced by the 1967 Arab–Israeli war (referring to General Assembly Resolution 2252 of 1967) and were unable to return.

In sum, the 2002 Note confirmed that three groups of Palestinians were in principle entitled to broader, legal protection. Firstly, those displaced for other reasons, for example individual persecution, would be entitled to protection under the 1951 Refugee Convention. Secondly, Palestinians outside UNRWA-assisted areas would be able to apply for 1951 Convention status.[30] Thirdly, states should consider the possibility of non-returnability of Palestinians to UNRWA-assisted areas for reasons of persecution and, where possible, extend alternative forms of legal protection.[31]

Confirming the responsibility to protect: ICJ advisory opinion of 2004
In July 2004, following a request from the United Nations Secretary General, the International Court of Justice in The Hague delivered an advisory opinion on the legal consequences of the construction of a wall in the occupied Palestinian territory.[32] As with every judgement it issues, the ICJ's conclusions in an advisory opinion are more than mere rhetoric. They represent the most authoritative statement of the content and applicability of international law. The court's judgement proved significant in a number of relevant aspects in confirming the responsibility to protect.

The court clarified that, notwithstanding the nature of the conflict, international human rights and humanitarian law were applicable in the occupied territories. Susan Akram and John Quigley analysed the advisory opinion, outlining key areas highlighted by the court:[33]

- There is a Palestinian people with a right to self-determination.
- The West Bank and Gaza, including East Jerusalem, are occupied territories under international law, and Israel is an occupying power with legal obligations.
- Israeli settlements breach international law.
- The Conventions (of International Humanitarian Law) are fully binding on Israel, and must govern all Israeli actions in the Occupied Palestinian Territories.
- Israel's occupation practices violate not only these Conventions, but also the Conventions of International Human Rights Law.

By this advisory opinion, the court made clear that construction of the wall in the occupied territories and in East Jerusalem was illegal and Israel should not only stop construction immediately, but also begin dismantling it.

Beyond the wall itself, the construction of settlements in the occupied territories (which Israel claims it is protecting in erecting the wall) was also declared illegal. The decision further declared that destruction of housing and property to construct the wall was illegal, and that Israel was obliged to make reparations for all damage caused by its construction.

But the court did not stop at Israel's obligations. The overwhelming consensus of the court was that all states were obliged not to recognize the illegal situation Israel has created and to refrain from any financial support to Israel in maintaining the illegally constructed wall. It also insisted that states party to the Geneva Conventions of 1949 had 'additional obligations to ensure Israel's compliance' with the Conventions. Finally, the court declared that the UN General Assembly and Security Council ought to 'consider further actions' against Israel to bring an end to the 'illegal situation'.

Israel responded by declaring that the advisory opinion was 'irrelevant', ignored its own High Court's order that certain sections of the wall be re-routed and dismantled, and continued its construction regardless.

Unfortunately, there has continued to be a persistent failure on the part of the international community to hold Israel to account. It has even continued supporting Israel and its military occupation, despite such actions quite clearly violating international law.

In short, despite the fact that the Palestinian/Israeli conflict has been at the top of the UN's agenda for over sixty years, the international community – with the notable exception of UNRWA and the UNHCR's revision of Article 1D – has so far failed in its responsibility to protect Palestinian refugees, although it is heartening to note that efforts continue.

Ongoing protection issues

The consequences of international authorities' failure to protect Palestinian refugees are well documented.[34] It is painfully evident in the fact that there still remains a strong need for international intervention in the form of UNRWA, which unfailingly continues to offer humanitarian assistance and basic social and economic rights, including education and health care services. However, its commendable efforts still fall short of what is needed.

Israel's unwillingness to recognize the application of international human rights and humanitarian law, and the international community's tolerance of this, has contributed to multiple violations against Palestinian civilians and particularly refugees. Israel's non-recognition of the right of return and exclusion from Israeli citizenship to Palestinian refugees, coupled with its control of movement in occupied Palestinian areas, has furthermore resulted in 55 densely populated bantustans. Most worryingly of all, civilian areas are regularly subjected to attacks by the Israeli security services, whether through policies of extra-judicial assassinations or by way of collective punishment.

Civil society responses: example of Badil

Badil Resource Centre on Palestinian Residency and Refugee Rights, established in 1997, has shown itself to be very effective in employing a range of human rights advocacy strategies, including direct and indirect actions.

Firstly, Badil invokes international law in producing research and documentation, which in turn supports campaigns and the development of position papers as well as documents in support of legal and advocacy claims. Secondly, it invokes international legal mechanisms in initiating direct and indirect claims before national and international authorities. For example, the organization has approached multiple authorities in the UN system, including the UNHCR's Executive Committee, the Committee on the Elimination of Racial Discrimination and the UN Human Rights Commission. Thirdly, Badil conducts human rights advocacy training, especially of NGOs and refugee communities. In this sense, the organization aims to close the gap between international legal principles and advocacy, both informing as to the content of international law and by sharing advocacy strategies.

Conclusions

With prevention of human rights and humanitarian law violations at the core of the responsibility to protect, the international community is vested with a renewed commitment to respecting international law and protecting vulnerable populations. This is increasingly recognized by the International Court of Justice.

Considering the court's more than sixty years of experience in delivering judgements on complex international disputes and advising the United Nations in the context of multiple international crises, Justice Rosalyn Higgins has confirmed that the law of state responsibility undeniably includes a responsibility to protect. Speaking in The Hague in 2004,[35] Justice Higgins noted that the court has made numerous references to the Vienna Convention on Consular Relations, for example in the *La Grande* case concerning Germany and the USA. The court has also determined that the legal consequences of illegal conduct insist not only that such conduct be reversed, but also that remedies be found to correct harm against individuals. Finally, the court has determined that there are certain obligations – *erga omnes* obligations – concerning protection of individuals from violations of human rights and humanitarian law: in other words, regardless of whether a state might have signed a particular treaty, individuals are entitled to certain standards of treatment by all states.

As Secretary General Kofi Annan has confirmed, defending against multiple dangers that threaten human security is a joint responsibility:

> No nation can defend itself against these threats entirely on its own. Dealing with today's challenges … requires broad, deep and sustained global cooperation. States working together can achieve things that are beyond what even the most powerful state can accomplish by itself.[36]

Annan's report 'In larger freedom' further confirms that the most challenging task of all is to reconcile the complex roles of and relationships between the now multiple stakeholders in international law, all of whom contribute to ensuring that the responsibility to protect is both recognized and respected. From the International Court of Justice, which seeks to resolve state disputes and advise the UN in international crises, to NGOs advocating that both states and the UN take more deliberate and principled action in the protection of vulnerable populations – all have a key role to play, particularly when – as unfortunately has happened in the case of Palestinian refugees – international authorities fail in their responsibility to protect.

Roles and responsibilities of various actors in the responsibility to protect

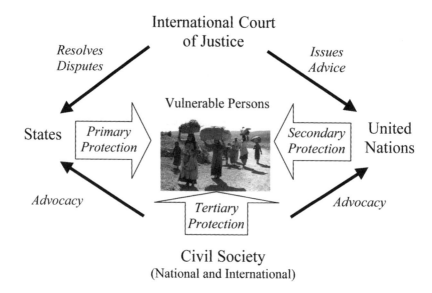

NOTES

1. David Barnhizer, ed., *Effective Strategies for Protecting Human Rights* (Ashgate, 2001).
2. Marco Sassoli, 'State Responsibility for Violations of International Humanitarian Law', *IRRC*, Vol. 84, No. 846 (June 2002), argues that 'the focus of implementing mechanisms is and must always be on prevention'.
3. 'Question of the Violation of Human Rights in the Occupied Arab Territories, Including Palestine: Report of the Special Rapporteur of the Commission on Human Rights, John Dugard, on the Situation of Human Rights in the Palestinian Territories Occupied by Israel since 1967', United Nations, 7 December 2004, Ref. E/CN.4/2005/29.
4. Sassoli, 'State Responsibility'.
5. Umesh Palwankar, 'Measures Available to States for Fulfilling their Obligation to Ensure Respect for International Humanitarian Law', *IRRC*, No. 298 (February 1994), pp. 9–25.
6. Ibid.
7. De Gaay Fortman has published extensively on this subject, including, 'Quod Omnes Tangit', Inaugural Address on Accepting the Msgr Willy Onclin Chair 2000–4 at the Catholic University of Louvain, in Rik Torfs, *Canonical Testament* (Louvain: Peeters, 2004), pp. 23–45; and 'The Human Rights Mission in an African Context', in Kwame Bediako et al., eds, *A New Day Dawning: African Christians Living the Gospel* (Zoetermeer: Boekencentrum, 2004), pp. 66–75.
8. The UN Declaration on the Right and Responsibility of Individuals, Groups and Organs of Society to Promote and Protect Universally Recognized Human Rights and Fundamental Freedoms, also known as the Declaration on Human Rights Defenders, was adopted by the UN General Assembly on 9 December 1998. See also 'First report of the special representative on human rights defenders', United Nations (E/CN.4/2001/94), 26 January 2001.
9. Protocol No. 11 to the Convention for the Protection of Human Rights and Fundamental Freedoms, *ETS* 155 (1998).
10. This principle, which effectively acts as a defence in any such claim, provides that the claimant must establish that there is no other country's court (forum) that is better suited to deal with the matter.
11. Although see *Altmann vs. Austria* (2004, USA), in which the Altmann family was successfully able to claim restitution of property confiscated during the Second World War that eventually fell into the custody of the State of Austria. In this case, Austria's claim of sovereign immunity did not prohibit restitution.
12. This section draws from J. Handmaker, 'Seeking Justice, Guaranteeing Protection and Ensuring Due Process: Addressing the Tensions between Exclusion from Refugee Protection and the Principle of Universal Jurisdiction', *Netherlands Quarterly of Human Rights*, Vol. 21, No. 4 (December 2003). See also R. Thakur and P. Malcontent, eds, *From Sovereign Impunity to International Accountability: The Search of Justice in a World of States* (UNUP, 2004).
13. 1984 Convention against Torture and Other Cruel, Inhumane or Degrading Treatment or Punishment, UNGA Resolution 39/46 of 10 December 1984 (entry into force June 1987).
14. These include the Nuremberg and Tokyo War Crimes Tribunals, established in the aftermath of the Second World War, the Rwanda Tribunal established in Arusha, Tanzania to adjudicate crimes committed during the Rwandan genocide of 1994, the International Criminal Tribunal for the Former Yugoslavia established in The Hague, and the recently established Sierra Leone Tribunal.
15. This section is adapted from J.Handmaker, 'Civil Society and International Law: Protecting and Promoting Human Rights in the Light of the July 2004 Advisory Opinion of the International Court of Justice', United Nations International Meeting on the Question of Palestine, UN Office at Geneva, 8–9 March 2005
16. Conversation with the author in Gouda, September 2004.
17. Examples of this in the context of highly contested conflicts such as Palestine/Israel are legion, covering everything from a failure to use the word 'occupation' (in describing the presence of Israel's military in Palestine), to a gross misuse of the word 'response/retaliation' (in explaining Israel's military aggression).

18. For example, the Presbyterian Church of the USA voted in 2004 to divest itself of any economic association with Israel on the basis of the Israeli government's violations of international humanitarian law, and various attempts have been made for city governments to divest.

19. During the first Intifada, civic structures were effective in a range of mobilizing efforts, from boycotting Israeli products (by growing their own vegetables) to staging well-organized and prolonged peaceful protests, which brought considerable international attention to the plight of Palestinians. Following the Oslo Accords between the PLO and Israel, the Palestinian Authority was established, replacing many of the preexisting civic structures with local government structures. Added to this, Israel's increasing stranglehold over the occupied territories has stifled what little existed of these civic structures.

20. J. Handmaker and A. Nieuwhof, 'Israel's Cry of anti-Semitism Blocks a Critical Dialogue', *Electronic Intifada*, 27 February 2004.

21. Source: UN Relief and Works Agency.

22. Convention (IV) relative to the Protection of Civilian Persons in Time of War, Geneva, 12 August 1949, Article 49, provides that 'Individual or mass forcible transfers, as well as deportations of protected persons from occupied territory to the territory of the Occupying Power or to that of any other country, occupied or not, are prohibited, regardless of their motive'.

23. See 'Land Grab: Israel's Settlement Policy in the West Bank', B'tselem, May 2002, at www.btselem.org.

24. Among many publications on this subject, see Lynn Welchman, 'A Thousand and One Homes: Israeli Demolition and Sealing of Houses in the Occupied Palestinian Territories', Al Haq, Occasional Paper No. 11, 1993, at www.alhaq.org.

25. Countless books and articles have been written about this. See www.reahamba.nl/palestine/biblio.pdf.

26. United Nations General Assembly Resolution 194 (III), 11 December 1948, Article 11.

27. UN Convention Relating to the Status of Refugees, 189 *UNTS* 150.

28. UN Security Council Resolution 242, 22 November 1967.

29. 'Note on the Applicability of Article 1D of the 1951 Convention relating to the Status of Refugees to Palestinian Refugees', UNHCR, Department of International Protection, October 2002.

30. Ibid., para. 7.

31. Ibid., para. 8.

32. 'Legal Consequences of the Construction of a Wall in the Occupied Palestinian Territory, Advisory Opinion', International Court of Justice, 9 July 2004.

33. Susan Akram and John Quigley, 'A Reading of the International Court of Justice Advisory Opinion on the Legality of Israel's Wall in the Occupied Palestinian Territories, July 2004'. Available at www.palestinecenter.org/cpap/pubs/update_on_wall_072004.pdf.

34. See www.zochrot.org; www.badil.org; www.reahamba.nl/palestine/biblio.pdf.

35. Lecture by Rosalyn Higgins, 'State Responsibility in the Case-Law of the International Court of Justice', Grotius Centre, University of Leiden, Campus Den Haag, 18 October 2004.

36. Kofi Annan, 'In Larger Freedom: Decision Time at the UN', *Foreign Affairs* (May/June 2005).

The International Legal Framework in Dealing with International Failure

Konrad Raiser

What to do when international authorities fail in their responsibility to protect? The question presupposes an agreement in the international community that the responsibility to protect people and populations who are exposed to acute risk with regard to their human security is a shared obligation of the entire international community. While reaching such an agreement is the objective of proposals and recommendations which are before the United Nations, it would be premature to assume an affirmative response. For an understanding of international relations that is based on the assumption that sovereign nations will always act according to their national interest and will accept international agreements only where they serve this interest, a general responsibility to protect people at risk, either through hunger, disease, environmental degradation or due to massive human rights violations or armed conflict, would appear to postulate a supranational accountability of states which enters into conflict with their sovereignty. The Charter of the United Nations was designed to establish a new system and understanding of international relations based on cooperation rather than on the pursuit of national interest. The present discussion about the recognition of the responsibility to protect as a shared obligation of the international community brings to the fore the tensions inherent in the conception of the United Nations, especially regarding the compatibility between the classical notion of sovereignty and the emergence of a binding framework of international law, particularly concerning human rights and human security.

What international authorities are we talking about? Reference would normally be made first to the United Nations. According to its Charter, the UN is founded to maintain world peace and international security, to strengthen the principle of equality and self-determination of peoples, to promote international cooperation for the solution of international problems in the economic, social, cultural and humanitarian field, and to further the respect for human rights and basic freedoms. In this sense, the UN is being considered as the overall international authority. It acts through its General Assembly, the Security Council, the Secretary General, the Economic and Social Council, the Trusteeship Council, and the International Court of Justice. The system of the UN includes in addition several commissions (e.g. for human rights and for sustainable development), programmes (e.g. for development and for the environment) and a number of specialized organizations with separate membership, like the WHO, ILO, FAO, UNESCO, etc. They form part of the UN as the overall international authority, based on the principle of intergovernmental cooperation. In addition to the UN there exist numerous additional intergovernmental organizations with a limited authority for international relations, beginning with the international financial institutions (whose links with the UN system are not clearly defined), regional organizations like the EU, OSCE, AU and OAS, and different regional bodies for the concerns of security, development, etc. Their links with the UN system are defined in Chapter VIII of the Charter, especially with regard to their role in the maintenance of world peace and international security. When the topical question for this session refers to international authorities it acknowledges that in principle all intergovernmental organizations should accept co-responsibility to protect. However, against the background of recent experiences, the issue concerns particularly the UN and most specifically the Security Council.

This leads to a further question: 'What do we mean by failure?' The response will depend on a clearer definition of the scope and eventual limits of the responsibility to protect. Much of the discussion has focused on when the Security Council can and should authorize interventions with the purpose of protection according to Chapter VI or VII of the Charter, and what options remain to act on the responsibility to protect in cases where the Security Council fails to reach a decision. The most dramatic cases have been the breakdown of the intervention in Sudan, the failure of the international authorities to act in response to the genocide in Rwanda, and the hesitations of the Security Council to authorize an effective intervention in the Darfur region of Sudan; these have to be seen together with the NATO intervention in Kosovo without authorization by the Security Council and the most recent failure of the US government to obtain Security Council authorization for its intervention in Iraq. In all these cases the criteria for decisions were those presently incorporated in the Charter – apart from questions of political interest and convenience, especially for the veto powers. The concept of the responsibility to protect broadens the criteria beyond the issues of world peace and international security to obligations under international humanitarian law and human rights conventions. In my earlier contribution on the ethics of protection I further broadened the scope by referring to human security in the comprehensive sense as the overall objective of protection. Obviously, this would change radically the basis for the judgement whether and when the international authorities have failed in their responsibility to protect.

For the purposes of our present discussion I will limit myself to the somewhat less ambitious understanding of the question as set out in the approach by ICISS. Under the heading 'When the Security Council fails to act' the Commission says:

> In view of the Council's past inability or unwillingness to fulfil the role expected of it, if the Security Council expressly rejects a proposal for intervention where humanitarian or human rights issues are significantly at stake, or the Council fails to deal with such a proposal within a reasonable time, it is difficult to argue that alternative means of discharging the responsibility to protect can be entirely discounted. What are the options in this respect?

The report then discusses two main options. First, an emergency session of the General Assembly of the UN under the Uniting for Peace procedure which was established in 1950 with regard to the Korean crisis, where the Security Council was unable to reach agreement. This is a complicated procedure designed for exceptional cases, but it was considered again with regard to the crisis in Kosovo. Second, intervention under the authority of a regional or sub-regional organization using the provisions of Chapter VIII of the Charter of the UN. Strictly following UN rules, an authorization by the Security Council is required here as well; this was not sought or given in the case of NATO's intervention in Kosovo, while authorization for the ECOWAS intervention in West Africa (Liberia and Sierra Leone) was sought and given ex post facto. The much earlier interventions of Tanzania in Uganda or of Vietnam in Kampuchea were tacitly given legitimacy, even though the UN rules had not been followed. The intervention of the USA and allies in Iraq, for which authorization had been refused by the Security Council, has correctly been termed 'illegal' by the Secretary General.

It is the realistic judgement of the Commission that it would be difficult to reach a substantial consensus in the international community about criteria which could legitimize interventions for the purpose of human protection outside authorization by either the Security Council or the General Assembly of the UN. On the other hand, we will continue to face situations, as in Rwanda, where the competent international authorities fail to discharge their responsibility to protect in view of a massive crisis for human security. In such cases there will be mounting pressures (or temptations) for individual states or 'coalitions of the willing' to take the risk of intervening on their own initiative. If they succeed and if they receive at least moral approval by world public opinion, there will be a significant loss of credibility of the Security Council and the collective system represented by the UN. If they fail, or if the intervention is clearly motivated by the national interest of the intervening powers, the whole system of international order for peace and justice will erode. As a consequence, there is an urgent need for a new framework for collective security strategy along the lines proposed by the HLP. The details of these proposals will certainly have to be discussed further, but tendencies like those expressed in the recent security doctrine of the US government which seeks to establish a right for a 'preemptive' intervention must be strongly resisted.

Much of the discussion is shaped by recent problematic experiences in Rwanda, Kosovo and Iraq; it has focused almost exclusively on the criteria and the conditions for military intervention in response to political and humanitarian crises, where no competent national authority was capable or willing to respond, or where the existing authority had itself become (co-)responsible for creating the crisis. Realistically, it should be recognized that the UN at present is severely limited in its capacities to assume to the full extent the responsibility to protect which is stated as a common obligation for the international community. The number of internal conflicts with severe threats to human security and the incidence of failed states where the structures of public order and authority have broken down have increased beyond the limit of what the UN in its present structure can responsibly deal with. Deliberations and decisions of the Security Council on appropriate measures for responding to these crises have been highly selective. There have been internal wars with dramatic loss of life, like the 27-year war in Angola, which have not been considered in the Security Council with regard to a possible intervention. Failure of the international authorities to act on their responsibility to protect may therefore be the consequence of sheer overload of the instrumentalities of the UN. The original intention of the Charter – that the UN should have a general staff committee which would advise the Security Council on all matters regarding the maintenance of world peace and international security and would coordinate and direct eventual military interventions – has never been implemented. Nor has the UN been provided with the military units to be used under its authority. It is unlikely that these provisions of the Charter will be implemented in any foreseeable future. It remains to be seen whether the proposals of the HLP to establish a peace-building commission and a peace-building support office will find the necessary support among the member states.

In view of these objective limitations which the UN is facing with regard to its ability to respond to mounting expectations that it should assume the responsibility to protect, it might be necessary to define more clearly the situations which should come under the responsibility of the UN. The Charter limits the authority of the Security Council to instances where world peace and international security are threatened. This criterion has been formulated with the classical case of interstate conflicts in mind. More and more the Security Council is meanwhile expected to act – and has acted – as well in response to dramatic cases of internal conflicts. The ICISS report uses the criterion of the just cause and argues that military intervention for human protection purposes would be justified in order to halt or avert the following:

- Large-scale loss of life, actual or apprehended, with genocidal intent or not, which is the product either of deliberate state action, or state inaction or inability to act, or a failed state situation.

- Large-scale 'ethnic cleansing', actual or apprehended, whether carried out by killing, forced expulsion, acts of terror or rape.

These conditions are then specified in greater detail. They would, if accepted, go a long way toward clarifying the scope of the responsibility of the UN and the Security Council, as well as their limits. These considerations are concerned with the extreme cases where the responsibility to protect might call for military intervention. Obviously, the UN and the Security Council have other options for response at their disposal under the Charter which have to be taken into account as well.

However, the responsibility to protect is not limited to governments and intergovernmental organizations, and even in conscience-shocking crises a military response may not necessarily be the most effective or most appropriate form of action. Many non-governmental organizations have in recent years developed effective models for civilian conflict management and conflict resolution which have not yet received sufficient public attention or support. Examples include the work of the Nairobi Crisis Initiative in East Africa, the efforts of the Life and Peace Institute in Somalia, the mediation activity of the St Egidio community in Mozambique, the influence of the Inter-Religious Council in Liberia and many other similar efforts. The basic principle of these responses is not intervention from outside, but rather the patient effort to strengthen the capacities of organizations of civil society in the country concerned to overcome the climate of polarization and militant antagonism and to work towards a negotiated end to armed violence. Empowering the people who are taken hostage by a given conflict to stand up against the warlords and to isolate them is a strategy which will not produce immediate results and may seem to prolong the suffering, but in the medium and long-term perspective is likely to be more successful than any outside intervention. It seeks to transform the conflict in the very approach chosen to manage it, by deliberately avoiding military confrontation.

Other examples could be cited of humanitarian agencies which have begun to integrate elements of civilian conflict management into their relief programmes. A first attempt of this kind was made by the ecumenical relief programme in response to the Rwandan crisis. The SecondII European Ecumenical Assembly at Graz (1997) considered proposals to create a special commission for conflict analysis and mediation. This somewhat accidental listing of instrumentalities created by non-governmental and particularly by religious organizations could be extended and would demonstrate that there are alternative options for non-violent, non-military forms of acting on the responsibility to protect.

So far, these ways of responding to situations of violent conflict which threaten human security have not received the attention and support they deserve. For their funding, most of them depend on private contributions or foundation grants. If only a fraction of the worldwide expenditure for armaments and military purposes would be made available to efforts for civilian conflict management and mediation, their effectiveness could be strengthened significantly. It should become an integral part of governmental and intergovernmental initiatives to build up the instrumentalities for the responsibility to protect, to train and equip persons for the task of civilian conflict management and mediation. The present trend to invest large sums of public funds in the establishment of high-tech rapid deployment forces is caught in the traditional logic of military response as the only effective solution to contemporary conflict. By comparison, far too little is being done to build up the necessary resources of competent civilian personnel who are able to work with people in conflict situations and to prepare the ground for conflict resolution. In many situations police personnel are more important than highly armed military units, but even now the UN has great difficulty in securing the necessary support from member states for its need for international police forces.

All these considerations lead to the conclusion that the adoption of the responsibility to protect as a general responsibility for governments and intergovernmental organizations, as well as the networks of civil society organizations, must find expression in a critical assessment of the instrumentalities and forms of action available. In order not to be misunderstood, I do not want to discount the special role of military intervention in extreme cases; however, there is a wide spectrum of possibilities to act on the responsibility to protect which need to be given visibility and support. This constitutes a new field of potential cooperation between the UN and non-governmental, civil society organizations whose special competence and potential need to be recognized and strengthened. Sometimes they have been given credit in the context of early warning, but they have not been used intentionally as competent actors in conflict response and resolution. The question of what to do when international authorities fail need not lead to an embarrassing silence, but could open the way for a new form of partnership between governmental and non-governmental agencies.

The Responsibility to Prevent
Prevention and Human Security

1.1 It is the fundamental responsibility of states to provide for the security and well-being of their people – in other words, to pursue human security by:

- providing for the physical safety of people;
- attending to their economic, social and health needs;
- respecting fundamental rights and freedoms;
- honouring the dignity and worth of all people.

1.2 To be faithful to the responsibility to protect people means above all prevention – prevention of the kinds of catastrophic assaults on individuals and communities that the world has witnessed in Cambodia, Rwanda, Sudan, the DRC, and other instances and locations of extraordinary human-made humanitarian crises.

1.3 When it becomes clear that states are failing, or risk failure, in the exercise of their responsibility to prevent, the international community has a duty to join the pursuit of human security before situations in troubled states degenerate to catastrophic proportions. This is the duty of protection through prevention of assaults on the safety, rights and well-being of people in their homes and communities.

Components of Prevention

2.1 The prevention of catastrophic human insecurity requires attention to the root causes of insecurity as well as to more immediate or direct causes of insecurity:

- Measures to address and mitigate root causes are necessarily long term.
- Measures to address direct causes or conditions of insecurity have more of the character of emergency responses and are necessarily more immediate and short term.

2.2 Prevention, by definition, requires action to address conditions of insecurity as they emerge, before they precipitate crises, which in turn requires specific prevention capacities:

- Early warning or identification of emerging threats or conditions of insecurity.
- A prevention toolbox: a set of practical measures and mechanisms to mitigate emerging problems effectively.
- The political will to act (to *use* the tools in the toolbox) before a crisis occurs: the political will to act even though conditions appear on the surface to be 'normal'.

2.3 To act before a crisis presents itself requires a special sensitivity to (a deeply rooted empathy with) and understanding of the conditions and needs of people, which in turn requires the active cooperation of civil society (especially faith communities, which are rooted in the daily spiritual and physical realities of people):

- Effective prevention must engage the perspective of those who seek or are in need of assistance in addressing conditions of growing insecurity.
- Special attention to the needs and conditions of the most vulnerable elements of society (including indigenous peoples, minorities, women and children) is also essential.

2.4 While prevention is in the first instance to be achieved at the national level, sub-regional, regional and international institutions and organizations are also indispensable to the implementation of an agenda of protection through prevention.

Long-Term Prevention Agenda: Addressing Root Causes
3.1 Broadly stated, the long-term agenda is to pursue human security, key elements of which are:

- Economic development (meeting basic needs)
- Universal education
- Respect for human rights
- Good governance, political inclusion and power-sharing
- Fair trade
- Control over the instruments of violence (small arms in particular)
- The rule of law by means of law-biding and accountable security institutions
- Promoting confidence in public institutions

Short-Term Prevention Agenda: Addressing Direct Causes
4.1 More immediate preventive attention to emerging security crises must include specific measures designed to mitigate immediate insecurities and to instill the reliable hope that national institutions and mechanisms, with the support of an attentive international community, will remain committed to averting a crisis of human insecurity:

- Focused economic measures with specific inducements, as well as threatened punitive measures, designed to address immediate vulnerabilities.
- Political and diplomatic pressures on national governments to embrace endangered populations.
- Human rights monitoring.
- Small arms collection.
- Reconciliation and mediation programmes.
- Security sector reform to rebuild confidence in security institutions and personnel.
- The attention of mass media to conditions of insecurity, as well as to efforts to address these insecurities.

4.2 Attention to direct threats to human security calls for gradually escalating and progressively more intrusive measures and interventions to encourage national authorities to act, to enable national authorities and institutions through capacity building, and to persuade states to frankly face and persist in addressing the threats and insecurities that governments may be more inclined to deny or avoid.
4.3 At the national level, governments should:

- Undertake self-monitoring to become aware of emerging threats.
- Establish mechanisms for alerting authorities and agencies to such emerging threats.
- Engage civil society and churches in assessing conditions of human security and insecurity.

- Initiate national dialogues, including dialogue with non-state actors, to acknowledge emerging problems and to engage the people in the search for solutions.
- Develop national action plans.

4.4 Sub-regional and regional organizations should also create early warning mechanisms, engage in discreet monitoring of security conditions within their region, and encourage the national authorities of affected countries to acknowledge and act on indicators of emerging threats.

4.5 At the international level, the United Nations Secretariat has a special role to play:

- Monitoring regional and national security conditions.
- Paying attention to particular indicators of human security, including changes in human rights conditions and the conditions of women and children (including female genital mutilation and human trafficking).
- Analysing trends.

4.6 The Secretary General, drawing on the Secretariat's monitoring and analysis, and in consultation with appropriate regional organizations and civil society, should provide the Security Council with regular (perhaps monthly) briefings on the security conditions in all regions of the globe, and on security conditions in individual countries of emerging concern.

Role of Faith Communities

5.1 Because faith communities and their leadership are rooted in the daily spiritual and physical realities of people, they have both a special responsibility and opportunity to participate in the development of national and multilateral protection and war prevention systems.

5.2 Churches and other faith communities have a particular responsibility to contribute to the early attention to conditions of insecurity. Prevention is the only reliable means of protection, and early detection of a deteriorating security situation requires the constant attention of those who work most closely with, and have the trust of, affected populations.

5.3 The churches are called to ministries of listening and accompaniment, making them an especially important resource for understanding and communicating the plight of the vulnerable and the needs of local communities.

5.4 Faith communities have a responsibility to contribute to the articulation of a vision of the state that embraces all parts of the population. A unifying vision of a state is one in which all parts of the population feel they have a stake in the future of the country. The churches' ministry of reconciliation and healing has an important role in advancing political unity and trust.

5.5 Church leaders can play a role in directly alerting national, sub-regional, regional, and international authorities to areas and communities of emerging distress and growing insecurity.

5.6 Churches should make a particular point of emphasizing the understanding of sovereignty as responsibility. Under the sovereignty of God we understand it to be the duty of humanity to care for each other and all of creation. The sovereignty exercised by human institutions rests on the exercise of the responsibility to protect each other and all of creation.

Mobilizing Resources for Security

6.1 Prevention requires material resources, and it is the responsibility of the churches, along with others, to draw attention to the disturbing fact that the world diverts extraordinary levels of wealth away from efforts to prevent war in order to prepare to fight wars.

6.2 Churches can help governments and publics to understand that the way people experience insecurity is not primarily through the threat of external military attack, but through the daily experience of unmet needs and violated rights and freedoms. Thus, 'security spending' must be understood to include spending to foster the kinds of economic, social and political conditions that provide for the day-to-day security of people.

When National Authorities Fail

We understand our aim to be to produce an aide memoire to the drafters of a WCC statement on the responsibility to protect, particularly on the issue 'when national authorities fail'. Our perspective is that of the churches in the ecumenical movement. Our addressees are the general public, political authorities (national and international), civil society, churches and other religious communities.

We divide our task into two parts:

1   Identifying the failure of national authorities.
2   Responding to the failure of national authorities

Identifying the Failure of National Authorities

Theological foundation and resources

What is the role of national authorities? What do churches expect from the state? There is a need for a renewed critical and constructive theological reflection on legitimate power, and the sovereignty of nation-states. Based on the biblical witness, faith in the Triune God, the churches first of all affirm life in its fullness for all. National authorities should be seen as serving people in the specific political realization – however provisionally – of that affirmation. The legitimate power (sovereignty) of the nation-state is dependent upon its conceived will and the capacity of national authorities to serve this overall affirmation/goal. Affirming life in its fullness for all means meeting the basic human needs – material (food, shelter, health, education, work, life in integrity with creation) and spiritual (freedom of thought and belief, participation in political and cultural process, etc.) – of all human beings in the community.

While affirming that the legitimate authority of the nation-state is dependent on its will and capacity to serve the overall goal of fullness of life for all, churches are mindful of the limitations of all human endeavours in a fallen creation. Optimally, the state is expected to aim at securing the space and conditions for the realization of this overall goal; as a minimum, it should not actively contradict, oppose or make impossible the realization of life in fullness for all.

Above all, 'securing the space and conditions' means respecting human rights and upholding security for all members of society and maintaining general order, through the rule of law. Whenever national authorities fail in this regard, they are found to be lacking. In theological terms, a state's failure is identified when national authorities directly contradict, work against or prohibit and inhibit life in its fullness for all (see Romans 13; Revelation 13).

The evangelical principle of providing justice and special attention to the poor and marginalized means that churches are particularly called to assess the function of the state from the point of view of powerless and marginal groups and persons. According to a Christian understanding, security is not the opposite of vulnerability. Vulnerability is a God-given condition of humanity, and an anthropological and ethical precondition. At the same time, it is human vulnerability that is the foundation of the right to protection.

Political analysis

The churches' view of national authorities as subject to the affirmation of life in its fullness for all makes it possible to welcome the proposed shift from seeing state sovereignty as primarily a matter of control, to a matter of protection. The concept of human security is a helpful indication of what national authorities are expected to provide. Failure can occur through state negligence, withholding basic services or directly inflicting harm in differing degrees. The assessment of state failure would depend on the degree of suffering inflicted as a result.

There is a distinction to be made between the lack of capacity and the lack of will on the part of national authorities for providing such protection. However, both lack of will and lack of capacity are failures that may call for appropriate measures from non-state actors, local and international. Local actors – among them the churches – have a key role to play in detecting these various forms and degrees of state failure. It should be noted that churches can be compromised or hindered in fulfilling this role adequately, both on external grounds (e.g. lack of religious freedom, a culture of impunity) and internal grounds (e.g. division and lack of responsibility, organized structures and funds; compliance with a culture of impunity). Some key indicators of failure include:

1   The disintegration of society, which may take the form of lack of law and order; lack of room and mechanism for peaceful conflict resolution; lack of respect for minority rights; lack of respect, framework or mechanism for civil society; a serious absence of the fundamental infrastructure necessary for meeting the basic needs of the population.
2   The situation of the most vulnerable groups in society, such as the poor, people with HIV/AIDS, indigenous groups, women and children, the elderly, differently abled persons, etc.

In all, churches should fully affirm the human security paradigm as a maximum standard for giving content to the state's responsibility to protect, or in theological terms for serving the affirmation of life in fullness for all. As a minimum requirement, churches should adopt the High Level Panel's concept of protection from avoidable catastrophe.

Cases
Specific examples can help show the different ways in which state failure can occur and how such failure may be detected. Cases such as Zimbabwe (withdrawal of access to food for political purposes), Rwanda (genocide), Colombia (lack of will for a political solution), Haiti (national disintegration, failure to meet basic needs) and Kosovo (repression of ethnic and cultural minorities) can be considered. It is nevertheless important to remember that each case is unique.

Guidelines for action
A WCC statement could specify expectations or guidelines for action by different actors:

By the international community
- Affirming the R2P norms and building capacity to fulfill that responsibility
- Monitoring
- Prevention
- Cooperation

By civil society
- Early warning

By the churches
- Solidarity with the groups at risk
- Ministry of listening

- Prophetic witness (political advocacy)
- Consider adopting policies like the WHO's resolution and recommendation on a violence prevention mechanism as a public health priority

Responding to the Failure of National Authorities

Theological foundation and resources

As pointed out above, the fundamental duty to protect belongs to the national authorities. However, protection as an affirmation of the fullness of life for all is also a Christian agenda: God is the Protector (Psalm 82). A theology of protection should be explored, placing particular emphasis on the cross in calling us to value vulnerability and solidarity with victims, and the role of God the Spirit in protecting, strengthening and renewing life visibly and invisibly. Human resilience in the face of catastrophe should be seen in terms of the empowering Holy Spirit.

This means that the role of protection belongs to both secular authorities and the church, in overlapping yet distinct ways. It is not the role of the church to take on the responsibilities of the state. Neither is it the role of the state to interfere in or take over the mission of the church for the nourishment of spiritual life and service for the coming kingdom of God. When national authorities fail, it is the task of churches to call them to their true responsibility. This should be done in humility, confessing the failures and shortcomings of the church and respecting legitimate state authority. Churches should be aware of the danger of self-inflation. There is a distinction between serving God and acting on God's behalf. At the same time it calls for boldness in addressing the specific failures of the authorities to fulfill their tasks or to respect the limits of their powers. Furthermore, churches, together with other religious communities and all people of good faith, have to work for the active creation of peace and protection. This includes diaconal service, solidarity with the afflicted, prophetic witness and specific action for justice, reconciliation and the restoration of community. Churches should strive to be an eye and a voice for those who suffer, always respecting their dignity and autonomous agency in working for the protection and affirmation of life in fullness for all. In the midst of suffering and hardship, churches are called to celebrate the good news of the coming of the kingdom of God with all God's children, thus affirming the hope of redemption and trusting in the saving power of God.

Political analysis

The WCC statement should:

- Endorse the framework of R2P.
- Enhance the capacity of the state to fulfill its R2P, looking at the consequences of economic globalization in weakening the state.
- Support UN reform and international civil society with a view to strengthening international community – not in opposition to national authorities, but as a way of confirming, complementing and controlling their role.

Relevant factors here include:

- UN reform
- Regional solutions
- Upholding and strengthening national states and their separate roles
- Strengthening democracy and the rule of law

- Capacity building
- Upholding and building state capacity
- Good governance
- Accountability
- International law
- Supporting tools for reconciliation and justice, such as the International Criminal Court
- Lessons from the roles and strategies of women in conflict situations

Guidelines for action
By the international community
- Consider non-military alternatives, toolbox, etc.
- Cf. presentations by Jeff Handmaker and Konrad Raiser

By civil society
- Using national and international legal frameworks to expose state failure and hold authorities responsible
- Cooperation

By the churches and other religious communities
- Call the government to faithfulness to their responsibility to protect.
- Call for truth and live by the truth: do not allow the truth to be hidden.
- Expect change, nurture change: do not be bound to the moment.
- Work vigorously for the forces that strengthen and uphold abundant life; work to reduce the forces that undermine them. This is an ongoing task.
- Work for reconciliation and community in the spirit of love and grace.
- Nourish the human consciousness in order for it to 'know when to be shocked'.
- Contribute to a culture of prevention, cooperation and unity as a global community.
- Contribute to good governance.
- Carefully consider the possible consequences of different measures to respond to state failure, in particular when considering the threshold for the use of military force.
- Encourage international accountability and transparency at all levels.
- Remain faithful and patient in processes of transition and reconstruction.
- Actively search for common ground, and particularly provide good cooperation with civil society.
- Engage seriously in interreligious dialogue for the sake of protection and peace.
- Enhance victims' rights for truth, justice and reparation.
- Call all people to conversion and transfiguration, searching to realize the kingdom values of loving one's enemy and establishing peace with justice for all.

Two crucial dilemmas that the churches are faced with:

- When to work silently, when to speak out?
- At what point to call for delegitimizing the state; when to continue to call it to duty?

Criteria for Intervention

General Observations

The purpose of intervention is protection, not the change of a political system or regime, nor the general maintenance of world peace and international security. The principle of a responsibility to protect is not so much concerned with international peace and security as with the human security of identifiable groups and individuals.

The question of the legitimacy of self-defence against an actual or imminent threat from another state under Article 51 of the UN Charter is to be considered outside the framework of a responsibility to protect.

In order to strengthen its protective aspect and the need for a disinterested implementation of any legitimate intervention, a multilateral approach should be taken. Such an approach should also strengthen the authority and mandate of the implementing forces.

From Prevention to Intervention

There is a continuum between the three phases of prevention, reaction and rebuilding. This needs to be considered and developed in order to achieve a more comprehensive understanding and approach to the responsibility to protect. Prevention can move over and into the reaction phase, and can also take coercive forms such as targeted sanctions, because they interfere with the internal affairs of a sovereign state. Many situations develop gradually, from one phase to the other. Thus, responses for protection need to be in tune with such developments. The least provocative response should be chosen in any given situation, so as to avoid escalation on the part of perpetrators. Measures that are too strong can cause a dramatic increase in violence.

There is a prevention aspect to all phases of a conflict or disaster. This is both a possibility for action and a complicating factor in discharging a responsibility to protect, relevant in all circumstances. There is even need for rebuilding and reconstruction at the beginning of any intervention, otherwise it may very well be counter-productive.

One dimension of prevention concerns the role of religious communities (e.g. with respect to the use of religious motives or religious identity in the development or escalation of conflict). Relations between religious leaders are in many societies a necessary platform for building political relationships, in particular after violent conflict and state failure. Seeking religious legitimation for a confrontational stance is often a political necessity, since it gives moral support. Such pressures can for instance deal with nationalism or ethnicity. Unfortunately, the ability of some religious communities to resist this temptation is limited.

The Just Cause Principle

ICISS should be commended for the prominence it gives to the principle of just cause. The subsequent precautionary principles verify and clarify whether a military response is the most appropriate method, given the presence of a just cause.

The application of the just cause criterion is complicated by two types of likely situations: (1) a situation characterized as a short but intensive peak in the loss of life, but not fully satisfying the conditions for a just cause; (2) a protracted situation of continuing loss of life, amounting in retrospect to levels that would meet the conditions for a just cause.

Translating moral concern into political action requires a certain procedure. The role of the media needs to be scrutinized in this context, since they are able to build up a morally compelling situation for a government, making it necessary to take action. However, translating a moral demand into political action is problematic: it is a process that requires to be mediated through the application of criteria based on procedures of accountability.

Operational Considerations

The idea that a military force is the most effective and able resource in ending violations and supporting the creation of a new political structure is highly dubious: Iraq is a case in point. Entities that play a key role in the rebuilding of critical democratic structures should resort to very little or no violence when trying to restore stability and peace in a society.

Essential civilian infrastructure (those functions that are critical for a civilian population in order for it to resume its responsibilities after a humanitarian disaster) must always be protected. This category also includes monuments and other physical manifestations relating to the history, religion and identity of the people. All of them should have the same protected status.

It is fundamental that governments train their troops in international humanitarian law (important also in respecting civilian infrastructure). Even UN-led troops have a poor knowledge of the rules of war. This is an essential dimension in the execution of the responsibility to protect.

When International Authorities Fail
How to Make International Systems More Effective

Observations

- Report of the Secretary General 'In larger freedom' (ILF) – humanitarian response remains woefully underfunded – rapid progress protecting internally displaced people (IDP) – more promising at regional level, but whatever happened to the Deng Principles?
- Human rights are central to the Charter, especially concerning equality of treatment.
- Cost of Gulf War was measured against cost of UN intervention. Dilemma: can't prove the need for intervention unless there is a crisis.
- Also need to work on long-term crises – countries with lowest per capita income are most likely to become embroiled in conflicts and forgotten by international system.

Broad suggestions

- Peace-building commission remains a possibility.
- Article 51 is adequate as currently formulated – prevent Iraq situation without backing under international law.
- ILF 135 – embracing responsibility to protect (R2P).
- Promoting accountability of Security Council – counter-balance them morally, if not politically.
- Holding collective states accountable – imperative duty on R2P.
- Development of intersectoral councils involving all relevant stakeholders (international, national and civil society) to address prevention, reaction and rebuilding.
- Support for role of International Court of Justice/International Criminal Court. ILF 203 – 208 – predictable response capacity (funding).
- Reaffirm importance of 1951 Refugee Convention and that people are increasingly internally displaced.

Specific recommendations

- UN must have standby capacity – idea of a preventive diplomacy fund should be explored – tsunami verified this was possible.
- Early warning, diplomatic, humanitarian, police, military.
- At UN, desk officers available for every country/region – referrals to it can be made informally, for example by NGOs.
- Human security should not be subject to the whim of individual vetoes.
- In particular, use of veto should not diminish Security Council's role in R2P.
- Well-founded and evidence-based genocide alerts (e.g. through advice by the genocide adviser) would make it inappropriate for veto to be exercised in relation to Security Council's obligation to R2P.
- It is essential for the General Assembly to maintain a role in discharging R2P.
- Criminal violations, massive and flagrant violations of rights – duty of UN to act.● High Level Panel should not introduce legal openings on unilateral intervention – but can be evaluated on a case-by-case basis.
- ILF 120 – instrument to monitor marking and tracing of small arms/light weapons.

- ILF 136 – protection of civilians (31 multilateral treaties).
- ILF 138 – impunity vs. IHL – encouraging international community to work with ICC and other international or mixed tribunals.
- ILF 139 – improving ICJ through greater resources, granting compulsory jurisdiction and using advisory powers.
- ILF 167–170.
- Recognize primary role/binding nature of the Security Council.
- Increases the representation of the Security Council (169A) – those who support the • UN financially, militarily and diplomatically.
- African permanent seat should go to one of top three contributors to UN.
- Any new member should be a non-nuclear state.

What States/Regional Systems Can Do to Make International System More Effective (Promoting Accountability)

Observations
- Many steps to isolate/put pressure on states (mainly non-military forms).
- Reform in the UK is being undertaken on humanitarian response system – British government recommended £100 million fund. Would be useful if UN had these resources up front at their disposal. Funds mustn't be 'hostage to CNN effect'.
- Strengthening role of non-aligned states.
- Requirement of states to monitor role of UN.

Broad suggestions
- Reminder to states to make UN system work as collective and as nation-states within it.
- Welcome West African small arms initiative – push for effective measures for marking and tracing and to limit the supply.
- HLP spoke of subsidiarity – trend towards regionalization – keep war-making power where it is. Keep threshold high, but regionalize lower-level engagements and strengthen regional interventions. Example: ECOWAS and regional warning systems.
- Often difficult for neighbours to take action, but regional systems might.
- Delegation by Security Council should be on case-by-case basis – Security Council can always take it back if things go wrong.

Specific recommendations
- Encourage greater financial commitment from wealthy and powerful states – needed for long-term prevention.
- ILF 110 – sanctions (monitoring mechanisms) – strengthen state capacity to implement sanctions.
- ILF 112 – interlocking system of peacekeeping capacities in context of UN and regional partnerships.
- ILF 210 – commitment for states to promote adoption of IDP principles to national legislation.
- ILF 211 – access to vulnerable populations.
- ILF 213 – improve capacity of AU to respond – Memorandum of Understanding on standby arrangements, especially peacekeeping operations.

Role of Civil Society

Observations
- How to bring players together, because of shared power of people coming together?
- How to encourage greater representation at international meetings?
- Confront power with truth.
- Better chance of developing good policies with broader participation of civil society.
- NGOs often have mandates that are too broad and an impact that is too diffuse.
- Need for accountability of NGOs and clarity of roles.
- Who is civil society?
- Talk of reconsidering how ECOSOC status is granted, including moving to Secretariat, but doubts as to whether this would make system more objective.
- Cardoso report on civil society – formal way of going through ECOSOC not so helpful since cannot take for granted this is where new ideas will come from.
- Civil society is involved in forming government protection policies and local civil society invokes international law in articulating its positions.
- Churches have capacity other structures don't have.
- They have an important role to play in fostering a culture of prevention, nationally and locally.
- They can only play a role in fostering a culture of prevention at international level if there is legitimacy or a critical mass.
- Examples: village in Peru, Palestine, Zimbabwe, where there is stronger awareness of key (local) issues such as domestic violence and treatment by police.
- Civil society not doing well in dialoguing with other aspects of civil society, particularly those it does not like.
- Religions/bodies within religions are sometimes part of the problem, but also potentially part of the solution – part of creating, prolonging conflict.
- 'Swedish Peoples' Parliament for Disarmament' (late 1980s):
- Set up to prepare response to disarmament efforts at the UN.
- 'Best guarantee for a progressive foreign policy is informed public opinion.'
- Succeeded in revoking the investigation procedure of conscientious objectors.
- Control of conflict diamonds good example of civil society and business working with UN.

Broad suggestions
- Churches can function as a 'worldwide web' of peace-building and human rights monitors and channelling information to UN political department and UN High Commissioner on Human Rights.
- On small arms, should be greater efforts at the demand side to balance efforts to curb the supply.
- There should be complementarity through differentiation of protection roles between collaborating NGOs.
- Good examples of NGOs (e.g. decisive on landmines and small arms issues). Good if implemented jointly with government/UN, but don't want NGOs competing for profile.
- NGOs exposed to a market where they are competing for profile (especially on conflict mediation/humanitarian assistance).
- R2P issues can't afford to be market driven.
- More difficult to create 'market' for prevention.

Specific recommendations

- Should be more of a possibility for NGO representatives to become more involved in policy and peace operations (women especially) – providing civilian aspect to HR and peace-building operations.
- Strengthen churches at regional level, especially as early warning mechanisms – special concern where churches are divided or part of the problem.
- WCC could strengthen its interaction with UN High Commissioner for Human Rights.
- In implementing SC Res. 1325, 2000:
- Women are recognized as actors in post-conflict rebuilding, rather than as passive victims.
- UNIFEM has fully fledged programme on peace and security and in post-conflict reconstruction/rebuilding processes.
- Capacity of police sector should be strengthened, in particular on crimes against women.
- Sexual exploitation by peacekeepers should be strongly rejected (also reflected in Secretary General's report).
- More women should be involved in peacekeeping – including gender units, to ensure they're effective.

Comments from Bertrand Ramcharan

Gareth Evans said in his presentation that R2P is an emerging norm of international law. If you go back to San Francisco when they were drafting the Charter, there was a great debate as to whether they would give the UN the role to promote as well as to protect. Agreement was not reached on the word 'protection'. You do not find the word 'protection' anywhere in the Charter. It took practice to develop this concept of protection. There was a time in the United Nations when you could not get, where you could not use the word 'protection'. How did the change come about?

In 1965, in the General Assembly, the new countries that were coming into the UN insisted: 'Let us deal with human rights violations in the colonies, apartheid in South Africa and any part of the world'. That led to an annual debate in the Commission on Human Rights on the question of violations of human rights. Not so long after, a confidential petition system came in, together with the criteria for dealing with situations with a consistent pattern of gross and reliably tested violations of human rights. Then the treaty systems came in as well, with petition procedures, followed by rapporteurs and other special procedures.

There is a concept called 'the human rights community'. The HR community must endeavour to discharge R2P. And I place within this HR community governments, international organizations, NGOs, civil society and academics.

What we did not discuss here is the role of human rights treaties. Governments must ratify the key treaties, they must operate the petition procedures and they must bring the treaties home (i.e. legislation and institutions). Then the treaties would lead us to a culture of human rights.

This culture of human rights is very important. For instance, when I was in the former Yugoslavia for peace negotiations, the hatred between Serbs and Albanians was such that I asked myself how could we move away from the fact that the Serbs were defeated on the plains of Kosovo polje in 1389? How does this culture of rights come about? Here, civil society and human rights education play a major role. It is important that there exists basic instruction on human rights in primary and secondary schools in every country of the world.

As for the role of governments, national protection systems must exist. The best thing we can do is to foster in every country a national protection system that works. This concept of a national protection system means that every country must be able to answer six questions:

1 Is the constitution of the country reflective of international human rights in the world? Is it taking in the culture of human rights?
2 Is the legislation in accordance with the international human rights system?
3 Are the courts able to draw upon international human rights norms?
4 Is the country teaching human rights in primary and secondary schools?
5 Does the country (especially a multi-ethnic country) have monitoring mechanisms to detect and head off potential grievances?
6 Does it have specialized human rights institutions that watch over the protection and promotion of human rights?

On the last point, the Swiss, who were having a debate on whether they should establish a national commission on human rights, asked me to go to a consultation. The question put to me was:

'Why do we need a national commission on human rights?' I replied that however good you think you are, it is important to be striving constantly for the protection and promotion of human rights. All countries must do this.

The Secretary General has asked the High Commissioner to compile a world report on human rights. I started the process of inviting every country to summarize in three or four pages the elements of its national protection systems. I received 35 replies. It was my intention to push for every country to give me a summary, which I would have published. This would have been used as a basis for dialogue with countries and to draw attention to issues on which resources might be spent to help the country to protect. This is important because the responsibility to protect needs to be exercised, to begin with, at the national level, then at regional and international levels.

We have had a fair measure of discussion on the role of international organizations. The idea of the High Commissioner for Human Rights started in Uruguay in 1947, with the idea that he or she would be an attorney general for human rights. The way that things have developed is that the High Commissioner should be a voice for human rights, speaking out in situations of violations. Organizations like the Red Cross do their bit on international humanitarian law, take initiatives and are discreet: they have access to situations, etc. All this is fine. But when it comes to discharging the responsibility to protect, the exercise of the voice of the High Commissioner in my view is very important. Let me give you two examples.

The Red Cross was visiting the Guantanamo detainees. It was making representation. For a while, because of the discretion of its methods, it couldn't speak out. It began to speak out because this was a matter of conscience. A High Commissioner for human rights, in consultation, with the passive understanding of the Red Cross, can speak out and can draw attention to a situation.

I lived this through in the situation in Iraq. In Iraq, the Red Cross was visiting prisoners of war. They had a partial understanding of what was going on in Iraq – things happened in this country that went beyond the treatment of prisoners. As a High Commissioner for Human Rights, I felt that whatever they were doing, I had to go out and I made a major report on human rights in Iraq that dealt with the totality of the situation. Here, I would ask you to think of the responsibility of the High Commissioner.

The High Commissioner on national minorities of the OSCE is operating behind the scenes, trying to act for the protection of national minorities. This is a good concept with some relevance for continents such as Africa and Asia.

The responsibility to protect is key for internally displaced persons. Refugees excepted, this is a group largely without protection. Governments do not accept that the international community has a role here, and there are some principles that have been worked out by Francis Deng, but right now no agency has responsibility for the protection of IDPs. There are approximately 24 million IDPs, as opposed to some 14 million refugees right now.

Millions of women are yearly affected by a trafficking and smuggling problem, and the traffickers are becoming more and more adept in their methods.

The church and NGOs such as Amnesty International, Human Rights Watch, etc., play a major role in protection. There is a need to strengthen the concept of alert – of alerting the international community to situations either of potential conflict or gross violation of human rights. There is a serious need to consider this issue by the NGO community.

In my work, I had to travel to central Asia, and I realized to my consternation that the human rights idea has not entered these countries. In places like Turkmenistan or Uzbekistan, we have to start from ground level. These countries are dealing with economic and social problems. In many developing countries, keeping in mind the economic problems the governments have, churches will play their role in promoting values of the church and human rights. Human rights education in the schools is something that can perhaps hold the human rights idea and give us a chance for promotion and protection.

When you come to systematize what you will do from the responsibility to protect perspective, you will need to think about all these categories of actors, of issues and of simple methods that can help us to promote and protect human rights in the long term. The High Level Panel and the Secretary General have thrown out some grand ideas, but the work of protection can sometimes require basic, practical action on the ground, step by step. The key is an effective national protection system in each country.

Comments from Ernie Regehr

Endorsing the Responsibility to Protect as a Global Norm

Churches seem to be in strong support of the emerging international norm of the responsibility to protect. This norm holds that national governments clearly bear the primary and sovereign responsibility to provide for the safety of their people. Indeed, a state's sovereignty is to some extent conditional on its capacity to carry out the responsibility to protect and serve the welfare of its people. When there is egregious failure to carry out that responsibility, whether by neglect, lack of capacity or direct assault, the international community has the duty to override sovereignty and to intervene in the internal affairs of the state in the interests and safety of the people.

Protection and Human Security

Churches also seem to be in broad agreement that it is the active and persistent pursuit of human security that offers the most reliable prospect for protecting people and preventing the kinds of human-made humanitarian catastrophes that we now witness in Darfur, DRC and Northern Uganda, and that we have seen in Rwanda, Southern Sudan, Cambodia, and in the many other locations and conditions of acute insecurity. The most immediate experiences of insecurity come in the form of unmet basic needs, political exclusion and the denial of basic rights, social and political disintegration, and the related escalation of criminal and political violence. Thus, the churches promote and participate in the delivery of measures that address and mitigate the ways in which people and communities experience insecurity. That means measures to ensure the physical safety of people, to meet basic economic, social and health needs, to respect fundamental rights and freedoms, to control the instruments of violence and prohibit the means of mass destruction, and to honour the dignity and worth of all people.

Protection and the Resort to Force

In calling on the international community to come to the aid of vulnerable people in extraordinary suffering and peril, churches are not prepared to say that it is never appropriate or never necessary to resort to the use of lethal force. This refusal in principle to preclude the use of force is not based on a naive belief that force can be relied on to solve otherwise intractable problems; rather, it is based on the certain knowledge that the primary consideration must be the welfare of people, especially those in situations of extreme vulnerability and who are utterly abandoned to the whims and prerogatives of their tormentors. The resort to force is first and foremost the result of the failure to prevent what could have been prevented with the appropriate foresight and actions, but having failed, and having acknowledged such failure, the world needs to do what it can to limit the burden and peril that is experience by people as a consequence. Just as individuals and communities in stable and affluent societies are able in emergencies to call on armed police to come to their aid when they experience unusual or extraordinary threats of violence or attack, churches recognize that people in much more perilous circumstances should have access to protectors. Churches are thus not prepared to say that armed force can never be effective in bringing at least a short-term reprieve from the assaults they endure.

So churches do not fudge or shrink from the issue of the resort to force for protection purposes. They acknowledge that in some circumstances it will be the only available option – an option that cannot guarantee success, but that must be tried because the world has failed to find and continues to be at a loss to find any other means of coming to the aid of those in desperate situations.

The Limits of Force

Churches do not, however, look to the exercise of lethal force to bring in a new order of peace and safety. By limiting the resort to force quite specifically to immediate protection objectives, churches acknowledge (indeed, insist) that the kinds of long-term solutions required – the restoration of societies to conditions in which people are for the most part physically safe, in which basic economic, social, and health needs are met, where fundamental rights and freedoms are respected, where the instruments of violence are controlled, and where the dignity and worth of all people are affirmed – cannot be delivered by force. Indeed, the limiting of legitimate force to protection operations is the recognition that the distress of deeply troubled societies cannot be quickly alleviated by either military means or diplomacy; and that in the long and painstakingly slow process of rebuilding the conditions for sustainable peace, those that are most vulnerable are entitled to protection from at least the most egregious of threats.

The use of force for humanitarian purposes is not the attempt to find military solutions to social and political problems, to militarily engineer new social and political realities; rather, it is intended to mitigate imminent threats and to alleviate immediate suffering while long-term solutions are sought by other means.

The Context of the Resort to Force

The use of force for humanitarian purposes must therefore take place in the context of a broad spectrum of economic, social, political and diplomatic efforts to address the direct and long-term conditions that underlie a crisis. Military interventions should be accompanied by humanitarian relief efforts, and should include the resources and will to stay with the people in peril until essential order and public safety are restored and there is a demonstrated local capacity to continue to build conditions of durable peace.

The Nature of Force for Humanitarian Purposes

The force that is to be deployed and used for humanitarian purposes must also be distinguished from military war-fighting methods and objectives. The ICISS report repeats this point several times. While noting that peacekeeping was designed to monitor ceasefires between belligerent states, the report says 'the challenge in this context is to find tactics and strategies of military intervention that fill the current gulf between outdated concepts of peacekeeping and full-scale military operations that may have deleterious impacts on civilians' (p. 5). Later, it makes the point that 'military intervention [for humanitarian purposes] involves a form of military action significantly more narrowly focused and targeted than all-out war fighting' (p. 37). Winning the acceptance of civilian populations, says the report, 'means accepting limitations and demonstrating through the use of restraint that the [military] operation is not a war to defeat a state but an operation to protect populations in that state from being harassed, persecuted or killed' (p. 63). It is more related to policing – though not necessarily in the level of force required, since it is inevitable that in some instances protection forces will face heavily armed, perhaps unrestrained adversaries. Military operations to protect people are analogous to policing in the sense that the armed forces are not employed in order to 'win' a conflict or defeat a regime. They are there only to protect people in peril and to maintain some level of public safety while other authorities and institutions pursue solutions to underlying problems. Such a specialized and restrained use of force requires specialized training, equipment and rules of engagement.

The Political/Moral Will to Act When Prevention Fails

There may therefore be circumstances in which churches actively call for the above kind of military intervention for humanitarian purposes. They are likely to be reluctant calls because churches (like other institutions and individuals) will always know that the current situation of peril could have been and should have been avoided. Churches in such circumstances should find it appropriate to recognize their own collective culpability in failing to prevent the crises that have put people in such peril.

A Responsibility to Protect:
Some Considerations for the Church

Shirley C. DeWolf

Our Theological Inquiry

It is clear that the responsibility to protect has been at the core of the church's mission since the beginning of Christendom. At certain pivotal moments in history, however, the practice of the church has not effectively reflected this central mission. There are many indications that the first decade of the twenty-first century is one of those decisive historical moments. Is our theological inquiry today urgent enough to meet the demands placed on the church by a world in serious trouble? Where does the motivation for this theological inquiry come from, and whose concerns and needs provoke it? Are we perhaps awakened to the urgency of our theological contribution only when the roar of the bidders on the international policy auction floor becomes too deafening to ignore?

Within our first-hand experience of widespread abuses of human rights, churches in Africa have become increasingly aware of the imperative to seek out a theology of human rights. We live on a continent where respect for the inherent and divinely endowed dignity of human life has always been the unquestionable foundation of community life. Now, under a multiplicity of threats, that respect is being vigorously eroded even as we watch. We interpret this as essentially a theological crisis. Thus we ask ourselves: does the international legal regime for the protection of human rights adequately replace what the continent appears to be losing from its traditions? How does an African Christian theology address this situation? Whose theology provides us with our take-off point?

Two quotations from Africans who have faced human vulnerability in its stark reality indicate the dilemma which theologians on our continent must deal with when we consider the responsibility to protect:

> Human life – as all life – is a gift from the gracious and ever generous Creator of all. It is therefore inviolable. We must therefore have a deep reverence for the sanctity of life … and must hold sway as God would hold sway – compassionately, gently, caringly, enabling each part of creation to come fully into its own and to realize its potential for the good of the whole … That is what invests us with our preciousness and from this stem all sorts of rights.[1]

> They broke down the door, they raped my wife. It was our fate, I think God predetermined it … God is the Creator, the Almighty, so even the war, it is God who made it to happen against us. I cannot be angry – I am his creation. I am powerless against God … We remember Noah. God was angry and drowned the people. Our punishment by comparison is mild.[2]

The gap between these statements from persons of faith is startling. How can the name of God be used to describe such utterly different beings? One voice speaks of a God who, with deep compassion for creation, has endowed humanity with rights than cannot be violated. The other two voices speak of a God who appears to terrorize, who uses power arbitrarily and in a bid to suppress the human spirit. And yet both these statements must be understood as statements of faith.

The first quotation comes from Desmond Tutu (Tutu: *Religious Human Rights and the Bible*), who accompanied his people through a protracted period of abuse by the apartheid regime of South Africa. Later, as he led the Truth and Reconciliation Commission, he was witness to some of the worst behaviour that human beings are capable of committing against other human beings. It was in that crucible that he developed a deep understanding of grace, and was able to say with conviction that to trample a person's dignity 'is positively blasphemous, for it is tantamount to spitting in the face of God'.

The second quotation is a combination of remarks from religious leaders at community level in Sierra Leone in the wake of the civil war that finally ended in 2002. The three people quoted have personally experienced serious human rights abuse and have witnessed the violation of their loved ones. They are struggling to integrate the horror of their experience into their faith. Their words may make us feel uncomfortable, may even shock us, but they must be accepted as genuine statements of faith. They are an explicit expression of the depth of pain in which they are trapped, beyond which at this moment they can see no feasibility. Like Job, these persons cry out: 'God has wronged me … He has stripped me of my honour … He uproots my hope' (Job 19:6–11). Job was rewarded for his faith, for after all the despicable things that happened to him, he refused to give up his faith in a God who must be more powerful than any form of evil. We hear the three testimonies from Sierra Leone as saying: 'We will attribute even that which crushes us to God, for any alternative concept of omnipotence is unthinkable. What we know from our experiences is that only God has rights; human beings have needs.'

Two statements, two perspectives on the same human experience. The first is a profession of hope refined through centuries of bold witness and reflection. The second is a profession of raw faith uttered in the heat of the fire. The gap between the first and second statements is the space in which an African theological investigation must take place as we consider the churches' agenda for protection.

It is important to recognize as a starting point for our quest for a Christian understanding of human vulnerability that it is an intentional God-given condition and not an accident. Neither is it a result of human sinfulness, for across the Christian theological spectrum most would agree that human creatures were never at any point completely above the precariousness of their cosmic environment.

Secondly, as we explore the meaning of the cross we are led to believe that, theologically speaking, vulnerability is not the opposite of power. It is astounding – indeed, it is a mystery – that the greatest of all power, the power of God's grace-filled love for humanity, a power which lies beyond the grasp of human imagination, is expressed in an act of utter defencelessness. The cry of Jesus from the cross – 'My God, why hast thou forsaken me!' – is something he learned from our side of the divine–human divide, and in that moment Jesus becomes truly human and God's plan for reconciliation touches down. Therefore, our respect and devotion for Jesus Christ on the cross give us a new perspective on human vulnerability. To be vulnerable is no longer a shameful thing, nor is to something to fill us with horror and dread. In the cross we can accept who we are and also who we are not.

Thirdly, Jesus' cry from the cross resonates from the same depth of anguish out of which we hear the cry from Sierra Leone: 'It is God who has made this happen – I am powerless!' But even as we recognize this, another gap becomes evident to which we have to give serious theological attention. God in Jesus Christ willed himself into a state of vulnerability by emptying himself, electing to take on the form of a slave and offering himself on the cross. This was a gift: God so loved that he gave. As a victim of extreme abuse in Sierra Leone, my poverty, my defencelessness against those who prey unjustly upon me, the rape of those dearest to me, the suppression of my human dignity, indeed my crucifixion, is not something that I choose to give. My vulnerability is not optional; it is absolute and it is inescapable. And in my own moment of greatest danger, if God pulls back his protection as part of some untransparent plan, I will accept that because God alone has rights and all I have are needs that depend on God's right of decision. The proverbial 'inviolability of right to life' is not in fact my right, but God's right, to give or to withdraw. Don't ask me to understand the grace-filled love part.

A theology of the cross must always be developed in light of the resurrection. If vulnerability and sacrifice (elected or imposed) become the central themes of our quest for greater understanding, we run the risk of glorifying our pain, failing to develop moral imagination, surrendering preventive action to the god of suffering, and locking ourselves and others into pious despair. The human experience is not only that of vulnerability; it is also that of overcoming vulnerability. The apostle Paul recognized this from his vantage point in a prison cell: know the hope to which you are called, he wrote, and how vast are the resources of his power open to you who trust in him, the power of the resurrection itself (Ephesians 1:18–20).

But the gap between the two confessions of faith that are stimulating this reflection begs our attention to another very important element of African theology. The same documentary film on Sierra Leone takes us to an interview with a Lutheran bishop, a man who is struggling honestly and painfully with this gap as it is represented on the one hand by his faith in the divine origin of human rights and on the other hand by the unconscionable acts of depravity that he is witnessing:

> Yes, I fear the sinful side of man. I witnessed seven people, including one old man … on a Sunday morning being beheaded in Bo. And I couldn't believe that that was being done by human beings to their companion human beings. That really drew some fear in me, some terror in me, the level to which we human beings can sink. And so I don't take lightly, I don't take lightly the presence of evil amongst us, in us, the extent to which evil can be incarnated in the human being.

Evil is an essential element in Africa's understanding of human vulnerability, both in traditional theologies and in modern Christian thinking. If we do not face the nemesis in the cosmos our theology is unbalanced, incomplete. An exploration of human rights driven by Western theological interests is likely to miss this.

So if I submit to my own abuse because I accept it as God's irrefutable judgement, am I faithfully conforming to God's unfathomable plan or am I conforming to the greed and maliciousness of people in whom evil is manifest? If I stand up and fight back the evil and at great risk to my community, am I grasping hold of that hope to which I am called, or am I breaking the protective barrier against evil that has helped my people to cope for generations? The theology expressed by the unnamed Sierra Leoneans earlier in this essay reflects a stamina built up over generations, without which communities that live with risk as a constant threat could not cope. Each new generation of children learns from birth to accept suffering as an integral part of life so that they can integrate negative experiences into their continuing life journey. The rules of resilience say keep your head down, don't go out on your own, blend into the crowd. The rules say accept, do not question, or your individualism will bring shame. And the rules say do not hope for that which is beyond feasibility. It is not surprising then if their theology should take the more non-confrontational route. Indeed, this is an indication of inner strength.

How then does the global Christian community hold together under such challenges? How can we make this vitally important theological sojourn together so that we help not only to shape the international policy on responsibility to protect, but also the human communities trying to protect themselves on the frontline?

The Lutheran bishop in Sierra Leone continues in the film to reflect on the atrocities he has witnessed:

> For a moment I asked myself 'Where is God?' and many times I have asked myself that question … There is always something that happens to show me that God is there. But we must have the courage to look.

The courage to look for God: that is our common agenda. If our theological inquiry is honest, it will require of all of us a commitment to enter spaces where we have not been before. It will require us to help each other shape questions out of cries of despair. It will mean that we find our common denominator in the most difficult of these questions, accept joint responsibility for both finding the answers and living with the consequences of our discovery.

A Ministry of Accompaniment

Policy formation around the responsibility to protect, being essentially an internationally coordinated response to an event or development in a specific location, must seek a valid entry point, both morally and legally. It is therefore interventionist in nature and must give considerable attention to avoiding the negative effects of interventionism while identifying the opportunities for positive penetration. The church's ministry reflects a different perspective and this requires deliberate cultivation lest it be lost by association.

The church's ministry with people in need of protection is grounded in a holistic and sojourning accompaniment of humanity throughout all of life, in good times and in bad. It is first and foremost a ministry in the most inclusive sense of that word. It does not begin when the community reaches a point of collapse, nor does it end after stability has been restored. One important implication of this premise is that the church does not define people by the negative circumstances that constrain them within certain periods of their lives, but by the strengths that are active within those people to cope with and overcome their circumstances. It is a belief in 'the One who is able to do immeasurably more than all we ask or imagine, according to his power that is at work within us' (Ephesians 3:20).

This leads us to recognize that the largest proportion of protection activity is carried out by the affected people themselves. It is they who have the greatest vested interest in their own survival and therefore are most highly motivated to find protection patterns that will work. As noted above, where populations know themselves to live in a perpetual state of insecurity they develop a culture of coping and resilience, endowing their children with adaptability and perseverance, teaching them survival skills and attitudes. Where vulnerability to life-threatening circumstances develops and increases over a period of time, people make daily adjustments to hold themselves as steady as possible – mental, physical, financial, social and spiritual adjustments. It is therefore incumbent upon the church to respect these coping mechanisms, recognizing the strength that they represent and assisting people to build upon them.

Such an approach would have major ramifications for both the purpose and the style of our ministry. For one thing, it means conceptualizing circular patterns of support.

Circles of support for communities in distress

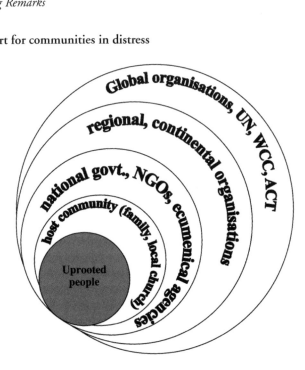

If indeed the greatest energy and most effective activity for protection happens within the community immediately affected, then they comprise the innermost circle, the one around which all others are built. The Mozambicans have a word that helps us with this conceptualization: dumbanenge. It means 'trust your own feet'. And when the burden becomes too heavy and your feet can no longer hold you up, turn to those who are familiar with your vulnerability out of their own life experience, because they will know how to uplift you without destroying your capacity. So the immediate circle of support around the centre is most often a local community in which vulnerable people embed themselves. This layer of support, the circle of hands-on caregivers, easily becomes overburdened, often suffers secondary trauma, and is rarely consulted in the greater Protection Plan. Within this immediate support band is a local infrastructure that would include religious congregations, schools, clubs and other instruments of social cohesion. The third circle of support would most likely be a district or national expression of the various institutions that serve society: government, NGOs and again the church. Beyond this layer lie the various regional and international circles of support.

The church exists at all levels in these circles of support, from the centre to the outermost layer. We must therefore conceive of these circles not as lines of demarcation and separation, but almost as layers of skin, each one adding strength to the layer inside it, and all together giving united support to the body in the centre. In our 'new configuration' of ecumenical expression, let us realize that its strength depends on how well this works. If our ecumenical conversation occurs only between circles 3 and 5, we will not be the church. If circle 3 is not listening to circles 1 and 2, then we delude ourselves that we are operating better than we are.

We cannot possibly do any of this without developing a ministry of listening. Recognized authority and expertise abounds, much more so in a state of emergency, and the clamour of opinions and communiqués invariably drowns out the voices in the centre circles. Religious communities provide the best potential for ensuring that the international protection regime is actually built upon the vision and values of those who seek protection.

But there is a long, long way to go before we fulfil this potential. The local congregation is supposedly the easiest point of access to the church by the community and vice versa; in fact, the local congregation often sees its role as being the most visible sign of the church's exclusivity, the border line between 'us' and 'them'. The local congregation by definition is embedded in the community and therefore expected to be the eyes and ears of the church in that situation; in fact, the eyes and ears of the congregation have often not been tuned for their task and therefore are trained inward. The nature of the local congregation supposedly makes it the least hierarchical and therefore the most participatory level of the church; in fact, it is often even more stratified and power-conscious than the society it is called to serve and therefore it seeks to control more than to respond. We need to spend time in the streets listening to rough language from people who don't know how to talk church-talk. We need to open up spaces for people to express anger, because anger is an essential survival tool. We need to give respect to the voices of frustrated children and youth and take seriously their vision on moving forward in a messed up, adult-dominated world. We need to understand why and how Jesus deliberately threw himself into the disorderly, unsafe, uncontrollable and confusing society of his time, risking his reputation to take new relationship, new order and new worth to people who were strategically excluded. A church without a resurrection attitude about everything we do again hardly qualifies for the name.

There is not the space here to go into a discussion on a theology of the living church, but clearly it is a fundamental consideration if the church is to take more seriously its protection responsibility. One thing must be mentioned in passing, since the WCC discussions on ecumenical reconfiguration intersect with the responsibility to protect in an important way. The merit of our global ecumenical witness depends squarely on the capacity of our local congregations to be what the church is meant to be. This means that our ecumenical dialogue on protection – or indeed on any matter – cannot stop with the national councils of churches as the bottom line for ecumenical collaboration.

NOTES

1. Desmond M. Tutu, 'Religious Human Rights in the Bible', from a report on the 1994 Atlanta Conference in the *Emory International Law Review*, Vol. 10, No. 1 (1996).
2. Extracts from interviews with three members of a community in Sierra Leone, taken from the World Council of Churches video *Roots of Violence* (2003).

Annex 1
The Responsibility to Protect:
Ethical and Theological Reflections

Guillermo Kerber

A report to the WCC Central Committee meeting in 2003, from the Commission of the Churches on International Affairs (CCIA) on the follow up of the 2001 WCC Central Committee document, 'The protection of endangered populations in situations of armed violence'.

Introduction

In February 2001, during its meeting in Potsdam, the Central Committee of the World Council of Churches adopted a document entitled 'The protection of endangered populations in situations of armed violence: toward an ecumenical ethical approach' (PEP). In its preamble, the Central Committee requested the CCIA to report back at a later date.

Last June a CCIA extended officers' meeting, gathered in Versailles, received a memorandum from the International Affairs, Peace and Human Security team (IAPHS) on this issue, discussed it, made some recommendations for redrafting and recommended to send the present report to the Central Committee to fulfil its requests.

This report, elaborated by IAPHS after consultation with the CCIA commissioners who attended the Versailles meeting, contains the following points:

1   A recall of the process that led to the PEP document.
2   A summary of the reactions from the churches and a reference list of other relevant documents related to this topic.
3   Some elements that could be part of the content of a follow-up process.
4   A proposal for next steps in the continuation of the reflection.

The Process Leading to the 2001 Central Committee's Document

PEP, adopted by the WCC's Central Committee in Potsdam in February 2001, is the most recent WCC document referring to this issue. The following paragraphs summarize the most relevant previous documents related to the subject.

The document should be seen in the framework of the WCC's documents related to war and the use of force, which can be traced back to the WCC's First Assembly (Amsterdam 1948). The Assembly stated clearly that 'war as a method of settling disputes is incompatible with the teaching and example of our Lord Jesus Christ. The part which war plays in our present international life is a sin against God and a degradation of man.' However, as PEP affirms, 'the perspectives of Christians on matters of war and the use of armed force differ radically and have time and again threatened the unity of the church.'

In 1948 no agreement was possible on how to answer this question. The most the Assembly could do was to restate the opposing positions.

(1) There are those who hold that, even though entering a war may be a Christian's duty in particular circumstances, modern warfare, with its mass destruction, can never be an act of justice.

(2) In the absence of impartial supranational institutions, there are those who hold that military action is the ultimate sanction of the rule of law, and that citizens must be distinctly taught that it is their duty to defend the law by force if necessary.

(3) Others, again, refuse military service of all kinds, convinced that an absolute witness against war and for peace is for them the will of God, and they desire that the Church should speak to the same effect.

We could suppose that these opinions, although more than fifty years have passed, are still present in Christianity. Pacifist positions within the churches and emblematically represented by the Historic Peace Churches confronted those who assumed the theory of just war. The discussion on the use of armed violence as the last resort remained a top issue. During the Cold War, however, these two positions somehow agreed that there was no possibility of a just use of nuclear weapons.

After the Cold War, the massive deployment of military force under UN Security Council auspices in the Gulf War revealed a deep division among the churches when it was debated in Canberra in 1991 during the WCC Seventh Assembly. While some justified the US-led intervention in the Gulf and its attacks on Iraq by the application of just war criteria, others asked: 'Can war now be an act of justice?'

In 1994 the creation by the Central Committee of the Programme to Overcome Violence pushed Christians who hold these different perspectives towards joint action 'to counter the rising tide of violence at all levels of contemporary society and promote a global culture of peace'.

In response to questions raised at the Central Committee in 1994 about whether and under what conditions the use of coercion is an acceptable tool to enforce human rights and the international rule of law in violent or potentially violent situations, the CCIA prepared for the Central Committee in 1995 a 'Memorandum and recommendations on the application of sanctions' and adopted a set of 'Criteria for determining the applicability and effectiveness of sanctions'.

In September 1999 the Central Committee adopted a 'Memorandum and recommendations on international security and response to armed conflict', which highlighted the dilemmas around humanitarian intervention, raised especially by the Kosovo experience.

Immediately before the Central Committee's statement on PEP, in April 2000, an ecumenical seminar took place in Bossey to discuss 'The ethics of humanitarian intervention'. Six CCIA commissioners as well as other invited participants and WCC and Lutheran World Federation staff reflected together. Parallel to the WCC's process, the LWF Council discussed a paper on 'Armed intervention to defend human rights' in June 2000.

A specialized CCIA reference group drafted the final document that was presented to the Central Committee for consideration. During the Central Committee meeting in Potsdam, the document was heavily discussed and redrafted and afterwards received and commended to the churches for further study, reflection and use.

As the process developed, it was clear that there was broad agreement on most of the matters. However, the notion of humanitarian intervention was strongly criticized and some differences remain within the ecumenical movement with respect to the use of armed force for the protection of endangered populations in situations of armed violence. Therefore, it was thought that the most important contribution of the churches was to help reshape and clarify the terms of the debate.

Responses from the Churches and Other Relevant Documents since February 2001
As previously stated, the Central Committee in Potsdam commended the document to the churches for further study, reflection and use and requested the churches to share the results of these studies with the CCIA. Very few responses were received by the IAPHS on this issue. This doesn't mean necessarily that churches have not studied it. As CCIA commissioners pointed out, in spite of the few responses, the issue remains a high priority for many churches. Given the political developments in Africa, for instance, the responsibility to protect is crucial, but in many cases churches don't have the appropriate means to respond to requests from the Central Committee. The responses that came are nevertheless very significant:

(1) A working group of the Commission on International Affairs of the Church of Norway Council on Ecumenical and International Relations prepared a study in 2000, which was presented in January 2001 and updated, translated into English and published in 2002. The study 'Vulnerability and security' deepens the relationships between these two concepts and focuses on the question of humanitarian intervention.[1] The document revisits the criteria for just war and questions whether they are useful for assessing the ethical legitimacy of humanitarian intervention. It presents the following criteria as the most important:

- Just cause
- Just intention
- Rightful authority
- Current rules for warfare to be complied with (*jus in bello*)
- Last resort
- Proportionality

The document states that although discussions continue on the validity of the criteria, they actually represent an important ethical framework for dealing with the topic. Although the criteria in themselves reject a general ethical legitimization of intervention, at the same time it is necessary to establish that such criteria cannot be sufficient. A more fundamental consideration of the relationship between human vulnerability and security, combined with a broad approach to the security problem, opens the way for a wider perspective.

The document ends by stating that the answer to the question 'What can the specific contribution of the churches be in the context of security policy?' can be summarized in two points: the victim's perspective and the service of reconciliation. The victim's perspective (Matthew 25:35) reinforces the human security concept that the document advocates. On the other hand, as peace and reconciliation are at the very core of the Christian message (2 Corinthians 5:18), on questions of security policy the churches must be the first to insist on peaceful solutions to confrontation and conflict. Reconciliation processes, however, are complicated. They require respect for truth and justice, remorse, forgiveness and a new beginning.

(2) The Evangelical Church in Germany (EKD) responded officially to the WCC in a letter to the CCIA director in November 2002, which echoed the previous reflections made by the church, especially in 'Steps on the way to peace: points of reference on peace ethics and peace policy'. EKD's study (SWP) relates the issue of humanitarian intervention to the broader perspective of security (defined with human security components). From this perspective, a reliable structure of peace includes the rule of law, ensuring the protection of freedom, economic balancing, international organizations and international law, and a culture of social manners and contact with minorities.

Hence, it includes conflict prevention, conflict resolution and post-conflict reconciliation. The concept of just peace (instead of just war) is presented as the basic idea of Christian peace ethics. This means there is a priority for non-military instruments in safeguarding peace. The document calls for the strengthening of the international peace system as intended and drawn up in the Charter of the United Nations. The universal acceptance and implementation of human rights is an important factor for strengthening the international peace system as a legal system.

The document also stresses that the use of military force should be a last resort (ultima ratio) and must remain a borderline case. It recognizes that the use of military force as ultima ratio has been vehemently criticized in internal church discussions; therefore, it needs to be analysed more carefully than previously. A number of criteria refer to proportionality and just war principles. Humanitarian intervention is defined as 'the military intervention with the reason and aim to contribute to the recognition and implementation of human rights in cases of serious violation of human rights and thus to grant protection and help to the victims of oppression and violence'.

The document ends by affirming that the dilemma of the use of violence or a radically pacifist position on the level of fundamental ethical discussion will not and probably cannot be resolved. Defensive war as well as collective defensive war can never be completely excluded. But in the prime task of peace promotion, policy must be pursued with strategies strengthening the promotion of democracy and economy.

Another EKD contribution was published later the same year – 'Guide our feet into the way of peace: violent conflicts and civil intervention' – that focused on the African context.

(3) Members of the Historic Peace Churches from different countries in the world met in June 2001 in Bienenberg, Switzerland, for an International Consultation and produced a study paper shared with the WCC: 'Just peacemaking: towards an ecumenical ethical approach from the perspective of the Historic Peace Churches'. The document expresses their concerns about the PEP document and offers a five-point response:

1   A biblically and theologically grounded pacifism regards seeking God's justice as central and integral to a non-violent philosophy of life. To state the issue as if we have to choose between non-violence and justice is a false dichotomy. The document sets forth a vision of justice that is holistic and social, distinguishing it from the view that emphasizes individual autonomy and freedom, the protection of private property and a narrow perspective on human rights, like freedom of speech and association. The biblical tradition of covenant justice, the documents adds, emphasizes social solidarity, religious liberty and comprehensive visions of human rights.

2   We can identify a number of normative practices for seeking justice within principled pacifism. A list of five available practices is illustrative of this: non-violent forms of defence and social transformation; citizens' corps of observers/interveners/advocates; acknowledging responsibility for violence and injustice and seeking repentance and forgiveness (e.g. the Truth and Reconciliation Commission in South Africa); training persons in the use of cooperative conflict methods and strategies; the church's witness and advocacy on behalf of the marginalized and those whose lives are threatened by injustice (e.g. the campaign to end sanctions in Iraq, etc.).

3   The use of violent force as a last resort to secure justice creates conditions that inhibit the achievement of justice. Too often, we work under the false assumption that, if we cannot find a non-violent solution to a conflict, the use of violent force will take care of the problem. Furthermore, the presumed humanitarian intervention may mask egoistic self-interests and the partisan political agendas of the parties who presume to intervene. Implicitly, the church has accepted the assumption that violent force is inevitable, and since it is inevitable, we must

support the preparation for that possibility. Last-resort thinking cuts short imaginative thinking and creative action to find alternative ways to make peace.

4   We call on the churches to emphasize the distinctive witness to the world that flows from our commitment to the Spirit of Jesus Christ and our identity as the Body of Christ in the world. We are disappointed, the document continues, that the language of the WCC study document is dominated largely by political analysis and prudential calculation about when resort to armed intervention might be justified and what restraints should be placed on it. We question whether the dominant language of the document can really help to develop an ecumenical ethical approach as suggested by the subtitle.

5   Both pacifists and those who reason with just war principles should make more modest claims about their ability to guarantee success. Though both traditions seek justice, neither tradition can guarantee that justice will be accomplished. Both traditions involve faith visions about how to 'secure' a future in which justice is more likely to be achieved. The pacifist commitment to non-violence is ultimately grounded in an eschatology of trust in the victory over evil of God revealed in Jesus' life, teachings, death and resurrection.

Outside the ecumenical movement, the International Commission on Intervention and State Sovereignty published its report 'The responsibility to protect' in December 2002, which targets the right of humanitarian intervention. It is not the intention of this essay to summarize the considerations of this report, but we would like to affirm that it should be studied in the next steps of the process.

Other institutions have also published interesting materials on this matter. For example, the US Institute of Peace published in July 2002 'The ethics of armed humanitarian intervention' by the Australian scholar C. A. H. Coady, while the Henry Dunant Centre for Humanitarian Dialogue published in February 2003 a report on 'Politics and humanitarianism: coherence in crisis?'

Final Considerations and Perspectives

After the 2001 Central Committee's document on PEP, we can identify three different development processes.

First, the 11 September 2001 terrorist attacks and their consequences led to a new consideration of the issue. The intervention in East Timor, the 'war on terrorism' and more recently the war against Iraq – which showed a new level of US unilateralism in the international arena and raised several questions on the role of international law and international institutions like the UN Security Council, and hence the function of humanitarian aid and military intervention – also reshaped the debate.

The second path is related to the churches. Some of them have taken the issue seriously and have produced important materials to continue the discussion. Others, as far as we know, although they have not commented on the PEP document, still consider the issue of great importance.

Third, the reports produced outside the ecumenical movement and referred to above show that the issue is also very important to other actors at governmental and non-governmental levels. Other contributions could certainly be found and included in a new study process. As for the content of such a process, some elements from the above documents can be highlighted:

Title

The next step of the study could be entitled 'The responsibility to protect: ethical and theological reflections'. The issue of protection has not only appeared in the title of PEP, shifting from 'humanitarian intervention' to 'the protection of endangered populations', but is also an important subject in other studies. It is in the title of the ICISS report and in the conclusion of the HD's report 'The UN and the protection of human life'. As the ICISS report puts it, protection includes prevention, reaction and rebuilding. Different aspects of conflict management and peace-building can be discussed. The EKD's study called for effective non-military means for the treatment and resolution of conflicts, in conflict prevention, measures of mediation and in post-conflict reconciliation.

Ethical and theological criteria for discernment

The ethical and theological perspective of churches should be highlighted. Though the criteria developed by PEP and others have been rejected by some, the need to further develop this approach is seen as necessary. This means making explicit the criteria for discernment in particular cases in which the action to be taken cannot be clearly foreseen. While humanitarian, governmental and non-governmental organizations, as well as scholars, continue to produce material (some of it quite good), only an ethical and theological analysis can reveal the unique role of churches.

Human security

The shift from security understood as something related only to states, to human security, has been an important process in the last decade. Human security includes the security of people: their physical safety, their economic and social well-being, respect for their dignity and worth as human beings, and the protection of their human rights and fundamental freedoms. Human security as a framework for considering the different implications of protection and intervention also needs ethical and theological elements. Most of the research papers of ecumenical, governmental and non-governmental bodies reject the terminology of humanitarian intervention. However, it is important to state clearly (as most have) why it is rejected and to place the discussion under the umbrella of human security. In present world circumstances the question as to what is the determining authority to decide on intervention remains crucial.

Sovereignty, human rights and international law

The conflict between respect for state sovereignty and protection of human rights remains at the heart of discussion on intervention and human security. The cornerstone of the international system was the principle of national sovereignty. The principle of non-intervention, on the other hand, although included in the United Nations Charter, has been broken several times, with intervention justified on the basis of serious human rights violations committed by a state against its own citizens as a threat to peace.

Issues of protection cannot be separated from respect for and promotion of human rights and the strengthening of democracy. As many documents have stated, measures to reinforce civil, political, economic, social and cultural rights, as well as a strong democracy, are perceived as central in prevention, mediation and reconciliation processes.

International law is not static, but in a constant process of evolution, and the new world configuration requires continuous reflection. The war against Iraq brought some issues to prominence: multilateralism and unilateralism, the role of the UN Security Council, the relationship between military intervention and humanitarian aid. Besides ethical criteria, legal and political criteria must be considered so as to go beyond the present situation. The specific roles of the International Court of Justice and the recently established International Criminal Court should also be included in reflection.

Just peace and the use of military force as last resort (*ultima ratio*)
PEP and other ecumenical documents stress the importance of developing the concept of just peace and just peacemaking. All the ecumenical documents emphatically underline the priority of non-military instruments in safeguarding peace and related the prior option of freedom from violence to the roots of the Decade to Overcome Violence. In church responses there is a divergence of opinion. While some try to specify criteria for the use of military force as a last resort, the Historic Peace Churches directly criticize this option. Recent discussions on just war and preemptive war should be included in a future study.

Proposal to the Central Committee
Having received a memorandum from IAPHS and discussed the issue in its extended officers' meeting last June, the CCIA would like to propose the following to the Central Committee:

1   To receive the present report as background information and as fulfilment of its request in Potsdam in 2001 to report back to the Central Committee.
2   To ask IAPHS to follow-up the study, within the spirit of the Decade to Overcome Violence, as 'The responsibility to protect: ethical and theological reflections', taking into account the new world scenario. A report should be shared at the next WCC Assembly. The study process should be undertaken in close collaboration with one or more ecumenical institutions already working on the issue. Academic institutions, especially from the South, should be involved and asked to deepen the study. A summary of two or three pages should be produced and made available for wider distribution and work among member churches and partners in the regions.

NOTES

1.   The document defines humanitarian intervention as 'the international use of force on the territory of other states and without their consent with the aim of (re-)establishing elementary human security when it has been grossly and persistently violated' (p. 29).

Annex 2
The Responsibility to Protect

Semegnish Asfaw

Indroduction

The changing geopolitical patterns of the late 1980s and early 1990s, characterized by the end of the Cold War, an increasing number of domestic wars, the erosion of sovereignty, the need to contain refugee flows resulting from civil wars, and the need to protect internally displaced people, led to more and more interventions for humanitarian purposes. Humanitarian intervention and assistance became a burning issue for the international community when foreign aid to populations in dire need was blocked for political reasons in several countries.

After a long and fruitful process of international negotiation, on 8 December 1988 the General Assembly of the United Nations adopted resolution 43/131 on 'Humanitarian assistance to victims of natural disasters and similar emergency situations'. This resolution was followed on 14 December 1990 by General Assembly resolution 45/100, which introduced the concept of relief corridors – a major cause of the evolution and development of the normative process of international law pertaining to humanitarian intervention. These two resolutions form the legal cornerstone of humanitarian intervention and assistance to populations in need.

However, their approach is mainly from the perspective of the intervening state, often creating uneasiness for intervened peoples, as the language of the 'right' or 'duty to intervene' is intrinsically confrontational. After a long series of consultations and negotiations in the international community, the new concept of the responsibility to protect was proposed by the International Commission on Intervention and State Sovereignty in its 2001 report. For the first time, the debate shifted from the viewpoint of the interveners to that of the people in need of assistance.

The responsibility to protect redefines sovereignty as a duty-bearer status rather than as an absolute power. In other words, states can no longer use the pretext of sovereignty to perpetrate human rights violations against their citizens with total impunity. Sovereignty has been reconceived in such a way that states have an obligation to protect their citizens and ensure their basic rights by preserving their dignity, well-being and safety.

The purpose of this report is to shape the debate of the seminar we are organizing. It will briefly assess some United Nations reports that have been adopted in relation to the responsibility to protect agenda, and then crystallize some controversial matters in relation to the topic.

The Responsibility to Protect and the United Nations

The ICISS report

During the 2000 Millennium General Assembly, the Canadian government and a group of major foundations announced the establishment of the International Commission on Intervention and State Sovereignty to help find consensus on how to approach the central question posed by the UN Secretary General Kofi Annan:

If humanitarian intervention is indeed an unacceptable assault on sovereignty, how should we respond to a Rwanda, to a Srebrenica – to gross and systematic violations of human rights that affect every precept of our common humanity?

The ICISS report was made public in December 2001. It shifted the debate on sovereignty vs. intervention from the 'right of humanitarian intervention' or the 'right to intervene' to a new formulation: the responsibility to protect. The responsibility to protect is a very innovative concept. It is primarily a change in perspective because it reverses the perceptions inherent in traditional formulations and adds a few of its own:

- It provides a new approach to national sovereignty that involves responsibilities and not just rights. In so doing, it implies an evaluation of the issues from the point of view of those seeking or needing support, rather than those who may be considering interventions.
- It stresses the moral imperative for the international community to act when the responsibility to protect citizens from serious harm is not being met. The primary responsibility for civilian protection rests with the state concerned, and it is only if the state is unable or unwilling to fulfil this responsibility, or is itself the perpetrator of human rights violations, that it becomes the responsibility of the international community to act in its place.
- It encourages a continuum of responsibilities from prevention to reaction, and then to rebuilding. The responsibility to protect means not merely the 'responsibility to react' but also the 'responsibility to prevent' and the 'responsibility to rebuild'. It directs attention to the costs and results of action versus no action and provides conceptual normative and operational linkages between assistance, intervention and reconstruction. The responsibility to rebuild is the need to mend or help mend a war-torn society.
- Last but not least, it emphasizes the need for prior preventive effort as the priority responsibility.

The responsibility to protect also implies a responsibility to react to situations of compelling need for human protection. When preventive measures fail to resolve or contain a situation, the international community may agree to adopt coercive measures, which may be political (an arms embargo and ending military cooperation and training programmes), economic (financial sanctions, restrictions on income generating activities) or diplomatic (restrictions on diplomatic representations, restrictions on travel).

It is only in extreme and exceptional cases that the responsibility to react may involve the need for military action. The principle of non-intervention must be taken as the starting point for the discussion of what constitutes an extreme case. This is the norm from which any departure has to be justified. It is the equivalent of the Hippocratic principle in medicine: first, do no harm.[1] The report establishes large-scale loss of life, 'ethnic cleansing' and other systematic violations of humanitarian law as the threshold just-cause condition for military action for humanitarian purposes. It also lists five criteria for military intervention as precautionary principles under the following headings:

- *Right authority.* Any military action for humanitarian purposes has to be taken under a legitimate authority. The UN Security Council is by far the most appropriate body to deal with and authorize military intervention for humanitarian purposes. Hence, unilateral military actions to alleviate human rights crises are not legitimate unless they have been authorized somehow by the Security Council. The Permanent Five should agree on a code of conduct on the use of their veto for actions aimed at stopping or averting significant humanitarian crises.

- *Right intentions.* The primary purpose and intention of the military intervention must genuinely be to halt or avert human suffering. Any use of military force aiming at benefiting the intervening state cannot be justified. Regime change is not a legitimate objective as such, although disabling that regime from harming its own people may sometimes be necessary.
- *Last resort.* Coercive military intervention for humanitarian purposes should be the very last option. Every diplomatic and non-military solution for the prevention or peaceful resolution of the humanitarian crisis must first be explored. It is only when the responsibility to prevent has been fully discharged that the responsibility to react militarily can be justified.
- *Proportional means.* The likely outcomes of the military intervention should not exceed or be worse than the magnitude of the original crisis. The scale, duration and intensity of the planned military intervention should be the minimum necessary to secure the humanitarian objective in question.
- *Reasonable prospects.* Military action can only be justified if it stands a reasonable chance of halting or averting the atrocities or suffering that triggered the intervention in the first place.

The High Level Panel report

In December 2004 the Secretary General's High Level Panel on Threats, Challenges and Changes released its report. It presents a total of 101 recommendations in furtherance of the conviction that 'the maintenance of world peace and security depends importantly on there being a common global understanding, and acceptance, of when the application of force is both legal and legitimate'. The HLP report is a programme for a more effective response to the threats of today's world. It stressed the interconnectedness of threats, broadened the definition of threats to peace and security by highlighting those posed by non-state actors and those undermining human security, and invited member states to accept shared responsibility for dealing with those threats.

Our shared vulnerability and the primacy of the rule of law are the overarching themes. The report stresses that no country must deal alone with today's threats, and no threat can be dealt with effectively unless other threats are addressed at the same time. Today's threats are interconnected, so that collective security is necessary in order to contain threats within national boundaries. The panel endorses UN-authorized preventive action, but not unilateral preventive action. That the use of force is legal does not mean that it is thereby also ethical and wise. Instead, the panel proposes five criteria of legitimacy: seriousness of threat, proper purpose, last resort, proportional means and balance of consequences.

Prevention is the work behind the scenes to solve problems before they become crises. The international community's primary challenge is to ensure that imminent threats do not materialize and distant threats do not become imminent. This requires early, decisive, planned, collective action against all the threats before they worsen. Hence, an emphasis is needed on development as a structural prevention approach, including the possibility of preventive military action.

With respect to internal conflicts, the panel endorses the responsibility to protect agenda. Due to our vulnerability to threats, sovereignty today also includes the state's responsibility to protect its own people and its obligations to the wider international community, alongside the privileges of sovereignty. Hence, too, the need to enhance state capacity in order to enable the state to exercise its sovereignty responsibly.

Much of the recent selectivity has come in the context of the so-called 'war on terror'. As Ramesh Thakur points out: 'The report's section on terrorism achieves a good balance between immediate threats and root causes, between short-term tactics and comprehensive strategies, between assistance and sanctions, and between local, national, regional and global efforts.'[2]

In Larger Freedom: Towards Development, Security and Human Rights for All
In March 2005 UN Secretary General Kofi Annan released a report dealing with what governments must commit to for achieving security in the coming years. The report builds on the December 2004 High Level Panel report and the January 2005 Millennium Project report. This report set the agenda for the world leaders' summit in New York in September 2005.

In his report the Secretary General embraces the emerging norm of the responsibility to protect and recommends that world leaders adopt the responsibility to protect agenda. He also proposes the creation of a peace-building commission and a peace-building support office in his Secretariat. He suggests that the commission report to the Security Council and ECOSOC in sequence, according to the stage of development of their peace-building work. The Security Council should adopt a resolution which will enshrine the principles to be applied in decisions dealing with the use of force and express its intention to be guided by them when deciding whether to authorize or mandate the use of force.

The Secretary General also recommends several steps for strengthening regional organizations and peacekeeping operations. He also encourages the General Assembly to act on the recommendations made by the High Level Panel on how to better engage civil society.

Without implementation, declarations ring hollow, explains the Secretary General. The normative framework has developed considerably over the last six decades. It is now time for the international community to move from an era of legislation to one of implementation.

The responsibility to protect agenda should be used as a basis for collective action against genocide, 'ethnic cleansing' and crimes against humanity. States are encouraged to ratify and implement all treaties relating to the protection of civilians. Cooperation with the International Criminal Court and other international war crimes tribunals should be promoted. The Secretary General also intends to strengthen the Secretariat's capacity to assist national efforts to reestablish the rule of law in conflict and post-conflict societies.

Discussions on Controversial Issues

Reactions to the ICISS report
Daniel Warner contends the ICISS report 'raised issues that it was unable to answer':[3]

> Responsibility, in legal terms, is both a process of imputation and a final result of determined responsibility … Having begun from the generating fact and the general recognition of that fact, the Commission searches for the relationship between the new environment and this generating fact to understand who is responsible for their prevention and who is responsible for the victims. Included within the new environment are both new sets of norms … and the possibility that those who are responding to the generating facts might be new actors, such as NGOs or the UNHCR. In other words, it is not just that we are not beginning from a state-centric system, but we are open to the possibility that the force behind the norms established and the description of the relationship between those norms and the fact that does not have to be done by states as well.[4]

Warner argues that the Commission moves away from a state-centric model by emphasizing the generating fact, but as it then moves towards imputing responsibility, returns back to the state-centric model and describes the implications of responsibility on sovereignty. According to Warner, international humanitarian assistance is not intervention in the internal affairs of a country, but merely amounts to substitution for the government. The government remains the first line of obligation and if it is unwilling or unable to fulfil its obligations, then it needs assistance to carry out its obligations.[5]

Warner goes so far as to claim:

The Commission blinked because it looked into an abyss. It recognized that while there are non-state actors that can justify intervention/assistance and even carry it out, it is also recognized that the 'international community' was incapable of systematically substituting for failed states ... Intervention/assistance is in fact substitution for the failed state because the local government has either abdicated or abandoned its obligations. It cannot be responsible, because it cannot respond. Intervention is a temporary activity until a legitimate authority is reestablished.[6]

In reaction to Warner's criticisms, Ramesh Thakur asserts:

I might accept this strange redefinition for failed state situations, but to conflate intervention into governmental substitution seems to me to stretch the meaning of words beyond the point of sustainability ... Warner's most serious charge ... is that the Commission was guilty of a failure of imagination and nerve in not moving beyond the Westphalian world of sovereign states.[7]

On sovereignty, Thakur explains:

The responsibility of protecting the lives and promoting the welfare of citizens lies first and foremost with the sovereign state. The international order is based on a system of sovereign states in the belief that it is the most efficient means of organizing the world in order to discharge the responsibility to the people of protecting their lives and livelihoods, and promoting their well-being and freedoms. In most cases this is better done by strengthening state capacity and resilience: the best guarantee of human rights is a world of competent, responsible and legitimate sovereign states ... Internally, sovereignty refers to the exclusive competence of the state to make authoritative decisions of government with regard to all people and resources within its territory. Externally, sovereignty means the legal identity of the state in international law, an equality of status with all other states, and the claim to be the sole official agent acting in international relations on behalf of a society.[8]

Thakur believes the United Nations is by far the best symbol and major instrument for moderating the use of force in the international community:

Reducing the entire debate simply to a question of UN authorization as a necessary condition for overseas military action is not good enough. If UN authorization is not a necessary condition, then either we accept the resulting international anarchy and the law of the jungle in world affairs, or we spell out the preferred alternative set of rules and the institutions and regimes in which they are embedded.[9]

On the consequences of the September 2001 terrorist attacks for the ICISS report, Thakur expresses his worry that 'ill-considered rhetoric of preemptive strikes, and of Iraq as an example of "humanitarian intervention", risks draining support from our report rather than adding to the legitimacy of such enterprises'.

Just War Theory

Michael Walzer presents two criticisms of just war theory:

- It moralizes war and hence makes it easier to fight. When we define the criteria by which war and the conduct of war can be judged, we open the way for favourable arguments.
- It frames wars in the wrong way. We need to distinguish between concocted reasons for war and actual reasons.

Walzer explains that just war theory is not an apology for any particular war, and it is not the reunification of war itself. It is designed to sustain a constant scrutiny and an immanent critique.[10]

To qualify as just, a war must be one of self-defence against aggression – a military assault on the territorial integrity and political sovereignty of a nation.[11] There may be several qualifications to this claim:

- *Anticipations.* A country may anticipate an aggression and initiate a first strike. However, a justified anticipatory first strike is one against a state that is already engaged in or expresses a manifest intent to harm. There should be a certain 'degree of active preparation that makes that intent a positive danger, and a general situation in which waiting or doing anything other than fighting, greatly magnifies the risks'.[12]
- *Counter-intervention in civil war.* In the case where a foreign state intervenes in a civil war in order to support one of the contending parties, it is morally legitimate for another nation to intervene militarily so as to eliminate the impact of the first foreign intervention and then leave the civil war to be determined by the balance of internal forces.
- *Humanitarian intervention.* It is morally legitimate for a state to intervene militarily within a country that is engaged in massive violations of human rights amounting to enslavement or massacre of significant numbers of people. Lesser violations of human rights do not justify a military attack that violates the territorial integrity of another nation.

Humanitarian interventions and peacemaking operations are first of all military acts directed against people who are already using force, breaking the peace.[13] In warfare, soldiers must aim fire only at legitimate, morally permissible targets. The distinction between combatants and non-combatants has a important moral significance: civilians must not be deliberately attacked or directly involved in hostilities. If soldiers violate the rules of war, then morally speaking they are criminals, whether the cause they are fighting for is just or unjust. This is the doctrine of double effect, so called because there are two effects to consider: intended and unintended. Michael Walzer applies the doctrine to non-combatant immunity. He argues that the killing or injuring of non-combatants is morally permissible when these conditions hold:

1. The act is good in itself or at least indifferent, which means, for our purposes, that it is a legitimate act of war.
2. The direct effect is morally acceptable – the destruction of enemy supplies, for example, or the killing of enemy soldiers.
3. The intention of the actor is good, that is, he aims only at the acceptable effect; the evil effect is not one of his ends, nor is it a means to his ends, and, aware of the evil involved, he seeks to minimize it, accepting costs to himself.
4. The good effect is sufficiently good to compensate for allowing the evil effect; it must be justifiable under [the] proportionality rule. There must be due proportion between the good intended effect and the evil foreseen but unintended effect.[14]

The Criteria for Intervention

In *Human Rights Crisis* the International Council on Human Rights Policy argues the crucial issue for human rights activist groups is not so much the intervention vs. sovereignty debate, but rather the tension between the obligation to protect victims and the unavoidable harm that military action causes. 'When, if ever, is it morally legitimate (and/or necessary) to advocate killing for human rights?'[15]

Humanitarian agencies have two major concerns:

- The morality and the legal justification of a military intervention. Here, the five criteria test is relevant.
- 'The use of the term "humanitarian" in the context of conflict. As noted already, impartiality is a fundamental principle for humanitarian organizations. Because military interventions are not impartial but preserve or change the balance of political power, some agencies – including the International Committee of the Red Cross and Médecins Sans Frontières (MSF) – have opposed all use of the term "humanitarian intervention."'[16]

From academia, Thomas Weiss holds that the ICISS report on the responsibility to protect sets the bar high for intervention: large-scale loss of life and large-scale 'ethnic cleansing'.[17] Two other candidates for inclusion were eliminated from the Commission's list of threshold conditions, namely the overthrow of democratically elected regimes (a criterion favoured by African states and regional institutions) and massive abuses of human rights (favoured by several Western proponents of outside intervention). However, the qualification of both thresholds as 'actual or apprehended' opens the door fairly widely to interpretation and extrapolation. Hence, justifiable causes can include overthrow of a democracy or violations of human rights, or even environmental catastrophe.

Weiss also explains that when humanitarian and strategic interests coincide, a window of opportunity opens for those seeking to act on the humanitarian impulse of the Security Council or elsewhere. We should not talk about humanitarian 'impulse' but humanitarian 'imperative'. Human values must be universal to be meaningful. The humanitarian imperative would entail an obligation to treat victims similarly and to react to crises consistently – in effect, to deny the relevance of politics, which consists of drawing lines and weighing effectiveness and available resources. Thus, while the humanitarian impulse is permissive, the humanitarian imperative would be peremptory.[18]

Legitimacy vs. Legality

Michael Glennon addresses issues of legitimacy and use of force, and international legal rules governing the use of force. On legitimacy, he explains:

'Legitimacy' is like 'morality', 'fairness' or 'justice' in that the standard it supposes to exist is entirely subjective; there is no commonly agreed upon test of legitimacy, nor is there any way of agreeing upon a methodology that would lead to the establishment of such a test. 'Legitimacy' is often used in the United Nations as synonymous with 'lawful', but the two terms have an entirely different meaning. Law is far less subjective, and its meaning is far less dependent upon the personal, political and philosophical predisposition of the interpreter. Law is intended to be objective and universal; its meaning is intended to be the same for all actors subject to it.[19]

Glennon explains that difficulties arise when law and legitimacy conflict, meaning 'when the law prohibits something that is seen as legitimate or permits something that is seen as illegitimate'.

According to Glennon, there is no universal condition under which the use of force is considered as legitimate. 'The use of force regime set out in the UN Charter has largely broken down, and ... states nowadays judge the propriety of using force not by whether such use is lawful but by whether it is wise.' There is no authoritative legitimacy with respect to the use of force.

On legality, Glennon asserts:

> The central problem is that rules governing the use of force by states have collapsed. The principal reason for that collapse is the absence of a consensus concerning when force ought to be used appropriately. Contributing to the fractured consensus are power disparities among member states, which give rise to disparate incentives to commit to legalist constraints, and a free-rider phenomenon that limits the willingness of member states to contribute to a genuine collective security regime.

According to Glennon, if the term 'aggression' is used in the Rome Statute establishing the International Criminal Court but is not defined, it is merely because there is no consensus among members of the international community on its definition. NATO's use of force against Yugoslavia in 1999 highlighted the extent of the divisions. In April 2000, 114 member states of the Non-Aligned Movement agreed that humanitarian intervention had 'no legal basis under the Charter'.

Fractures within the international community severely undermine the effectiveness of legal regulation of the use of force. However, to function properly, law requires a consensus on basic values concerning the subject matter of the regulation. When that consensus evaporates, working rules become paper rules. As British Foreign Secretary Jack Straw put it, 'If you have a set of rules which conflict with reality, then reality normally wins'. That, unfortunately, is what has happened to the use of force rules embodied in the Charter: the rules have fought a losing battle with geopolitical reality.

Because the Security Council has been used, misused and bypassed several times, Glennon claims there are simply no rules any more, and that the whole UN Charter system is no longer viable. The hegemonistic position of US power and the failure of the Security Council structure to reflect it should be frankly recognized. As a solution, Glennon suggests:

> Reform efforts must originate primarily with individual member states ... The best that the UN can therefore do is to help lay the groundwork for the creation by member states of conditions in which the use of force can realistically be regulated by law ... The UN can continue to test the waters to see whether the international community is any closer to a consensus. The General Assembly is the perfect laboratory in which to do so, and a trial balloon of the sort floated by the Secretary General in his 1999 address is the perfect medium for doing so.

Collective Security and Armed Humanitarian Intervention

According to Thomas Weiss, the most basic transformation in Security Council powers is that civil war and internal strife have been accepted as threats to international peace and security and may be the basis for Chapter VII enforcement. The Appeal Chambers of the ICT of the former Yugoslavia stated it is the 'settled practice of the Security Council and the common understanding of the UN membership in general' that a purely internal conflict constitutes a 'threat to the peace'

(*Prosecutor vs. Tadic*, IT-94-1-AR72, October 1995, para. 30). Consequently, the Security Council has declared substantial flows of refugees and internally displaced peoples as threats to international peace and security, as well as 'serious' or 'systematic, widespread and flagrant' violations of international humanitarian law within a country. Such a position is strongly supported by humanitarian agencies. However, this expansion of situations under the rubrics of 'threats to international peace and security' is not considered in a positive light by all.

On collective security and humanitarian intervention, Weiss explains:

> Humanitarian interventions open the proverbial Pandora's Box of addressing a wide range of goals. By their very nature humanitarian interventions reconfigure the political landscape of war-torn societies, create new needs, and lead to 'mission creep' ... 'Collective security' is a state-centric theory that posits an automatic international response by all UN members against a clearly identified aggressor state (unless it is a permanent member or an important ally). The theory has never worked in practice (Korea and the Gulf War are possible exceptions). Moreover, a serious question arises whether a concept that applies against an invading state can be adapted to places where individual human beings are threatened – especially by failed states or non-state actors. Human protection is distinct from state security.[20]

Regarding humanitarian intervention, the ICISS report suggested instead 'military intervention for human protection purposes'. The meaning of both is clear: the use of military coercion against the expressed wishes of political authorities to protect and sustain civilian populations. The shift from the rights of outsiders to those of affected populations is appealing, and the responsibilities (if not obligations) of outsiders to protect them is persuasive.[21]

Preemptive and Preventive Wars

Michael Walzer explains that a war fought before its time is not a just war.[22] As for the Iraq war, Walzer argues it is preventive, not preemptive, meaning it is designed to respond to a more distant threat. A preventive war alludes to distant and speculative threats, whereas a preemptive war refers to an imminent, close and near threat which should be dealt with. Distant dangers can be avoided by diplomacy, mediation or other peaceful means of conflict resolution.

Walzer resists the argument that force is a last resort because the idea of lateness is often merely an excuse for postponing the use of force indefinitely.[23] He explains that force is not a matter of all or nothing, and it is not a matter of first or last (or now or never): its use must be timely and proportional. In any case, he concludes 'whether or not war is properly the last resort, there seems no sufficient reason for making it the first'.[24]

The Iraq War

In five essays written during the Iraq crisis, Michael Walzer condemned the war while it was still in the offing, as it was being conducted, and after the occupation began. The United States' conduct, he concluded, was *injustum ad bellum, injustum in bello, injustum post bellum*. Legitimacy and closure are the two criteria against which wars' endings can be tested. These are the hardest tests to meet.

Walzer explains that members of the Bush team were looking for an excuse to adopt an anticipatory war strategy for dealing with terrorists everywhere. Even humanitarian intervention was not justified in Saddam's case, since his major human rights violations against the Kurds and after the 1991 war were over, not ongoing, and invasion to punish rather than prevent atrocities is very hard to justify.

In January 2004 Human Rights Watch released a report on 'War in Iraq: not a humanitarian intervention'. Ken Roth, its author, submits the Iraqi case to several criteria similar to those listed in the ICISS report, in order to test the humanitarian nature of the military intervention. Roth argues that the question was not whether Saddam Hussein was a ruthless leader, but rather whether the conditions were present at the time of the intervention that would justify humanitarian intervention:

> But the substantial risk that wars guided by non-humanitarian goals will endanger human rights keeps us from adopting that position ... since allowing the arguments of humanitarian intervention to serve as a pretext for war fought mainly on other grounds risks tainting a principle whose viability might be essential to save countless lives.122122

With time, the initial justifications given for the Iraq war lost much of their force: weapons of mass destruction have not yet been found; no significant link between Saddam Hussein and international terrorism has been discovered; the difficulty of establishing stable institutions in Iraq is making the country an insecure place for promoting democracy in the Middle East.

According to Roth, 'the invasion of Iraq failed to meet the test for a humanitarian intervention'. The level of killing in Iraq at the time of the war was not of an exceptional nature that would have justified such intervention; intervention was not the last reasonable option to stop Iraqi atrocities, as the inspectors were still doing their job. Humanitarian concerns were not the primary motivations of the intervention. The conduct of the war itself did not fully comply with international humanitarian law requirements. The military intervention was not approved by the Security Council.

The Darfur Crisis

In the Human Rights Watch report for January 2005, Michael Clough describes various civil society efforts and Security Council resolutions adopted in response to a humanitarian crisis that has not been recognized as genocide despite the high level of human rights violations and killings. He concludes:

> Even in the shadow of Rwanda, the Security Council in 2004 failed to muster the collective will necessary to act quickly and decisively to end the humanitarian catastrophe in Darfur and hold accountable those who are responsible for creating it. This is not likely to change unless and until the United Nations accepts the principle, as recommended by the International Commission on Intervention and State Sovereignty and the High Level Panel on Threats, that all states have a 'responsibility to protect' civilians faced with avoidable catastrophes, including mass murder and rape, ethnic cleansing by forcible expulsion and terror, and deliberate starvation and exposure to disease. Recognizing the responsibility to protect would provide the Security Council with the basis it needs to act in the face of a determined refusal by a sovereign state to protect its own citizens.[26]

Clough notes that despite the impressive corpus of norms aimed at protecting civilians in conflict, 'the United Nations is still an association of sovereign states committed to traditional principles of international order and constrained by the ability of the five permanent members of the Security Council to veto collective action'. Most UN member states hold to the state sovereignty principle when a conflict arises. This traditional principle is reaffirmed by the December 2004 High Level Panel report, which reiterates sovereign states' role as frontline actors in dealing with international threats:

The norm of non-intervention in the 'internal affairs' of a sovereign state flows directly from the principle of state sovereignty – and few norms are more fiercely defended by most UN member states than this norm. Many governments, especially those in Africa, Asia and Latin America, understandably regard it as one of their few defences against threats and pressures from wealthier and more powerful international actors seeking to promote their own economic and political interests. But the non-interference norm has also been used by barely legitimate governments to block international efforts to end gross abuses of their citizenry. That is what happened in the case of Darfur: Khartoum used sovereignty, first, as a veil to hide its brutal campaign against African villagers; and, later, as a shield to fend off calls for international action to protect its victims.[27]

Clough argues that the veto power of the permanent members of the Security Council gives them 'a unique power to protect and promote their national interests at the expense of global interests'. In the case of Darfur, China's 40 per cent share of Sudan's main oil producing field was one impediment to stronger action by the Security Council

In an open letter dated 18 February 2005, the R2P-CS project of the World Federalist Movement asked UN Secretary General Kofi Annan to protect civilians in Darfur and urged 'the United Nations to take immediate and strong action to stop the humanitarian crisis and flagrant human rights violations taking place in Darfur'. The WFM urged the Security Council to protect the people of Darfur, and asked members of the Security Council not to use their veto against any resolutions which may help alleviate the suffering in Darfur. In so doing, it reminded us:

> The Security Council was established to 'ensure prompt and effective action by the United Nations' for maintenance of international peace and security. According to the UN Charter, the Security Council, in carrying out its duties, acts on behalf of all members of the United Nations. Refraining from the use of the veto for matters involving large-scale loss of life or human rights abuses would advance the fundamental purpose of the Council.

The WFM concluded: 'The use of veto by the permanent members of the Security Council must not impede the responsibility of the international community to take all necessary steps to halt the ongoing human rights abuses in Darfur.'

Conclusion

This report has summarized the current debate on the responsibility to protect agenda. While the UN's normative process for this agenda is flourishing, discussions and controversies on the issue continue. This is a good sign, for it shows that the matters at stake are worth pursuing. Our seminar will focus on four major aspects of the responsibility to protect agenda: the importance of prevention, the subsidiary role of the international community *vis-à-vis* large-scale human rights violations, the criteria for intervention and the steps to take when international authorities fail.

Although not all member churches share the same views about war in general, for the World Council of Churches prevention is the priority. In other words, military reaction to a human rights crisis should not be the primary option. All preventive and protective measures should be exploited and employed first. The church plays a major role in identifying early signs of an eventual humanitarian crisis and taking preventive measures, or at least informing others early enough for them to take action.

As Fe'iloakitau Kaho Tevi rightly notes, prevention work calls for foresight and detailed knowledge of the ills and root causes of conflicts:

The church should first and foremost be the eyes and the voice of the suffering. In this role, the church should be called to expose the unjust structures that promote suffering ... Addressing the root causes of injustice is the role of the church. In many countries, the churches are doing the silent work on the ground to prevent conflicts. They do it because they consider it as a calling, not a job. There is some fundamental difference in this approach and motivation to do activities that prevent conflicts. In some ways, the Christian calling to be prophetic could mean a way of life rather than an employment. But the question to a Christian is whether the two are mutually exclusive. I claim that it should not be so. Being a Christian is not a Sunday affair, nor should preventing conflict be a Monday to Friday affair.[28]

Prevention must receive priority attention. As little harm as possible is done when potential threats to security are identified and defused at an early stage before conflict escalates:

But even where prevention has failed, the orientation toward protection of the endangered population remains defensive; it may have to be content with eliminating the immediate threat with as little harm as possible, without claiming to have removed the root cause once and for all. The objective normally should be to restore the capacity and willingness of the authorities of the given state to provide for human security relying on their own forces. The international community can influence and further this process in various ways, including diplomatic, legal, political and financial/economic measures of incentive or pressure. These measures belong to the standard instrumentalities of a preventive strategy, but they remain important even in cases of imminent or actual threat to human security. The responsibility of the international community should be only *subsidiary*, while the primary responsibility to protect remains with the authorities of the sovereign state and its forces of order.[29]

A number of criteria for intervention were listed by the ICISS report that seek to regulate the use of force for humanitarian purposes. Those criteria (mostly inspired by Christian just war theory) serve to illuminate unjustified, unauthorized or unilateral armed intervention for 'humanitarian purposes'.

When international authorities fail to respond adequately to a large-scale human rights and humanitarian crisis, who should take action to deal with the crisis? What lessons should be learnt from past experiences and failures? What should be the role of churches? These are just some of the things that should be dealt with by this seminar.

NOTES

1. See Lopeti Senituli, 'The Right of Humanitarian Intervention: Human Rights and Human Security in the Asia and Pacific Region'. Paper presented at a conference in Taiwan, 2003.
2. Ramesh Thakur, 'Reshaping the Concept of Shared Responsibility for Global Security', newsletter of United Nations University, March–April 2004.
3. Daniel Warner, 'Responsibility to Protect and the Limits of Imagination', *International Journal of Human Rights*, Vol. 7, No. 3 (2003), p. 154.
4. Ibid., p. 155.
5. Ibid., p. 156.
6. Ibid., p. 157.

7. Ramesh Thakur, 'In Defence of the Responsibility to Protect', *International Journal of Human Rights*, Vol. 7, No. 3 (2003), p. 164.

8. Ibid., p. 165.

9. Ibid., p. 170.

10. Michael Walzer, *Arguing About War* (New Haven, CT: Yale University Press, 2004), p. 22.

11. 'Michael Walzer on Just War Theory – Philosophy 87', at www.philosophy2.ucsd.edu/~rarneson/Courses/87MichaelWalzeronjustwartheory.pdf.

12. Ibid., p. 11.

13. Ibid., p. 73.

14. Ibid., p. 11.

15. International Council on Human Rights Policy, *Human Rights Crisis: NGO Responses to Military Interventions* (Vernier: ATAR Roto Press, 2002), p. 24.

16. Ibid., p. 24.

17. Thomas G. Weiss, *Military–Civilian Interactions: Humanitarian Crisis and the Responsibility to Protect*, 2nd edn. (Lanham, MD: Rowman & Littlefield, 2005), p. 201.

18. Ibid., p. 203.

19. Michael J. Glennon, 'Legitimacy and the Use of Force', at www.un-globalsecurity.org/pdf/Glennon_paper_legit_use_of_force.pdf.

20. Thomas G. Weiss, 'Collective Security and Humanitarian Intervention', at www.un-globalsecurity.org/pdf/Weiss_paper_hum_intervention.pdf.

21. Ibid., p. 21.

22. Walzer, *Arguing About War*, p. 161.

23. Ibid., p. 160.

24. Ibid., p. 147.

25. Ken Roth, 'War in Iraq: not a humanitarian intervention', *Human Rights Watch World Report 2004*.

26. Michael Clough, 'Darfur: whose responsibility to protect?' *Human Rights Watch World Report 2005*.

27. Ibid., p. 27.

28. Fe'iloakitau Kaho Tevi, 'Role of the Church in Conflict Prevention and Peace Building'. Paper presented at a seminar in Fiji.

29. Konrad Raiser, 'The Responsibility to Protect'. Contribution to a public seminar in the context of an International Affairs and Advocacy Week, New York, 13 November 2003.

Annex 3
Selected Bibliography

Semegnish Asfaw

Reference Reports

'The Responsibility to Protect', Report of the International Commission on Intervention and State Sovereignty, December 2001.

'A More Secure World: Our Shared Responsibility', Report of the High Level Panel on Threats, Challenges and Change, December 2004.

'In Larger Freedom: Towards Development, Security and Human Rights for All', Secretary General Report, March 2005.

Books

Church of Norway, *Vulnerability and Security*. Study prepared by the Commission on International Affairs in Church of Norway Council on Ecumenical and International Relations. 2002.

Holzgrefe, J. L. and Robert O. Keohane (eds), *Humanitarian Intervention: Ethical, Legal and Political Dilemmas*. Cambridge: Cambridge University Press, 2004.

Runzo, Joseph, Nancy M. Martin and Arvind Sharma (eds), *Human Rights and Responsibilities in the World Religions*. Oxford: Oneworld Publications, 2003.

Taylor, Thomas and Robert S. Bilheimer, *Christians and the Prevention of War in an Atomic Age: A Theological Discussion*. Geneva: World Council of Churches, 1962.

Walzer, Michael, *Arguing About War*. New Haven, CT: Yale University Press, 2004.

Webster, Alexander F. C. and Darrell Cole, *The Virtue of War: Reclaiming the Classic Traditions East and West*. Salisbury: Regina Orthodox Press, 2004.

Weiss, Thomas G., *Military–Civilian Interactions: Humanitarian Crisis and the Responsibility to Protect*. Lanham, MD: Rowman & Littlefield, 2005.

NGO Publications

International Council on Human Rights Policy, *Duties Sans Frontières: Human Rights and Global Social Justice*. Vernier: ATAR Roto Press, 2004.

International Council on Human Rights Policy, *Human Rights Crisis: NGO Responses to Military Interventions*. Vernier: ATAR Roto Press, 2002.

Articles, Study Papers, Theses, Reports and Speeches

'Accepting "Our Shared Responsibility."' 36th United Nations Issues Conference. Sponsored by the Stanley Foundation, Arden Conference Centre, Harriman, NY, 11–13 February 2005.

'Canadian Action Agenda on Conflict Prevention.' Report issued by Canadian Conflict Prevention Initiative, December 2004.

Coady, C. A. J., 'The Ethics of Armed Humanitarian Intervention.' United States Institute for Peace, July 2002.

Cole, Darell, 'Good Wars', *First Things* 116, October 2001, pp. 27–31.

Elshtain, Jean Bethke, 'Just War and Humanitarian Intervention', *Ideas, from the National Humanities Centre*, Vol. 8, No. 2, 2001.

Enns, Fernando, 'Seeking the Welfare of the City: Public Peace, Justice and Order', *Ecumenical Conversation*, Akron, PA, August 2004.

Evans, Gareth, 'When Is It Right to Fight?' *Survival*, Vol. 46, No. 3, Autumn 2004, pp. 59–82.

'Investing in Prevention: An International Strategy to Manage Risks of Instability and Improve Crisis Response.' UK report released by the Prime Minister's Strategy Unit, February 2005.

Klassen-Wiebe, Sheila, 'What are the Key Theological and Ethical Considerations that Should Inform Church Recommendations Related to the International Community's Obligations to Come to the Aid of Vulnerable Populations?' June 2004.

Levitt, Jeremy I., 'The Responsibility to Protect: A Beaver Without a Dam?' Reviewing International Commission on Intervention and State Sovereignty. *Michigan Journal of International Law*, 2003, pp.153–77.

'Michael Walzer on Just War Theory – Philosophy 87. www.philosophy2.ucsd.edu/~rarneson/Courses/87MichaelWalzeronjustwartheory.pdf.

Raiser, Konrad, 'The Responsibility to Protect: Contribution to Public Seminar in the Context of an International Affairs and Advocacy Week', New York, 13 November 2003.

'The Responsibility to Protect: Ethical and Theological Reflections.' WCC Document, 2003.

Senituli, Lopeti, 'The Right of Humanitarian Intervention: Human Rights and Human Security in the Asia and Pacific Region.' Paper presented at a conference in Taiwan, 2003.

Slim, Hugo, 'Dithering Over Darfur? A Preliminary Review of the International Response', *International Affairs*, Vol. 80, No. 5, 2004, pp. 811–33.

Slim, Hugo, 'Protecting Civilians: Putting the Individual at the Humanitarian Centre.' In *The Humanitarian Decade: Challenges for Humanitarian Assistance in the Last Decade and into the Future*, Vol. 2. New York: OCHA, 2004, pp. 153–81.

Slim, Hugo, 'Why Protect Civilians? Innocence, Immunity and Enmity in War', *International Affairs*, Vol. 79, No. 3, 2003, pp. 481–501.

Sommaruga, Cornelio, 'La responsabilité de protéger.' Opening statement, 9th Annual Humanitarian Conference, Webster University, Geneva, 22 April 2004.

Tardy, Thierry, 'The United Nations and Iraq: A Role Beyond Expectations', *International Peacekeeping*, Vol. 11, No. 4, 2004, pp. 591–607.

Tejeda, Commandant Gustavo, 'De l'ingérence humanitaire à la responsabilité de protéger.' Mémoire de géopolitique sous la direction de Messieurs Jean-Luc Pouthier et Jean-Jacques Roche, CollÈge Interarmées de Défense, May 2003.

Tevi, Fe'iloakitau Kah, 'Role of the Church in Conflict Prevention and Peace Building.' Paper presented at a seminar in Fiji.

Thakur, Ramesh, 'In Defence of the Responsibility to Protect', *International Journal of Human Rights*, Vol. 7, No. 3, 2003, pp. 160–78.

Warner, Daniel, 'Responsibility to Protect and the Limits of Imagination', *International Journal of Human Rights*, Vol. 7, No. 3, 2003, pp. 154–9.

Internet Links (as of 20 April 2005)

From www.foreignaffairs.org (Foreign Affairs)

Evans, Gareth and Mohamed Sahnoun, 'The Responsibility to Protect', November/December 2002.

Feinstein, Lee and Anne-Marie Slaughter, 'A Duty to Prevent', January/February 2004.

Glennon, Michael J., 'Why the Security Council Failed', May/June 2003.

Luck, Edward C., 'Stayin' Alive: The Rumors of the UN's Death Have Been Exaggerated', July/August 2003.

From www.amnesty.org (Amnesty International)
Sané, Pierre, 'Soldiers in the Name of Human Rights', 14 June 2000.

From www.globalpolicy.org (Global Policy Forum)
Evans, Gareth, 'Why Nobody is Doing Enough for Darfur', *Financial Times*, 3 August 2004.

From www.hrw.org (Human Rights Watch)
Clough, Michael, 'Darfur: Whose Responsibility to Protect?' *Human Rights Watch World Report 2005*, January 2005.

Roth, Ken, 'War in Iraq: Not a Humanitarian Intervention', *Human Rights Watch World Report 2004*, January 2004.

From www.icg.org (International Crisis Group)
Evans, Gareth, 'After the Tsunami: Prospects for Collective Security Reform in 2005.' Institute of Southeast Asian Studies (ISEAS) Regional Outlook Forum 2005, Singapore, 6 January 2005.

Evans, Gareth, 'Darfur and the Responsibility to Protect', *The Diplomat*, August–September 2004.

Evans, Gareth, 'International Law and the United Nations: The Use of Military Force.' 5th Annual Foreign Policy Conference on The Role of International Law and the United Nations in a Globalizing World, Berlin, 24 June 2004.

Evans, Gareth, 'Preventing Deadly Conflict and the Problem of Political Will.' Montague Burton Professor of International Relations Lecture, 2002.

Evans, Gareth, 'The Responsibility to Protect and September 11.' UNU/Canadain Government Seminar on the Responsibility to Protect, 2004.

Evans, Gareth, 'The Responsibility to Protect: Humanitarian Intervention in the 21st Century.' Wesson Lecture in International Relations Theory and Practice, Stanford University, CA, 2002.

Evans, Gareth, 'The Responsibility to Protect in 2005.' Annual Society and Defence Conference, Salen, Sweden, 16 January 2005.

Evans, Gareth, 'Uneasy Bedfellows: "The Responsibility to Protect" and Feinstein–Slaughter's "Duty to Prevent."' Commentary on Lee Feinstein and Anne-Marie Slaughter's 'A Duty to Prevent' (*Foreign Affairs*, January/February 2004). American Society of International Law Conference, Washington, DC, 1 April 2004.

Evans, Gareth, 'Waging War and Making Peace.' Annual Hawke Lecture, Bob Hawke Prime Ministerial Centre, University of South Australia, Adelaide, 2003.

Evans, Gareth, 'When Is It Right to Fight? Legality, Legitimacy and the Use of Military Force.' Cyril Foster Lecture, Oxford University, 10 May 2004.

Evans, Gareth, 'The World Should Be Ready to Intervene in Sudan', *International Herald Tribune*, 14 May 2004.

From www.ploughshares.ca (Project Ploughshares)
'Civil Society Meeting on the Responsibility to Protect: Final Report.' NGO roundtable on the responsibility to protect co-organized by Project Ploughshares and the World Federalist Movement – Institute for Global Policy (WFM-IGP), Ottawa, 8 April 2003.

Berry, Glyn, 'Sovereignty as R2P', *Ploughshares Monitor*, Spring 2004.

Fast, Larissa, 'Protecting the Vulnerable', *Ploughshares Monitor*, Winter 2002.

'Norms and the Responsibility to Protect.' Canadian Conference Centre, Meeting Report, Ottawa, 7 April 2003.

From www.unu.edu (United Nations University)

Thakur, Ramesh, 'The Peril of Pre-Emptive Thinking', newsletter of United Nations University, November–December 2002.

Thakur, Ramesh, 'Reshaping the Concept of Shared Responsibility for Global Security', newsletter of United Nations University, March–April 2004.

From www.japantimes.com (Japan Times)

Thakur, Ramesh, 'Contradictory US Triumph', 1 June 2003.

Thakur, Ramesh, 'US Test of UN Relevance', 9 February 2003.

Thakur, Ramesh and Andrew Mack, 'The United Nations More Relevant Now Than Ever', 23 March 2003.

From www.hdcentre.org (Centre for Humanitarian Dialogue)

Slim, Hugo, 'The Church, Military Forces and Humanitarian Identity in War.' Caritas Internationalis Humanitarian Seminar on Relations with the Military, Vatican City, 4 December 2003.

From www.ourworld.compuserve./homepages/jim_forest

Behr-Sigel, Elisabeth, 'Orthodoxy and peace', from www.ourworld.compuserve.com/homepages/jim_forest/behrsige.htm.

Harakas, Fr. Stanley S., 'Not Just War in the Fathers', from www.ourworld.compuserve.com/homepages/jim_forest/Justwar.htm.

Ovsiannikov, Fr. Sergei, 'Peace and Conflict in Scripture and History', from www.ourworld.compuserve.com/homepages/jim_forest/Bible.htm.

From www.incommunion.org (Orthodox Peace Fellowship)

'War and Peace', from www.incommunion.org/articles/the-orthodox-church-and-society/viii.

'Plea for Peace from the Orthodox Peace Fellowship in North America', from www.incommunion.org/articles/news-reports/iraq-appeal.

Azar, Michael G., 'Orthodox Americans, the Orthodox Peace Fellowship, and Iraq', from www.incommunion.org/articles/iraq/orthodox-americans-the-opf-and-iraq.

Forest, Jim, 'Following Christ in a Violent World', from www.incommunion.org/forest-flier/jimsessays/following-christ-in-a-violent-world.

Harakas, Fr. Stanley S., 'The Teaching on Peace in the Fathers', from www.incommunion.org/articles/essays/peace-in-the-fathers

From other websites

Archer, Robert, 'Human Rights and Global Social Equitability', from .

D'Arcy, Bishop, 'Just War Criteria Have not been Met', 26 February 2003, from .

Dagorn, René-Eric, '"In Gun We Trust": la re-géopolitisation du monde', from .

DeForest, Mark Edward, 'Just War Theory and the Recent US Air Strikes Against Iraq', 1996, from .

Falk, Richard, 'Defining a Just War', 29 October 2001, from .

Falk, Richard, 'Legality to Legitimacy: The Revival of the Just War Framework', from .

Glennon, Michael J., 'Idealism at the UN', *Policy Review*, No. 129, February–March 2005, from .

Glennon, Michael J., 'Legitimacy and the Use of Force', from .

Harrison, Fr. Andrew, 'A "Just" War?', Winter 2003, from .

'Just War Tradition', from .

Meilaender, Gilbert, 'Michael Walzer, *Just and Unjust Wars* (1977)', *First Things*, 101, March 2000, pp. 52–3, from .

Mills, Garry, '"What is a Just War?" Reviewing Michael Walzer's *Arguing About War*', 18 November 2004, from .

Novak, Michael, 'Asymmetrical Warfare and Just War', from .

Novak, Michael, 'Civilian Casualties and Turmoil', 18 February 2003, from .

Novak, Michael, 'Michael Novak Argues that Iraq Attack is "Just War"', *The Times*, February 2003, from .

'Peace and War in the Eastern Orthodox Church: A Message from Fr. Paul', from the December 2002 and January 2003 *Messenger*, from .

Raymond, Brother John, 'The Just War Theory', from .

Slye, Ronald C., from the Seattle University School of Law, reviewing Michael J. Glennon's *Limits of Law, Prerogatives of Power: Interventionism After Kosovo*, from .

'Theology and Culture', from .

'The United States in the World – Just Wars and Just Societies: An Interview with Michael Walzer', *Imprints, A Journal of Analytical Socialism*, Vol. 7, No. 1, from , 2003.

'War and Peace: What Does Orthodoxy Teach Us?', an AGAIN Interview with Fr. Alexander F. C. Webster, from .

'War and Peace', in 'The Orthodox Church and Society', from .

Weiss, Thomas G., 'Collective Security and Humanitarian Intervention', from www.un-globalsecurity.org/pdf/Weiss_paper_hum_intervention.pdf.

Zinn, Howard, 'A Just Cause, Not a Just War', December 2001, .

Annex 4

The Responsibility to Protect: Milestones to Porto Alegre

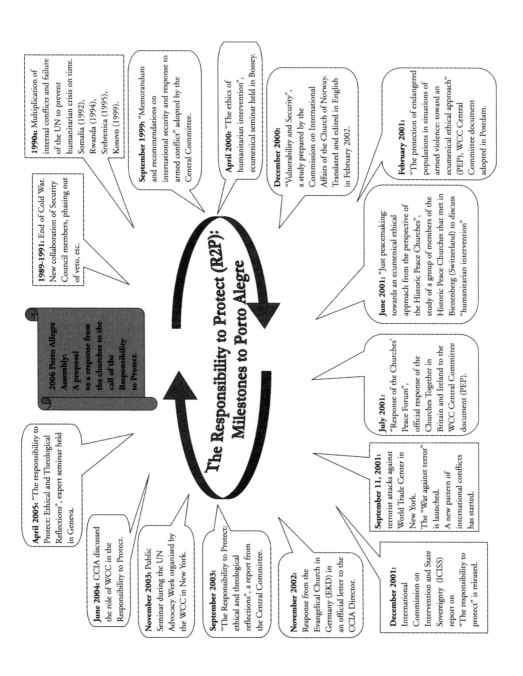

1990s: Multiplication of internal conflicts and failure of the UN to prevent humanitarian crisis on time. Somalia (1992), Rwanda (1994), Srebrenica (1995), Kosovo (1999).

September 1999: "Memorandum and recommendations on international security and response to armed conflict" adopted by the Central Committee.

April 2000: "The ethics of humanitarian intervention", ecumenical seminar held in Bossey.

December 2000: "Vulnerability and Security", a study prepared by the Commission on International Affairs of the Church of Norway. Translated and edited in English in February 2002.

February 2001: "The protection of endangered populations in situations of armed violence: toward an ecumenical ethical approach" (PEP), WCC Central Committee document adopted in Postdam.

1989-1991: End of Cold War. New collaboration of Security Council members, phasing out of veto, etc.

The Responsibility to Protect (R2P): Milestones to Porto Alegre

2006 Porto Allegre Assembly: A proposal to a response from the churches to the call of the Responsibility to Protect.

June 2001: "Just peacemaking: towards an ecumenical ethical approach from the perspective of the Historic Peace Churches", study of a group of members of the Historic Peace Churches that met in Bienenberg (Swizerland) to discuss "humanitarian intervention"

July 2001: "Response of the Churches' Peace Forum", official response of the Churches Together in Britain and Ireland to the WCC Central Committee document (PEP).

September 11, 2001: terrorist attacks against World Trade Center in New York. The "War against terror" is launched. A new pattern of international conflicts has started.

December 2001: International Commission on Intervention and State Sovereignty (ICISS) report on "The responsibility to protect" is released.

November 2002: Response from the Evangelical Church in Germany (EKD) in an official letter to the CCIA Director.

September 2003: "The Responsibility to Protect: ethical and theological reflections", a report from the Central Committee.

November 2003: Public Seminar during the UN Advocacy Week organised by the WCC in New York.

June 2004: CCIA discussed the role of WCC in the Responsibility to Protect.

April 2005: "The responsibility to Protect: Ethical and Theological Reflections", expert seminar held in Geneva.

Annex 5
The Responsibility to Protect: Timeline

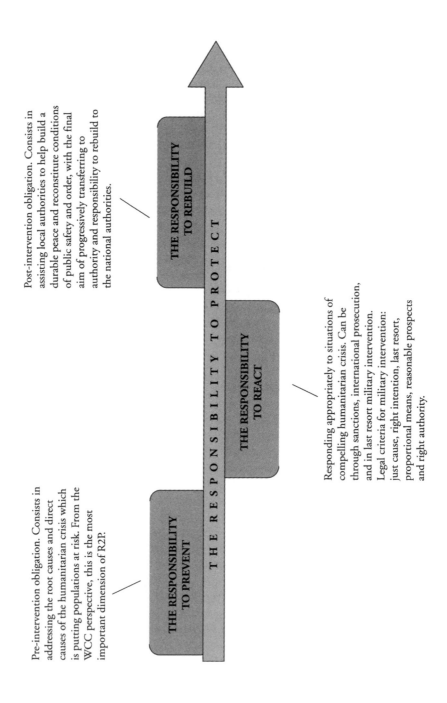

Pre-intervention obligation. Consists in addressing the root causes and direct causes of the humanitarian crisis which is putting populations at risk. From the WCC perspective, this is the most important dimension of R2P.

THE RESPONSIBILITY TO PREVENT

THE RESPONSIBILITY TO REACT

Responding appropriately to situations of compelling humanitarian crisis. Can be through sanctions, international prosecution, and in last resort military intervention. Legal criteria for military intervention: just cause, right intention, last resort, proportional means, reasonable prospects and right authority.

THE RESPONSIBILITY TO PROTECT

Post-intervention obligation. Consists in assisting local authorities to help build a durable peace and reconstitute conditions of public safety and order, with the final aim of progressively transferring to authority and responsibility to rebuild to the national authorities.

THE RESPONSIBILITY TO REBUILD

Annex 6
Difference Between Preventive and Preemptive Actions

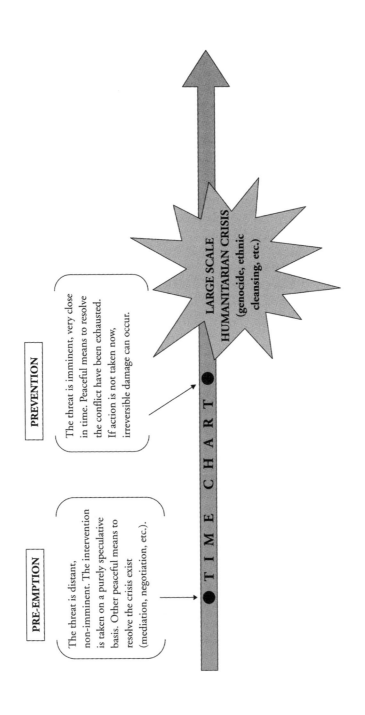

PRE-EMPTION

The threat is distant, non-imminent. The intervention is taken on a purely speculative basis. Other peaceful means to resolve the crisis exist (mediation, negotiation, etc.).

PREVENTION

The threat is imminent, very close in time. Peaceful means to resolve the conflict have been exhausted. If action is not taken now, irreversible damage can occur.

TIME CHART

LARGE SCALE HUMANITARIAN CRISIS (genocide, ethnic cleansing, etc.)

Annex 7
Participants

Dr Jean-Luc Blondel
Personal Advisor to the ICRC President
International Committee of the Red Cross
Switzerland

Ms Nicole Deller
Program Advisor
World Federalist Movement – Institute
for Global Policy
United States of America

Rev. Shirley C. deWolf
Lecturer
Africa University
Institute for Peace, Leadership and
Governance
Zimbabwe

Hon. Gareth Evans
President & CEO
International Crisis Group
Belgium

Mr Jeff Handmaker
Rea Hamba Advice
Netherlands

Dr Arnold Neufeldt-Fast
Ausbildungs- und Tagungszentrum
Switzerland

Prof. Kjell-Ake Nordquist
Associate Professor
Uppsala University
Sweden

Rev. Dr Konrad Raiser
Germany

Dr Bertrand Ramcharan
United Nations Office at Geneva (UNOG)
Palais des Nations
Switzerland

Mr Ernie Regehr
Director
Project Ploughshares
Canada

Mr Yuri Ryabykh
Russian Orthodox Church
Danilov Monastery
Russian Federation

Ambassador Mohamed Sahnoun
United Nations Office at Geneva (UNOG)
Palais des Nations
Switzerland

Dr Hugo Slim
Policy Director
Centre for Humanitarian Dialogue
Switzerland

Dr Cornelio Sommaruga
Geneva International Centre for
Humanitarian Demining (GICHD)
Switzerland

Dr Sturla J. Stalsett
Church of Norway
Commission on International Affairs
Norway

Bishop Michael Kehinde Stephen
Secretary of Conference
Methodist Church Nigeria
Nigeria

Dr Thierry Tardy
Course Director, European Training
Course
Geneva Centre for Security Policy
(GCSP)
Switzerland

Dr Grant White
Principal
Institute for Orthodox Christian Studies
United Kingdom

Dr Roger Williamson
Associate Director
Wilton Park
United Kingdom

WCC staff

Rev. Dr Samuel Kobia
General Secretary

Ms Geneviève Jacques
Director of Programme

Rev. Hansulrich Gerber
Coordinator for Decade to Overcome
Violence Programme

**International Affairs, Peace & Human
Security team**

Mr Peter Weiderud
CCIA Director & Team Coordinator

Mr Melaku Kifle
Programme Executive, Africa, including
Focus on Africa

Dr Guillermo Kerber
Programme Executive, Latin America &
Caribbean, Impunity, Justice &
Reconciliation

Mr Clement John
Programme Executive, Asia & Pacific,
Human Rights & Religious Freedom

Mr Jonathan Frerichs
Programme Executive, Middle East,
Peacebuilding & Disarmament

Ms Patricia Bruschweiler
Administrative Assistant

Ms Semegnish Asfaw
Consultant

World Council of Churches
150, route de Ferney
PO Box 2100
1211 Geneva 2
Switzerland
Work tel:+41.22.791.61.11
Work fax:+41.22.791.6406
Website: www.wcccoe.org

Apologies

Mr Manuel Quintero Perez
General Secretary
Frontier Internships in Mission
Switzerland

Rev. White Rakuba
Coordinator
Action by Churches Together (ACT
International)
WCC/LWF Emergency
Switzerland